A Community on Trial

A Community on Trial

The
Jews of Paris
in the
1930s

David H. Weinberg

The University of Chicago Press

Chicago and London

DAVID H. WEINBERG received his Ph.D. from
the University of Wisconsin in 1971. He is now
associate professor of history at Bowling
Green State University.

An earlier version of this work was published
in French as *Les Juifs à Paris de 1933 à 1939*,
©1974 by Calmann-Levy

The University of Chicago Press, Chicago 60637
The University of Chicago Press, Ltd., London

81 80 79 78 77   5 4 3 2 1

Library of Congress Cataloging in Publication Data

Weinberg, David H   1945-
    A community on trial.

    Originally presented as the author's thesis, Univer-
sity of Wisconsin, 1971.
    Bibliography: p.
    Includes index.
    1. Jews in Paris—History. 2. Paris—History—
1870-1940. I. Title.
DS135.F85P427 1977   944'.36'004924   77-2999
ISBN 0-226-88507-0

Contents

Introduction

Of the many complex issues raised by the historical investigation of the Holocaust, none has been studied more intensively than the European Jewish response to Nazism. Some scholars, in confronting the awesome tragedy of the Final Solution, have emphasized the passivity of European Jewry as reflected in the willingness of Jewish community leaders to negotiate with German authorities and in the seeming indifference of concentration camp victims to their plight. Others, seeking to counter the view of dehumanized Jew, have stressed physical resistance and in particular Jewish participation in the various anti-Nazi movements organized in occupied countries. More recently, accusatory and apologetic accounts of the Jewish Response have given way to more cautious historical analyses of the complex moral and political issues involved in the relationship between victim and victimizer during the Nazi period.[1] Yet, whatever the emphasis, almost all studies of the Jewish Response have limited themselves to the war years and to the implementation of the Final Solution. Little attention has been paid to the period directly before the war when attitudes of European Jews were being shaped in response to the growing Nazi threat.

The period from 1933 to 1939 is a watershed in modern Jewish history. The catapulting of the "Jewish question" into the public arena occasioned profound soul-searching among European Jews and in particular among those Jews who had been uprooted from their homelands as a result of Nazi persecution. The events of the 1930s raised not only immediate questions of the dangers of anti-Semitism and of the appropriate Jewish response but also far-reaching concerns reflecting on the very nature of Jewish identity and on the Jewish future in the Diaspora.

Nowhere was this more evident than in Paris, whose geographical position on the European continent made its Jewish inhabitants directly aware of the tragedy unfolding there. Too often viewed as merely a stopping-off point in the journey from the Old World to the

New, Paris in the 1930s boasted the third largest Jewish community in the world, surpassed only by New York and Warsaw. Unlike those of New York and Warsaw, the Paris community contained a sizable proportion of both western European—that is, native French—and eastern European Jews, the latter having arrived in the capital after fleeing anti-Semitic outrages in their homelands. The clash of these two groups, often described simplistically as that of assimilant versus ghetto dweller, led in fact to a wide and bewildering variety of Jewish identities and responses to the Nazi threat. Together, they form a microcosm of European Jewish attitudes in prewar Europe.

The present study of Paris Jewry in the years 1933 to 1939 represents a contribution to the growing historical literature of European Jewry in the interwar years. As a work in social history, it seeks to understand the challenge facing a vibrant Jewish community which must strike a balance between its own internal needs and the demands of the larger society in which it finds itself. As an investigation into the prehistory of the Holocaust, it attempts to examine the reaction of the major ideological and cultural elements in European Jewry to Nazism in a period in which the "Jewish question" existed but genocide was not its only "solution."

No study can hope to encompass the entire Jewish population of Paris. At the same time, I do not wish to restrict my work to the statements and activities of the more prominent and articulate Jewish intellectuals in Paris in the 1930s, such as Léon Blum and Emmanuel Berl, who had only tangential contact with the mass of Jews. In dealing with Paris Jewry, therefore, I have chosen to concentrate on the organized Jewish community, that is, on the myriad of Jewish-oriented groups and societies that existed in Paris before World War II. The role of organizations in the Paris Jewish community is a crucial one and will be discussed in detail in chapter 3. One may note here, however, that as a general rule those Jews in Paris who consciously identified themselves with other Jews tended to join organizations that reflected their particular beliefs and attitudes. This was particularly true among eastern Europeans Jews, whose societies or *landsmanshaftn* served as a means both of maintaining ties to the homeland and of defense against the new and often hostile environment. As such these societies are also significant as a measure of immigrant resistance to acculturation into French society. The tendency toward organization was much less marked among native French Jews, many of whom felt little or no attachment to Jewish life. Nevertheless, those who maintained a

Jewish identity generally joined the *Association consistoriale israélite de Paris* (hereafter referred to as the *Consistoire de Paris*), the largest religious organization among Paris Jewry, or one of its affiliate groups.

The emphasis upon organizations reflects more than the use of a convenient research tool to gauge the attitudes and opinions of Paris Jewry. Organizations were the basic building blocks used by both native and immigrant Jews to solidify the Paris Jewish community against the threat of anti-Semitism. For native Jews, benefiting from 125 years of uninterrupted organizational development in Paris, the 1930s brought a growing disenchantment with established communal institutions. The Consistoire de Paris, tied to a narrowly religious definition of Jewish identity, seemed ill-equipped to answer the problems posed by a native population which, rejecting religious belief and ritual, was groping for a more "relevant" Jewish posture to counter the Nazi threat. For many, the solution lay in a revitalization of the old communal structure through an accommodation with the new immigrants from eastern Europe, so different in background from western European Jews yet increasingly influential in Paris if only because of their numbers. For others, and particularly native Jewish youth, the needs of Paris Jewry called for the creation of new structures more militant in their defense of Jewish interests than the overly cautious Consistoire.

Most eastern European Jews in Paris rejected native institutions outright. Instead, they hoped to create a new Jewish community resulting from the blending of Jewish life as molded in the *shtetl* and the progressive atmosphere of the French capital. The exact nature of the balance between eastern and western Europe was a subject of bitter debate among immigrants, for if some looked longingly back to the tightly structured communities of Poland, others welcomed the relative freedom of France. As with their native coreligionists, debate over communal structure was inextricably tied to the problem of anti-Semitism and the pressing need to mount an appropriate Jewish defense. Here too, organizations played a crucial role both as the spokesmen for the differing views within the immigrant community toward the question of acculturation in France and as the first lines of defense against the Nazi onslaught.

Thus, for both native and immigrant Jews in Paris in the 1930s, the problem of communal organization went far beyond a mere concern over internal structure and administration. Bound up as it was with questions of Jewish identity and Jewish response and set against the backdrop of the disintegration of Jewish communities in central and eastern Europe, it is the major theme running through the history of Paris Jewry in the period between 1933 and 1939.

Given the nature of my study, it was perhaps unavoidable that questions would be raised after the book's publication in France as to its relevance to the so-called "debate" over the Jewish Response. Thus, more than one reviewer drew parallels between the activities of the Jewish community in the 1930s and the role of the *Union générale israélite de France* under Vichy rule. Similarly, in public forums and private discussions, interested questioners seemed mainly concerned with whether my conclusions supported or refuted Hannah Arendt's thesis concerning Jewish complicity in the Final Solution. The publication of my work in the United States where the debate had its origins and where it continues unabated impels me to clarify my position.

There is no question that some Jewish elements in Paris in the thirties were convinced of the viability of physical defense and shaped their activity accordingly. A historian viewing the events with forty years' hindsight, however, must conclude that there was little that Jews could have done directly before and during the Holocaust to physically prevent their annihilation. My study of the response of the Paris community to Nazism therefore assumes Jewish impotence and will offer little satisfaction to those seeking to praise or condemn elements within the European Jewish community for their action or inaction in the face of Nazism.

In contrast to those participants in the debate who would limit the question of the Jewish Response to the polarities of physical resistance and passivity, I see the central issue as that of psycho-logical resistance, an awareness of the new and terrifying nature of Nazi anti-Semitism and a commitment to maintain one's humanity and Jewishness in the face of the concerted effort to deny them both. My concern in the study, therefore, is more with the attitudes of Paris Jewry than with the actions that resulted from them. Yet the activities of the various elements within the community are not without significance. Viewed from the perspective of psychological resistance, they are an important indicator of the readiness of organizations and organizational leaders to educate the Jewish community to the dangers of Nazi anti-Semitism. In linking my evaluation of community activities to the question of community consciousness, I have assigned responsibility and blame in those instances in which community leaders failed to create a common awareness of the Jewish plight.

The failure to unify the native and immigrant communities before the war, which is the major theme of the book, should be understood in this context. A unified Jewish community would have made little difference in the success or failure of the implementation of the Final Solution in Paris. It would, however, have performed a vitally important psychological function by providing the basis for a commitment to maintain Jewish solidarity against the Nazi enemy. If my study offers anything to the debate over the relationship between native and immigrant Jews in France during the Vichy period, then, it is the central importance of the failure to create a commonly accepted understanding of the Jewish plight in the years directly before the outbreak of war.

The study consists of three major parts. The first three chapters deal with population, professions, and organizations of Paris Jews in the 1930s and provide an insight into the economic, social, and political structure of the community. The fourth chapter examines the nature of Jewish identification among Jews in Paris in an attempt to show the marked ideological differences separating natives and immigrants and indeed dividing both groups internally. In the final three chapters, these differences are discussed as they relate to the contrasting analyses of anti-Semitism within the community and attitudes toward the question of a Jewish response. It is hoped that such an approach will provide a meaningful understanding of the Paris Jewish community both as a vibrant entity in itself and as a useful case study of the attitudes of prewar European Jewry.

A word must be said about the sources used in my research. A number of reviewers of the French edition have criticized the work for being too insular, ignoring documents and sources of the larger French society which influenced the decisions and actions of Paris Jewry in the 1930s. The sheer volume of material that I uncovered during the course of my research forced me to limit my documentation and concern to the Paris Jewish community itself. While recognizing the need to incorporate general documentation for a broader understanding of Paris Jewry and its relationship to the host society, I also felt that, given the growing gap between French and Jewish interests and the resultant isolationism that marked Paris

Jewish consciousness in the period directly before World War II, it was important that voices within the community be given greatest emphasis. Nevertheless, like the study of the Holocaust, the study of the pre-Holocaust era must be viewed within the context of both general and Jewish history, and I look forward to expanding the scope of my study in the future.

In approaching my study, I was surprised to find that there are few secondary works on the Paris Jewish community in the interwar period. With the exception of a number of impressionistic works on French and Parisian Jewry, such as Rabi's *Anatomie du Judaïsme français* (Paris: Editions de Minuit, 1962) and Michel Roblin's *Les Juifs de Paris* (Paris: Editions A. et J. Picard, 1952), French Jewish historians have shown a singular uninterest in the study of French Jews between the two world wars. Even general works tend to ignore the crucial period between 1918 and 1939. Bernhard Blumenkranz's *Histoire des Juifs en France* (Toulouse: Edouard Privat, 1972), for example, accords only 11 pages (out of 469) to the interwar years. The editors of the *Guide juif de France* (Paris: Editions Migdal, 1972), a major source of information on contemporary French Jewish society, could not find even one significant event in the period between 1919 and 1940 to include in their chronology of French Jewish history!

The main sources for information on the Paris Jewish community in the 1930s are the various newspapers and journals published by natives and immigrants. Of the many I looked at, a number deserve special mention. *L'Univers israélite*, although not the official organ of the native community, provides the most complete coverage of French Jewish activities in the period. Its close ties with the Consistoire de Paris make it a fairly authoritative source for the attitudes of native Jewish leaders in the 1930s. Journals like *Archives israélites*, issued by dissident members of the Consistoire, and *La Revue juive de Génève*, which had extensive coverage of French Jewish affairs, gave added depth to the study. In the immigrant press, French-language publications like *Le Journal juif*, *Samedi*, and *Affirmation* offer valuable information on older immigrants and their more militant sons and daughters.

Of equal importance is the Yiddish press and specifically the three Yiddish dailies published in Paris in the 1930s. *Pariser Haint* (Paris Today), the largest of the Yiddish dailies, was Zionist oriented and generally sympathetic to the *Fédération des sociétés juives de*

France, the major immigrant organization in Paris before World War II. In the absence of primary sources on this most important organization, the *Haint* provides valuable insights into the thinking of immigrant leaders. The *Haint* also carried articles by immigrant militants who, although vehemently anti-Communist, were dissatisfied with the moderacy of the Fédération's position concerning the plight of European Jewry. *Naie Presse* (New Press), the Communist daily, is important for an understanding of Jewish social and economic conditions in Paris in the 1930s. It assumed great importance in the mid-thirties when, as we shall see, Jewish Communists took an active role in the life of the community. Finally there is *Unzer Stime* (Our Voice), published by Paris Bundists beginning in 1936. Although less influential than the other two newspapers, it is an important source for an understanding of Jewish left-wing activity. Other short-lived Yiddish journals, such as *Hebdo-Pariz* (Paris Weekly) and the *Illustrierte Yiddishe Presse* (Illustrated Yiddish Press), were used to supplement the incomplete runs of the three major newspapers.[2]

The war saw the destruction of many valuable documents of the prewar Jewish communities in Europe. In France native Jews, centrally organized and relatively wealthy, were able to collect many of their papers and to store them in a secluded chateau outside Paris in the last days before the outbreak of the war. The archives of the Consistoire de Paris thus retains a fairly complete collection of letters, minutes of meetings, and unpublished manuscripts which were quite useful in my research.[3] The archives of the *Alliance israélite universelle*, subject to a fifty-year ban, remained closed to me.

Immigrant archives for the period are in a sorrier state. Scattered among different organizations, relatively poor, and less conscious of their "historical" importance for future generations of scholars, immigrants found little time in August 1939 to store their documents for safekeeping. The archives of the Fédération des sociétés juives de France are still hidden in a cave outside Paris with no plans by the organization to unearth them. Similarly, documents on the Jewish subsection of the *Parti communiste français* (PCF) as well as on the Yiddish-language sections of the *Confédération générale du travail unitaire* (CGTU) are allegedly deposited in a garden somewhere in Paris but as yet remain unfound.[4] What survives today in the way of immigrant sources is a handful of letters, brochures, and flyers collected by enterprising individuals during the war and smuggled out of France to what was then Palestine and to the United States. [5]

My attempts to supplement written sources with oral documentation met with only partial success. Most of the survivors of the prewar period whom I attempted to interview are no longer active in the organizations they once led. Though all were more than willing to share their recollections with me, there were only a few who could remember details which seem so terribly important to a historian viewing events with forty-years hindsight. Some had forgotten the period, having considered their role to be slight and certainly not worthy of historical analysis. Others were left with only bitter memories, important for an understanding of the flavor of the period but shedding little factual light. Most of the individuals mentioned in the book unfortunately remain only names to me, no longer alive and forgotten by their one-time comrades whom I did manage to ferret out. (I would therefore like to apologize beforehand for any misspellings of names or misconceptions of roles of particular individuals within the community.) Despite the many difficulties, I gleaned much useful information from the interviews I was able to obtain. I can only hope that the publication of the book will bring other participants forward, if only to correct my analysis and to offer new information.

The extensive use of Yiddish sources has forced me to resort to a complicated method of transliteration. Where possible, I have followed the rules of spelling devised by the YIVO Institute for Jewish Research. The sole exceptions are (1) the names of newspapers which listed their Roman letter transliterations on their mastheads according to a system geared to French pronunciation (hence, *Pariser Haint* rather than *Parizer Haynt*, *Naie Presse* rather than *Naye Presse*, and so on); (2) words originally derived from Hebrew that have assumed a standard English spelling (for example, Yom Kippur, Succoth, and so on). Proper names spelled in Yiddish were transliterated phonetically unless I found a French or English equivalent. Finally, although there is no rule governing capitalization in Yiddish (since there are no capital letters), I have chosen to use a system close to that of French: capitalization of proper nouns and of the first noun (and adjectives which precede it) in a title.

In the course of my research, many people have helped me to track down well-hidden sources, documents, and personalities. Special thanks should go to the many archivists and librarians that I have encountered: Mme. Yvonne Lévyne at the Alliance israélite universelle; M. Noé Gruss at the Bibliothèque nationale; M. Gérard Nahon at the archives of the Consistoire de Paris; Mr. Ezekial Lifschutz at the YIVO Archives; and Mr. Hillel Kempinsky at the Bund Archives. I also received valuable assistance and guidance from Professor Harvey Goldberg, my major professor at the University of Wisconsin. I am especially indebted to Professor George Mosse of the University of Wisconsin and Professor Georges Haupt of the *Ecole pratique des hautes études*, who took an active interest in my research and who were both instrumental in having my work published, and to M. Roger Errera, editor of the Diaspora Collection of Calmann-Lévy, who was a constant source of encouragement and advice in the preparation of both the French and English manuscripts. The secretarial staff of the History Department of Bowling Green State University deserves special praise for successfully typing a manuscript whose intermingling of three languages often confused even the author. I should also like to thank the National Foundation for Jewish Culture, the Memorial Foundation for Jewish Culture, and Bowling Green State University, whose generous grants enabled me to go to Paris to do research. Finally, I am deeply grateful for the understanding and patience of Judy, Joshua, and Rachel, who shared in both the joyful discoveries of research and the painstaking process of composition.

Notes

1. The work which is most generally associated with the criticism of Jewish passivity is Hannah Arendt's *Eichmann in Jerusalem: A Report on the Banality of Evil* (New York: Viking, 1963). Though not a major concern of her essay, Arendt's thesis that the existence of Jewish councils greatly facilitated the roundup and extermination of Jews occasioned vociferous debate among Holocaust historians. A representative work which emphasizes Jewish resistance is Yuri Suhl's *They Fought Back* (New York: Crown, 1967), a collection of personal reminiscences by Jewish partisans. Among the more recent works which attempt to avoid the extremes of condemnation and apologetics, Isaiah Trunk's *Judenrat* (New York: Macmillan, 1972) stands out as a model of Holocaust historical scholarship.

2. Of the myriad of publications within the community, only three—*Pariser Haint*, *L'Univers israélite*, and *Naie Presse*—can be said to have had a general readership which transcended special interest and parochial appeal. At its peak in the 1930s, *Pariser Haint* had a circulation of some 10,000, while *Naie Presse* claimed 8,000, and *L'Univers israélite*, 6,000. Circulation figures are deceptive, however. It was not uncommon for Jewish papers to be passed from hand to hand, one newspaper serving

the needs of four or five people. In addition, the readership of the three newspapers fluctuated greatly in the 1930s, partly because of intense competition, especially between the two Yiddish papers, and partly because of the changing appeal of their varying positions on the solution to the Jewish plight. *Naie Presse*, for example, attained its circulation of 8,000 during the early months of the Popular Front. By 1937 its readership had dropped to 5,000 with the waning of Jewish enthusiasm for the Blum government and fears of rising xenophobia with the French Communist movement.

3. Since my visit to the archives in 1969–70, the Consistoire de Paris has instituted a fifty-year ban on all its documents.

4. The information on the archives of the Fédération was supplied to me by M. Rajak, the organization's librarian. The information on the documents of the Jewish subsection and of the Yiddish-language sections was supplied to me by M. David Diamant, chief archivist of the Institut Maurice-Thorez.

5. The YIVO (Yiddish Scientific Institute) Library in New York contains an impressive collection of documents on immigrant Jews in Paris in the 1930s. Of particular importance are the Bielinky Archives, an uncataloged collection of manuscripts, letters, and articles written by Jacques Bielinky, a Russian Jew who had close ties with both the native and immigrant community in Paris in the interwar period. Some material may also be found at the Bund Archives in New York, though, not surprisingly, most of it pertains to the activity of the small but active Bundist group in Paris.

1   Population

Although traces of Jewish settlement can be found as early as Roman times, the modern continuous Jewish inhabitation of the French capital begins in the seventeenth century. Thanks to a policy of informal toleration initiated by Louis XIV and continued by his successors, individual Jews were allowed to settle and to carry on business in Paris, though community structures and activities were forbidden. By the French Revolution, Jews in Paris had become confident enough of their position to argue publicly for Jewish emancipation in Assembly debates. Jews could be found in every revolutionary faction, an important indication of their growing involvement in the larger Paris community.[1]

The proclamation of Jewish emancipation in 1791 brought an influx of Jews to the capital. The first to arrive were Sephardic Jews of Spanish and Portuguese origin from the neighboring territory of the Netherlands, many of whom could trace their ancestry back to Jews who were forced to flee France after the expulsion of 1394. To these were soon added a small number of well-to-do Sephardim from Bordeaux and Provence who were quick to take advantage of the business opportunities offered by an expanding government bureaucracy and by the growing commercial interchange between Paris and the provinces during the Napoleonic Era and the Restoration. In general, however, Sephardic immigration remained small and the influence of the Sephardic community in Paris actually diminished during the nineteenth century. Over one-quarter of the Paris Jewish population in 1789, Sephardim numbered only a little over 1,000 in a population of 40,000 a century later.[2]

By far the largest proportion of Jews settling in Paris during the nineteenth century were Ashkenazim of German origin, most of whom were born in the eastern provinces of Alsace and Lorraine. The Ashkenazic immigration began early in the century in response to the growth of anti-Semitic movements in eastern France. Alsatian Jews chose Paris as their place of refuge because they believed that anti-Jewish sentiments would never flourish in the cosmopolitan atmosphere of the French capital. Economic reasons also played a role in the migration of Ashkenazic Jews. Many were dependent upon profits from goods sold on credit, a situation that in the unstable economic climate of the eastern provinces made them constantly at the mercy of price fluctuations and the whims of suppliers and clients. Others found themselves threatened by the introduction of modern economic institutions into rural Alsace and Lorraine. The small Jewish creditor and shopkeeper in the Alsatian countryside was particularly hard hit by the spread of bank branches and department store outlets throughout France during the Second Empire.[3] Fleeing economic dislocation, they gravitated toward Paris whose expanding economy allowed some to maintain their preindustrial roles and others to start anew in more modern business ventures.

Thanks largely to this influx, the Paris Jewish community grew from 500 in 1789 to over 6,000 at the beginning of the Restoration. In the period after 1815, Alsatian Jews were joined in Paris by German Jews from the left bank of the Rhine who had enjoyed the benefits of rights granted to Jews under Napoleonic rule. Faced with the prospect of a reimposition of restrictions on Jewish activity in the wake of the Prussian takeover, they chose to come to France and to Paris in particular. By 1859 the number of Ashkenazic Jews in Paris stood at about 12,000, a significant enough number to warrant the transfer of the *Ecole rabbinique* or Rabbinical Seminary from Metz to Paris.[4]

The most important influx of Jews from Alsace and Lorraine, however, occurred after 1871, when the two provinces were annexed by Germany. Emotional ties to France as well as the thought of losing their rights with the advent of German rule sent thousands of Jews fleeing westward to Paris and its suburbs.[5] Between 1872 and 1881 the Paris Jewish population grew from 24,000 to 40,000 and eclipsed the two provinces as the major area of Jewish settlement in France.[6] Because Jews were not actually forced to leave Alsace and Lorraine, many immigrants were able to bring their capital with them and in time succeeded in relocating their businesses in Paris. Others, leaving their belongings behind in their rush to emigrate, found new sources of wealth in the capital.[7] By the turn of the century, Alsatian Jews had become the dominant element in the Paris Jewish community, a position they were to maintain until well into the 1920s.

No one really knows when the first eastern European Jews settled in Paris. A journalist writing in a Paris Jewish newspaper in the 1930s created a minor sensation when he claimed that he had discovered a number of "Pollacks" in the membership lists of various Jewish social organizations in the French capital as well as traces of a Polish *landsmanshaft* in the early 1800s, but his conclusions have been questioned by more serious scholars of Franco-Judaica who cannot find detailed documentation of eastern European Jewish settlement before the 1850s.[8] Though the exact date of the first settlement may never be known, it is undeniable that there was a small but steady trickle of eastern European immigrants to Paris in the early and mid-nineteenth century. Most of them were Poles, Russians, and Rumanians fleeing abortive revolutions or anti-Semitic pogroms. Others came in search of economic betterment. Still others sought to partake of the rich intellectual and cultural life of Paris. Exact figures are unavailable, but one may venture the guess that by 1881 the number of eastern European Jews in Paris stood at a few thousand.[9]

The eastern European Jewish community in the French capital was enlarged substantially by a massive wave of immigration in the 1880s. The combination of political repression following the assassination of Tsar Alexander II in 1881 and pogroms throughout Russia and the Ukraine in the 1880s and 1890s sent many Russian Jews fleeing westward. By 1900 some 8,000 of them had settled in Paris.[10] A decade later the figure had risen to over 18,000 in the wake of the massacres of Jews in Kishinev and Zhitomir and of the failure of the Revolution of 1905. In the intervening years before 1914, Russian Jews were joined by Rumanians and Galicians fleeing pogroms in their own countries. On the eve of World War I, eastern European immigrants numbered over 20,000, two-fifths of the Jewish population of Paris.[11]

By far the largest influx of eastern European Jews to Paris occurred between the two world wars. Russians fleeing the Revolution of 1917, Poles, Hungarians, and Lithuanians hoping for a better life in the unfettered atmosphere of western Europe, Polish activists escaping punishment for illegal political activity, Rumanians seeking educational opportunities—all were welcomed directly after the war by a France desperately in need of manpower. To these must be added the substantial number of Jews fleeing Nazi persecution in the 1930s. The actual number of immigrants is unknown. Many entered illegally and thus were never recorded in government statistics. Others, although officially listed as immigrants, remained in Paris for only a short while, eventually continuing on to the United States or returning to their homelands. In the 1930s French immigration policy, which was generally liberal in its acceptance of refugees but made few allowances for their continued stay, only increased Jewish transiency.[12] An extrapolation of the often conflicting figures reported by those who have studied the period places the number of eastern European Jews who settled in Paris in the years between 1918 and 1939 at no more than 70,000.[13]

Adding together the figures for eastern European Jews who settled in Paris before World War I with those of Jews who settled between the wars yields a figure of 90,000 eastern European immigrants living in Paris in the 1930s out of a total Jewish population of 150,000.[14] Of these, some 50,000 were Polish, about 15,000 Russian, 11,000 Hungarian, 10,000 Rumanian, and 1,500 Lithuanian and Latvian with the remainder scattered among various nationalities.[15] The almost zero birthrate among native Jews during the period after 1880, coupled with the continuous influx of immigrants, meant that by the 1930s eastern European Jews had achieved a sizable majority in the Paris Jewish community.[16]

Scholars studying the patterns of Jewish immigration to Paris have tended to ignore the Sephardic influx from North Africa and from the Near East. Once again the exact number of immigrants is unknown. Records show a steady stream of Jews from North Africa throughout the nineteenth century and particularly after the proclamation of the Crémieux decrees in 1870, which granted Algerian Jewry full French citizenship.[17] Jews from the Ottoman Empire (the Balkans, Crete, Salonica, Anatolia, and Bulgaria) began arriving in noticeable numbers during and after the outbreak of nationalistic revolts in their homelands in the late nineteenth and early twentieth centuries. There was little contact between older North African immigrants and the newer immigrants from the Near East. While Algerian Jews arriving in Paris in the mid-nineteenth century tended to affiliate with the Consistoire de Paris,[18] more recent immigrants from other areas in North Africa as well as from the Near East banded together into small groupings throughout Paris. A federation of Sephardic organizations was established in 1930, but its main purpose seems to have been to bring the message of the Consistoire to skeptical immigrants from North Africa and the Ottoman Empire Although eventually to become the dominant element in both Parisian and French Jewish life in the 1960s, the Sephardic community was only in the process of organization in the 1930s and numbered no more than 15,000.[19]

Most native Jews in the 1930s lived in one of two general areas of Paris. Jews arriving from Alsace in the nineteenth century tended to settle in the central and eastern sections of Paris, especially in the ninth, tenth, eleventh, and twelfth *arrondissements*. It was here that the major Jewish synagogues and social institutions were built and are still to be found today. An examination of the burial figures of the Consistoire de Paris for the month of March from 1933 to 1939 reveals that almost a third of those buried lived in these four *arrondissements*. Already before World War I, however, there was a noticeable migration of more affluent natives to the western areas of the city. It is not surprising, therefore, that the same burial figures show that over one-third of the deceased lived in the sixteenth, seventeenth, and eighteenth *arrondissements*. The figures also reveal movement still further westward into the near suburbs of Paris, a trend which resulted in the building of a number of suburban consistorial *temples* in the 1920s and 1930s.[20]

Immigrant Jews tended to concentrate in three main areas. The so-called "Pletzl" in the fourth *arrondissement*, a network of small narrow streets near the Saint Paul Metro stop, was generally the first home of newly arrived immigrants. Once an aristocratic quarter, the area was a veritable ghetto in the 1930s containing the least assimilated and poorest elements of the immigrant Jewish population. Belleville, an area encompassing portions of the nineteenth and twentieth *arrondissements*, attracted working-class and artisan elements of the immigrant populace. More politically active than the religious "Pletzl," Belleville was the main center of left-wing activity among immigrant Jews.[21] A third area, less clearly defined, ran from the Bastille to the Place de la République. Here were found the main shops and *ateliers* (workshops) of the clothing and textile trades, which employed many Jews. Other areas of immigrant settlement included the Porte de Clignancourt and the Porte de Saint-Ouen, inhabited largely by Hungarian and Polish peddlers and antique dealers frequenting the Flea Market, and Montmartre with its strong concentration of Rumanian and Russian artisans and intellectuals. Some Russian immigrants, arriving before World War I and subsequently successful in business, followed native Jews to the richer western quarters of the city such as Passy, Auteuil, and Porte Saint-Cloud. For the most part, however, eastern European Jews remained in the poorer eastern and central portions of Paris.[22]

The concentration of Parisian Jews into a limited number of areas was a mixed blessing for the Jewish community. On the one hand, geographical concentration tended to reinforce the natural ties of religion and ethnic tradition that underlay the cohesiveness of the community. On the other, the tendency of native and immigrant Jews to settle apart from each other only increased the hostility between the two groups. While natives feared that the creation of immigrant "ghettos" would only increase the "visibility" of Jews and thus help to feed xenophobic feeling, immigrants viewed the movement of natives to western Paris as further proof of the latter's desire to assimilate.

By the 1930s the Paris Jewish community had become one of the most important Jewish communities in the world. The fact that its growth after the French Revolution stemmed from a continual influx of new immigrants rather than an increase in the birthrate among resident Jews, however, meant that it was also one of the most unstable. The successive waves of immigration, first from within France, then from Germany, then from Russia, and finally from eastern Europe, injected new blood into the community but also occasioned profound convulsions among its established members. Each new wave of immigration meant an organizational restructuring of the community to fit the needs of the new arrivals. Each new immigration also meant a change in social and economic position, in religious practice, and in some cases in behavioral patterns. The problem was compounded by the fact that each successive wave dwarfed the preceding one, so that Sephardic Jews were soon surpassed in numbers by Alsatian Jews, who in turn were surpassed by immigrants from eastern Europe.

The constant flow of immigration throughout the late nineteenth and early twentieth centuries meant that the community was in a continual state of transformation. Under these conditions it was difficult for any group to firmly ensconce itself in positions of power and prestige within the community. Nevertheless, by the 1930s a basic social structure could be discerned whose divisions followed closely the shifts in population that characterized the Jewish settlement in Paris in the period after the French Revolution.

Notes

1. For a synopsis of Jewish settlement in the three centuries preceding the French Revolution, see Arthur Hertzberg's *The French Enlightenment and the Jews* (New York: Columbia University Press, 1968), pp. 12–247.

2. Michel Roblin, *Les Juifs de Paris* (Paris: Editions A. et J. Picard, 1952), p. 52. The figure of 40,000 Jews in Paris at the turn of the century is confirmed by Theodore Reinach, a contemporary of the period. According to a census conducted by the *Consistoire central* in 1897, there were 45,000 Jews in the capital. The two figures are cited in the excellent work by Michael R. Marrus, *The Politics of Assimilation: A Study of the French Jewish Community at the Time of the Dreyfus Affair* (New York and London: Oxford University Press, 1971), pp. 30–31. Marrus suggests that taking into account the inaccuracies of the Consistoire's census, the figure may have been as high as 50,000.

3. *Histoire des Juifs en France* (Toulouse: Edouard Privat, 1972), pp. 309, 312.

4. Jules Bauer, *L'Ecole rabbinique en France, 1880-1930* (Paris: Presses universitaires de France, 1930), p. 145.

5. A dramatic description of one Alsatian Jew's reaction to the events of 1871 was provided by Sylvain Halff, secretary-general of the Alliance israélite universelle, in an article written in the organization's journal in November 1934 after the death of his predecessor, Jacques Bigart. Halff described Bigart's impressions in the following manner: "In the meantime, the war came unexpectedly—the other war—the war of 1870. Soon there was the foreign invasion, which he saw with his own eyes, and for which he retained a hatred and nightmarish memories to the end of his life. Then, the defeat, the drama of the small *patrie* orphaned from the larger [*patrie*] which must now serve as the enemy's border.... For Jacques Bigart, passionately French from his youth, the decision was never in doubt. He had to leave" (*Paix et Droit*, November 1934, p. 4).

6. Robert F. Byrnes, *Antisemitism in Modern France*, vol. 1 (New Brunswick, N.J.: Rutgers University Press, 1950), p. 50. According to Byrnes, the Jewish population of Alsace-Lorraine decreased by more than 10,000, or 25 percent, in the period between 1871 and 1910 (ibid.).

7. Although not concerned with Paris, Jean Richard Bloch's *"& Co."* (New York: Simon and Schuster, 1930) is a masterful fictionalized account of one Alsatian Jewish family's successful business relocation in France after 1871.

8. One researcher has also found a number of Polish Jews among a group of soldiers who remained in Strasbourg after the Napoleonic Wars, but it is not known whether any of them eventually settled in Paris (Arnold Mandel, "Di Yidn in Frankraykh," *Algemayne Entsiklopedie: Yidn*, vol. 4 [New York: Dubnow Fund and CYCO, 1950], p. 628).

9. Roblin states that in 1881 Alsatians made up 90 percent of the Paris Jewish population (Roblin, p. 136). The remainder, some 4,000, included not only eastern Europeans but also native and Oriental Sephardim.

Probably the most famous eastern European Jew who came to Paris in the mid-nineteenth century was Leo Fraenckel, a leading participant in the Paris Commune of 1871. Like many politically active Jews in the French capital in the nineteenth century, however, Fraenckel did not actually settle in Paris but instead sought temporary refuge there.

10. Paris was chosen above other cities of refuge by many bourgeois Russian Jews because of their close attachment to French culture. In a survey of immigrant Jews in Paris conducted in the early 1960s, the majority of Russians interviewed claimed that they had known French before they arrived (cited in Ida Benguigui, "L'Immigration juive à Paris entre les deux guerres," thesis submitted for a *Diplôme d'études supérieures* at the *Faculté des Lettres et des Sciences humaines*, Université de Paris, 1965, p. 152).

For an account of one Russian Jewish family's arrival in Paris, see Romain Gary, *Promise at Dawn* (New York: Harper, 1961).

11. Figures for non-Russian eastern European immigrants in Paris before World War I are spotty. Roblin consulted the statistics on foreigners living in the Department of the Seine issued by municipal officials in 1901 and somehow arrived at the following figures for foreign Jews: about 1,000 Jews from the Austro-Hungarian Empire and anywhere from 584 to 3,532 Rumanian Jews! (Roblin, p. 66).

According to *L'Univers israélite* (May 13, 1938), there were 6,000 immigrant Jewish volunteers from Paris in the French Army in World War I, 1,200 of whom were killed in action. The figures were undoubtedly inflated to counter xenophobic feeling in France in 1938, although they do attest to the cohesiveness of the immigrant community on the eve of World War I.

12. This was particularly true of the wave of German Jewish refugees who arrived in France in the 1930s. Figures are lacking, although most researchers place the number of German refugees arriving in Paris in the period between 1930 and 1939 at about 50,000. Few, however, remained in the capital. By 1939 there were said to be only about 10,000 German Jews in Paris. These estimates are taken from Roblin, p. 73; Zosa Szajkowski, "Dos Yidishe Gezelshaftlikhe Leybn in Pariz tsum yor 1939," in *Yidn in Frankraykh*, ed. A. Tcherikover, vol. 2 (New York: YIVO, 1942), p. 244; HICEM, *Dix années d'émigration juive (1926–1936): Rapport présenté à la Conférence d'émigration juive les 20 juin–1 juillet 1936* (Paris: HICEM, n.d.), p. 52, in the section on France.

Because of the transient nature of their stay in Paris, German Jews never succeeded in establishing firm roots in the Paris Jewish community. I have therefore chosen to deal with German Jews in the capital only as they interacted with the more established members of the community. German refugees published a daily German-language newspaper, the *Pariser Tageblatt*, in Paris in the 1930s, and it remains a major source of information on their activities. For a discussion of German Jewish organizations in Paris in the 1930s, see *La Terre retrouvée*, March 23, 1936.

The lack of official statistics on Jewish immigration to Paris has led researchers to attempt a number of rather imaginative though not always successful methods of determining the immigrant population. For discussions of methods and problems in immigrant demography, see the following works: *Les Etrangers de religion juive en France*, a document edited by a "specialist" under the auspices of the *Centre d'études de Lyon* (Lyon: Centre d'études de Lyon, 1942), p. 5; Yaakov Yisroel Fink, "Bamivkhan," *Yahaduth Tzarfath* (Paris: Machberoth, 1951), p. 57; Charlotte Roland, *Du Ghetto à l'Occident: Deux générations yiddiches en France* (Paris: Editions de Minuit, 1962), pp. 37–38; Zosa Szajkowski, *The Growth of the Jewish Population of France* (New York: Conference on Jewish Relations, 1946), pp. 179, 297; and Roger Berg, "Juifs de Paris," *La Terre retrouvée*, February 15, 1948.

13. Roblin, p. 73. Arthur Ruppin, *The Jews in the Modern World* (London: Macmillan, 1934), p. 60.

14. Roblin claims that there were some 80,000 "Slavic" Jews in Paris in 1939 (Roblin, p. 89). Ruppin concludes that there were about 100,000 eastern European Jewish immigrants who came to France between 1880 and 1930 (Ruppin, p. 62).

It must be pointed out that the figure of 90,000 refers only to immigrant Jews who had settled in Paris and does not include the large floating population of refugees— numbering as many as 40,000—who remained in Paris for only a short while.

15. For detailed figures on the national origins of Jewish immigrants in France, see the various sections on eastern European countries in HICEM, *Dix années d'émigration juive*. The study of national origins of Jewish immigrants is complicated by the fact that many immigrants did not come directly from their country of birth. A study by M. Dobin in 1932, for example, revealed that of 15,000 Jewish immigrant workers and artisans registered at a labor bureau, over 4,000 had first settled in another country before arriving in France (M. Dobin, "Yidishe Immigrantn-Arbeter in Pariz," *YIVO Bleter*, January–May 1932, p. 395).

16. Roblin claims that the percentage of Alsatian Jews in the Paris Jewish community decreased from 90 percent in 1880 to 15 percent in 1940 (Roblin, p. 137). The figures are highly dramatic but undoubtedly wrong. My calculations place the number of native Jews in 1940 at about 30 percent.

For a discussion of the birthrate among Jews in Europe in the 1930s, see L. Hersh, "Yidishe Démografie," in *Algemayne Entsiklopedie: Yidn*, vol. 1 (Paris: Dubnow Fund, 1939), pp. 351–52, 379–80.

17. Roblin, p. 68.

18. The influx of Algerian Jews into the Consistoire was so great toward the end of the nineteenth century that the religious body was led to set aside its then newly built synagogue on rue Buffault for the observance of Sephardic ritual.

19. Various philanthropic organizations were also created during this period, but they soon became faithful members of the Fédération des sociétés juives de France, the largest eastern European immigrant organization in Paris. The same may be said for the Sephardic youth groups and veterans' organizations founded in the 1930s.

Because of their fragmented social organization and their small numbers in the prewar period, Sephardic Jews will be treated in the study only as they related to the larger native and eastern European immigrant organizations. For studies of the Sephardic community in Paris in the 1930s, see the articles in *La Terre retrouvée* (April 25, 1936) and *L'Univers israélite* (May 4, 1934).

20. The figures are taken from an examination of the burial records found under the rubric NN-*Inhumations* in the archives of the *Association consistoriale israélite de Paris*, henceforth to be referred to in the footnotes as ACIP.

21. The origin of the name *Pletzl* is unknown, although it probably is a diminutive name for the Place Hospitaliers–Saint-Gervais, a street corner in the Jewish area formed by the intersection of rue des Rosiers and rue des Hospitaliers–Saint-Gervais.

The immigrant areas of settlement in the 1930s presented a grim picture of poverty and disease. Arnold Mandel, in his novel *Les Temps incertains* (Paris: Calmann-Lévy, 1950), p. 35, graphically captures the miserable living conditions of newly arrived immigrants in Belleville: "Seas of putrescent water, urine heated in the flaming sun, stagnate in the narrow courtyards. Up above, women sew silently in rooms, while tubercular humorists press pants."

The impoverishment of immigrants is also reflected in the fact that in 1935, 7 percent of the inhabitants of the "Pletzl" were said to be tubercular (figure cited in *Naie Presse*, April 30, 1935).

22. A satirical article in *Hebdo-Pariz* on April 12, 1935, commented upon the relationship between geographical settlements and social standing among Paris Jews. In Paris, the article noted, things are the reverse of what happens in a *beth midrash* (house of learning): the common people sit on the east side while the rich sit on the

west. (It was traditional in synagogues and houses of learning in eastern Europe for the eastern portion, closest to Jerusalem, to be reserved for rich Jews.)

For a discussion of Jewish settlement by *arrondissement* as reflected in the unreliable Nazi census of 1941, see Roblin, p. 81, and Joseph Klatzmann, *Le Travail à domicile dans l'industrie parisienne du vêtement* (Paris: Imprimerie Nationale, 1957), pp. 89–91.

2   Professions

A study of the professions of Parisian Jews in the 1930s reveals that, as a general rule, the earlier an individual arrived in the capital, the higher his social status.[1] This is most clearly seen when one compares the statistics on native Jews (in large part comprised of descendants of earlier immigrants from Alsace and Lorraine) with those on eastern European immigrants. Almost 50 percent of all native Jews in Paris in the 1930s were engaged in large-scale commerce as commercial representatives, commission agents, and wholesalers. Natives also made up over 75 percent of the Jewish bankers of Paris. In contrast, no more than 15 to 20 percent of the immigrant population was involved in commerce, and over half of those—8,000 in 1938—barely eked out livings as peddlers of second-hand goods. Twenty percent of the native Jews were engaged in industry, largely in ownership or managerial capacities in the textile, jewelry, and precision machinery trades. All in all, the native population provided only 5 percent of the Jewish labor force, the major proportion of workers coming instead from the immigrant populace. Thus, of the 60 percent of eastern European Jews engaged in either industry or artisan trades, over 83 percent—some 50,000— were employed as workers in *ateliers* or as home laborers in the garment and textile trades. Similarly, while only 8 percent of immigrant Jews were to be found in the liberal professions, the figure for native Jews stood at 25 percent and included 60 percent of the Jewish lawyers, 25 percent of the Jewish dentists, 30 percent of the Jewish doctors, and 75 percent of the Jewish educators.[2]

By far the most marked social divisions among the various elements in the Paris Jewish community in the 1930s were to be found in the fields of commerce and industry. At the top of the Jewish social hierarchy stood the wealthiest members of the community, the bankers and financiers. Only a few of the large Jewish banking families that had attained wealth and influence in the nineteenth century were still active in French economic life in the

1930s. Of the three major families—Fould, Pereire, and Roth-schild—only the latter maintained close ties with Paris Jewish communal life. Members of established banking houses had been joined in the mid-nineteenth century by wealthy Alsatian and German Jews who achieved financial and commercial prominence during the economic boom of the 1850s and 1860s. Although many of these *parvenus* had disappeared from French economic life by the 1930s, influential families such as the Dreyfusses and the Bischoff-sheims survived to play important roles in Parisian commerce as well as in the Jewish community.

Despite the preponderance of commercial wealth among the "notables" in the community, a growing number of Jewish indus-trialists were beginning to make their mark in French heavy manufacture after World War I. Second- and third-generation Frenchmen, often converted or assimilated into Paris bourgeois society, they generally avoided affiliation with the organized Jewish community and its more traditional social elite. Those who chose to publicly identify themselves as Jewish, such as the Deutsch de Meurthes, with their substantial oil and aeronautical interests, tended to retain family business as well as religious ties and thus were more easily accepted by the established financial and commer-cial leadership of the community.

A rung lower on the social scale stood a small but significant group of native Jews engaged as financial consultants, agents, and stock brokers. Less financially secure than the bankers and finan-ciers, this stratum saw a continual influx and outflow of French Jews on their way up or down the economic ladder. By far the most numerous element among native *commerçants* were merchants and wholesalers supplying raw material and machines or distributing finished products. Merchants of cloth and textiles were particularly numerous, and native dry goods stores could be found scattered throughout the central and eastern sections of Paris. Similarly, native-owned stores selling fine jewelry, wearing apparel, and leather goods were prominent along the *grands boulevards* of the capital. A few French Jews were also involved in the department store chains that were beginning to develop in Paris in the period before World War II.[3] Still others managed hotels, restaurants, and cafes in the areas of Jewish settlement.[4]

Many of the older immigrants from Russia and eastern Europe who had settled in Paris on the eve of World War I had been petty merchants and peddlers in their homelands. Upon their arrival in

the French capital they often set up store in the Jewish neighborhoods to service the needs of the growing immigrant community. In
time, many were able to join French Jews as *commerçants* in the
textile and garment trades. As the immigrant community expanded,
so did the opportunities for commercial exploitation. By the 1930s
these early eastern European immigrants were to be found in almost
every aspect of commerce from antiques to travel agencies. In
contrast to native merchants, however, older eastern European
immigrants tended to restrict their business ventures to the immigrant community. Although often financially successful, few of them
dared to compete with French concerns servicing the Paris populace
as a whole. Wealthy enough to assume community responsibility yet
not established enough to acquire full respectability within the
native community, older immigrants often occupied middle-echelon
positions in the Consistoire and the Alliance.

Unlike older immigrants, eastern Europeans who arrived in the
1920s and 1930s and became engaged in commerce were generally
forced to do so because of the economic crisis in France in the 1930s.
Arriving without ready capital, unable to speak the language, and
unsuccessful in obtaining employment, many eked out livings by
buying secondhand goods, repairing them, and then selling the
finished products at the open markets of Paris.

The plight of these secondhand peddlers or *brocanteurs* had been
described by Joseph Klatzmann in his excellent work on home-
laborers in the Paris clothing trade.[5] Arriving at the market place
with a small suitcase of old clothes, housewares, and trinkets, the
immigrant peddler would have to wait patiently until an empty place
became available. If he were not a frequent seller at the particular
market, he would have to bribe officials to gain a place. Forced to
stand long hours in the rain and cold, he often experienced days in
which he sold nothing at all. His problems were compounded by the
existence of itinerant peddlers who brought goods into local areas
and by older immigrants who, arriving under more favorable
economic conditions, had managed to establish stores in local
neighborhoods.

The existence of differing waves of immigration thus tended to
create social divisions among eastern Europeans themselves. Nowhere was this more evident than in the so-called "Jewish" trades—
textile and clothing. Although Alsatian Jews were actively involved
in the commercial aspects of the "Jewish" trades as suppliers of raw
material and distributors of the finished products, most of the

patrons (employers) and shopkeepers were Russian and Polish Jews who had arrived in Paris in the late nineteenth and early twentieth centuries. Artisans and petty merchants in the "Old Country," these Jews quickly established small *ateliers* and shops in the French capital.[6] Blessed with favorable economic conditions after World War I, they were instrumental in the development of the clothing and textile trades. In the early twenties, they were joined by other Polish Jews who were especially active in the tailoring, hat making, and leather trades. Thriving on cheap labor supplied by new immigrants eager for work, these early immigrants from eastern Europe rose quickly on the social and economic scale. Small *ateliers* grew into factories; small shops into *maisons de couture* (fashion houses). By the mid-twenties, Russian and Polish Jews comprised over half of all the *patrons* in the clothing and textile trades.[7]

The eastern European immigrant who came to Paris in the late twenties and early thirties thus found "Jewish" trades only too willing to employ him. Yet many of the new arrivals, having left jobs in large urban industries, did not wish to engage in what they regarded as "regressive" labor.[8] Instead, they sought employment in the mines of the Nord and in factories in the larger cities, thereby hoping to join together with French workers. In many cases, Jewish immigrants were hired while still in eastern Europe by agents of French industrialists sent to contract laborers in a period of extreme labor shortage. Immigrants also benefited from agreements entered into by the French government that facilitated the hiring of foreigners. The economic crisis of the late twenties and early thirties, marked by large-scale unemployment and scarcity of jobs, put an end to the dreams of these would-be "Jewish proletarians" and forced them into the "Jewish" trades as home-laborers.[9]

The plight of the home-laborer or *façonnier* is the distinguishing characteristic of the Paris "Jewish" trades in the 1930s. Of the more than 50,000 immigrant Jews in the clothing and textile trades, only about 22,500 were actually employed as wage earners in *ateliers*. Most of the work was done by the more than 10,500 home-laborers whose seemingly independent existence belied a vicious and cruel exploitation.[10]

The unwilling transformation of the newly arrived immigrant into a home-laborer stemmed from two interrelated factors: the need to work and the inability to procure it legally. Unlike the more prosperous Jews who had arrived before World War I, the immigrant arriving in the late twenties and early thirties generally had to

viduals, it was difficult to differentiate between worker
, and *patron* and home-laborer. True, a tripartite
ween natives, older immigrants, and newer immigrants
scerned, but the lines separating the three groups were
igid by the opportunities for advancement provided by an
economy. It is only in the early thirties, when jobs became
the rights of immigrants were severely curtailed, that we
rst real signs of class consciousness in the clothing and
es. But the crucial role of the *façonnier* in the production
role accentuated in the 1930s, leads one to the conclusion
Jewish" trades, as much of the French economy during
d, were more relics of a preindustrial past than harbingers
n industrialism.[20]

rom the clothing and textile trades, eastern European Jews
o be found in a number of small crafts concentrated in the
eas of settlement in Paris. In particular, mention should be
the jewelry and watch trades, the former employing some
ws, the latter about 200.[21] As in the clothing trade, the basic
in both trades was made by newer immigrants (in the rue de
area near the "Pletzl"), sold in bulk by older immigrants
rue Cadet, an area of early eastern European Jewish
nt), and finally sold to the general public by natives (on the
a Paix off the *grands boulevards*).

her trade concentrated in Jewish areas was furniture making.
ubourg Saint-Antoine quarter near the Bastille, for example,
ed several hundred furniture factories employing over 2,500
workers. Unlike immigrant Jews in other trades, however,
urniture workers were older immigrants who had acquired
kills only after having come to Paris. Eastern European Jews
lso active in the sale of furniture, comprising 75 percent of all
s in Paris.[22] Many immigrants in the trade made large
es buying old furniture, reworking and varnishing it, and then
g the refurbished product to rich American tourists as genuine
es!

e social divisions among Parisian Jews in the 1930s meant that
were actually two Jewish communities. One community,
ring around the natives and some older immigrants from
ia and Poland, consisted mainly of *haut* and *moyen bourgeois*
engaged in large-scale commerce and industry. The other,
e up of eastern European immigrants, was largely *petit bour-*
s in make up, consisting mainly of artisans and workers em-

borrow extensively from friends in order to pay for his transportation to Paris. Having left his family behind, he immediately sought to obtain money for their passage. Aside from family concerns, he had to have a certain amount of money on hand so as not to be arrested as a *clochard*. If he swallowed his pride, he may have gone to the various Jewish organizations established by native Jews to deal with the massive influx of impoverished immigrants. But as the history of these organizations attests, officials generally advised newly arrived immigrants to leave the country, in some cases even offering to pay the cost of their transportation.[11]

In his search for employment, the newly arrived immigrant faced formidable obstacles. Ignorant of French and of Parisian life in general, he found it difficult to go out and find work himself. Arriving in the midst of great unemployment, he could hardly expect to find a well-paying and secure job. Even if he were fortunate enough to find employment, he would still have to obtain an identity card and a work permit from unsympathetic government authorities. Without these documents, he could not venture freely into the street, for he feared arrest and subsequent expulsion as an undesirable alien. If he finally did manage to secure a work permit, he ran the risk of being fired and replaced by an "illegal" immigrant only too eager to work for lower wages.

By far the most formidable obstacle which the immigrant in Paris faced in the 1930s was the myriad of regulations and restrictions imposed by the French government on alien labor. The history of antiforeigner legislation in France is an involved one and cannot be explained in detail within the limitations of the study. Although there were various restrictions on the naturalization of aliens in the late twenties and early thirties, it was not until the end of 1934 and the beginning of 1935 that the first law affecting already settled immigrants was enacted. These decrees, issued under the regime of Pierre Laval, placed quotas on the employment of aliens in certain trades and generally made it difficult for immigrants who had not yet secured citizenship to secure employment.[12] In October 1935 further restrictions were placed upon aliens seeking to establish new businesses, and government officials were given the right to refuse readmission to any alien who had left France. Immigrants were given a brief reprieve by the laws passed under Léon Blum's Popular Front government in October 1936 which effectively reversed the Laval decrees. The fall of Blum's government in July 1937, however, brought a reenactment of restrictive legislation culminating in the notorious antiforeigner laws passed after Munich in November 1938. Although the French government did not expressly forbid refugees from entering the country until 1939, its policy of restrictive legislation made it impossible for them to remain. It is no wonder, then, that one observer compared the immigrant's life in the 1930s to that of a man "bicycling on butter."[13]

What seemed endless misery to the newly arrived immigrant proved a boon for older immigrant *patrons* in the clothing and textile trades. The mass of immigrants desperately in need of employment yet unable to procure it legally served as a ready supply of cheap labor for unscrupulous employers. In hiring an immigrant without a work permit, the *patron* only ran the risk of a small fine which was compensated by the low wages he paid out. Under the putting-out system, the *façonnier* worked in the privacy of his home through an unofficial agreement with the employer. Thus he could not be traced easily by government authorities in search of "illegal" laborers. Subject only to a verbal agreement, he was not covered by government regulations pertaining to working conditions or wages. Nor would he dare voice his grievances, for he feared being replaced or being turned over to the police. For the employer the use of *façonniers* also meant the elimination of workers and often of *ateliers* themselves. Why continue paying rent and upkeep for *ateliers*, he reasoned, when by establishing a putting-out system one could do away with them completely?

And what of the home laborer's living and working conditions? Forced to live on subsistence pay, his home and his place of work generally was a single room in one of the ramshackle hotels of Belleville.[14] Because of the size of the machines he used, he barely had room to cook or to sleep. Rare was the room that had adequate closet space, fresh air, and running water. Unencumbered by working-hour limitations and paid poorly for the material he made, he often spent days and nights working over his machine. The cramped quarters, the poor lighting, the feverish attempt to produce as much as possible in the shortest amount of time led to countless accidents and numerous deaths.[15] Even during peak periods, the *façonnier* was forced to take on other jobs in order to survive.[16] At other times of the year, he had no work at all. Uncovered by state regulations, he could not receive unemployment benefits. When he did manage to find work during these so-called "dead seasons," he was accused of conspiring with employers against workers.

Despite the blatant exploitation of home laborers by *patrons*,

attempts to organize *façonnier*
being identified as an "illegal" l
join any groups. Afraid of losing t
had little interest in demanding
conditions. When strikes involving
in June 1936, they petered out r
went to work for other *patrons* rath
were replaced by other immigrants

By far the most important factor
home laborers was the complexity
"Jewish" trades. In actual fact, tl
laborers. One type, the so-called *ou*
material he used but depended only
assist him in his work. Most immigr
this category. A second type, the *entr*
material he worked on but did employ
The *façonnier* thus represented a so
patron and worker. Although more
unionized worker, he never lost hope
own *atelier*. Caught between the conflic
worker, he could never clearly define his

Workers in *ateliers* were no less aff
relationships. Jewish activists on the Left
class hostility that supposedly existed betw
in the "Jewish" trades. Yet many wor
hoped to become *patrons* themselves some
to save enough money eventually did set
Those that did not often worked side by s
partners in production if not in manag
employer and worker banded together in s
large *maisons de couture* that placed order
the atmosphere of a small shop, social
between worker and employer. Similar back
overrode conflicts of class. Immigrant wom
portion of the working contingent, were par
ideas of *klal yisroel*—the notion that Jews are
past tradition and history.[19]

In the end, the confusion of working relatio
trades stemmed mainly from their artisan
situation where management, production, a
often in the hands of one individual or a sma

skilled indi
and *patro*
division be
could be d
made less
expanding
scarce and
find the f
textile tra
process, a
that the
this perio
of moder

Aside
could als
Jewish ar
made of
1,000 Je
product
Temple
(on the
settlem
rue de

Anot
The Fa
contair
Jewish
most f
their s
were a
dealer
fortur
sellin
antiq

Th
there
cente
Russ
Jews
mad
geo

ployed in the "Jewish" trades. With the exception of the more politically militant natives and immigrants, however, most Jews did not see the conflict between the two communities in economic terms. Even those who sought to apply a Marxian analysis to the conflict were forced to confront the anomalous social structure of Paris Jewry which, with its large number of middle-class *entrepreneurs* and artisans and relatively few workers, resembled an inverted rather than the upright pyramid typical of industrialized societies. At most, natives feared that the concentration of immigrants into a small number of trades would only help to increase anti-Semitism in France while immigrants demanded that natives make use of their elevated social status to influence government officials to aid refugees fleeing from Nazism. In the end, though, the division that existed between natives and immigrants centered less around conflicts of economic interest than around differing attitudes toward Jewish identity and the appropriate Jewish response to the Nazi threat.

Notes

1. The major exception to this rule were the German Jewish refugees fleeing Nazi persecution in the 1930s, of whom two-thirds had either been engaged in academic professions or owned businesses of their own in their native country (figure taken from C. L. Lang, "Second Start in France," in *Dispersion and Resettlement* [London: Association of Jewish Refugees in Great Britain, 1955], p. 21). The severe economic crisis facing France during this period forced many of them to take menial jobs upon their arrival in Paris.

2. The figures on native Jews are taken from Roblin, pp. 136–38; and A. Menes, "Yidn in Frankraykh," *Yivo Bleter*, January–May 1937, p. 350. The figures on immigrant professions are extrapolated from the conflicting reports in Roblin, pp. 102–3; *Almanach juif, 1931*, ed. La Colonie Scolaire (Paris: La Nouvelle Generation, 193?), pp. 24, 31; and Menes, "Yidn in Frankraykh," p. 348.

The statistics on Jewish peddlers are taken from an article in *Naie Presse*, June 14, 1938.

In studying professions, one should not overlook the 5,000 to 10,000 immigrant Jewish students in Paris during this period. For discussions of Jewish students, see *L'Univers israélite*, December 30, 1932, June 9, 1933; and *Naie Presse*, October 31, 1934.

3. Probably the most important Jewish-owned department store in the 1930s was Galeries LaFayette, which is still one of the largest retail outlets in Paris.

4. A typical example of a Jewish *commerçant* active in the Consistoire was Léon Edinger, the president of the administrative commission for all of the consistorial synagogues. A Chevalier of the *Légion d'honneur*, Edinger was the head of an important commercial firm and the president of the *Chambre syndicale du commerce et de la nouveauté*. As "an active and committed 'israélite,' heir to pious family

traditions," he was responsible for the administration of the rue de la Victoire synagogue, president of the mutual-aid society, *Les Enfants de Sion*, and treasurer of the *Union des sociétés israélites de secours mutuels*, a loose federation of mutual-aid societies affiliated with the Consistoire. (Information taken from an article in *L'Univers israélite*, December 30, 1932.)

5. Klatzmann, p. 122.

6. According to Léon Berman in his *Histoire des juifs de France des origines à nos jours* (Paris: Librairie Lipschutz, 1937), p. 477, most of the Russian Jews who came to Paris after 1880 were hatters and tailors by profession.

7. Georges Mauco, *Les Etrangers en France* (Paris: Librairie Armand Colin, 1932), p. 300.

8. A study conducted by Charlotte Roland among immigrants in Belleville in 1960 reveals that those arriving in the capital after World War I tended to come from large urban centers, while those arriving before the war came largely from small villages and towns (Roland, pp. 218–19). This difference in place of origin explains not only the penchant of newer immigrants for factory employment but also their distaste for those aspects of Jewish life in Paris that smacked of the *shtetl*, or small eastern European town—*landsmanshaftn, shuls* (small synagogues), burial societies, and so forth.

9. A series of reports issued by the *Oeuvre d'assistance par le travail aux immigrants juifs*, a native-run relief organization in Paris in the 1920s and 1930s, reflects the plight of the new immigrants. In a report covering its activity between October 1926 and October 1927, the Oeuvre noted that of 865 immigrants applying for employment, 294 were placed in the metal, electrical, and construction industries while only 92 were placed in the clothing trades. Among so-called "specialists," 33.7 percent were hired in the heavy industries while only 10.6 percent found employment in the "Jewish" trades. Already in 1930, however, there were signs of an impending change. Thus placement in the provinces in 1930, where many of the openings in heavy industry were to be found, was way down. In Paris itself, 35 immigrants were hired in the metal industry, 15 in construction, and 44 in the clothing trades. The report covering the period between January and March 1933 reflects the drop in available positions in heavy industry and the subsequent shift to the "Jewish" trades. Thus, within Paris, the organization was able to place only 5 in construction, 20 in metals, and 32 in the clothing trades. (All of the reports are to be found in the YIVO Archives: Yidn in Frankraykh—Plitim, migratsie, hilf organizatsies.)

10. An extrapolation of figures cited in Roblin, p. 104, and statistics presented at the Jewish Pavillion of the 1937 International Exposition held in Paris as reported in *Naie Presse*, August 15, 1937, and *La Terre retrouvée*, October 1, 1937.

11. In her book, Charlotte Roland notes that only 28 percent of first-generation immigrants interviewed went to Jewish charitable organizations upon arriving in Paris. Almost all of them claimed that they were politely but firmly told to leave the country. (Roland, p. 232.)

12. The antiforeigner legislation, particularly those laws directed against immigrants entering illegally and immigrant artisans, also precluded any hope eastern European Jews may have had of eventual naturalization. In the period between 1928 and 1938 naturalizations of all foreigners decreased by more than half, while the percentage of Jews naturalized decreased by more than two-thirds. For detailed figures on Jewish naturalization, see *Les Etrangers de religion juive en France*, pp. 14–16.

13. *Naie Presse*, November 30, 1938.

14. A study conducted in 1930 by La Colonie Scolaire, a philanthropic organization run by older immigrants, revealed that it was not uncommon for an immigrant family of six to eight people to live in a single room (cited in *Almanach juif, 1931*, p. 10).

15. By far the most hazardous trade was *caoutchouc*, or rubber raincoat production. The extensive use of benzine and other noxious chemicals often resulted in severe burns, lung ailments, and even asphyxiation.

16. An extreme case of multiple employment was that of a *façonnier* cited in a study of professions of immigrant Jews in Paris published in 1932. Aside from his work at home in the evening, he also was employed as a secretary of a museum in the morning and a day-laborer in the afternoon. For a list of the most frequently found job combinations, see M. Dobin, "Di Profesies fun di yidishe immigrantn in Pariz," *YIVO Bleter*, August–December 1932, pp. 30–32, 36–37.

17. For an examination of the role of home-laborers in the clothing-trade strikes of June 1936, see Klatzmann, pp. 109–10.

18. For an example of such a strike action, see *Naie Presse*, September 3, 1935. The headline of the lead article, "Against the *Maisons* or Against the Workers?" reflected the dilemma facing many *entrepreneurs* in the "Jewish" trades.

19. For a discussion of the effect of *klal-yisroeldike* doctrines on female workers, see *Naie Presse*, February 27, 1934.

20. A strong case can be made for the argument that the conditions of Jewish workers and artisans were actually worse in Paris than they had been in eastern Europe. Although wages were undoubtedly lower in their homelands, Jewish artisans had been organized in strong professional unions and, as the example of newer immigrants showed, a significant Jewish proletariat was beginning to form with close ties to non-Jewish workers. In Paris, as we have seen, it was difficult to organize immigrant laborers, and the concentration of Jews into a few trades tended to isolate them into what one writer called "an economic ghetto of the Jewish masses" (*Naie Presse*, December 29, 1935).

The confusion of work roles in the clothing trades befuddled even serious scholars of the period. Jacob Lestschinsky, an eminent authority on the social and economic conditions of Jews, noted in his article on Jewish economic conditions published in the *Algemayne Entsiklopedie* in 1939 that there were 50,000 Jewish "proletarians" in France, a figure that undoubtedly included Jewish *façonniers* in the clothing and textile trades. See Jacob Lestschinsky, "Yidishe Ekonomik," in *Algemayne Entsiklopedie: Yidn*, vol. 1 (Paris: Dubnow Fund, 1939), p. 433.

21. *Naie Presse*, November 29, 1934.

22. *Naie Presse*, November 28, 1934.

3   Organizations

The social division between natives and immigrants was only one of many fissures within the Paris Jewish community in the 1930s. Unique among Jewish settlements on the European continent, the Paris community contained a sizable number of both western and eastern European Jews differing not only in national origin but also in attitudes toward Jewish identity and the appropriate response to Nazism. The variety of attitudes among Paris Jewry was reflected in the hundreds of Jewish organizations that existed in the French capital in the decade before the outbreak of World War II. Organizations within the community served not only as institutionalized structures for religious, cultural, social, and political identification but also as forums in which the basic ideological and tactical positions of natives and immigrants were thrashed out. In a period of crisis created by the onset of Nazism, Jewish organizations were also seen by their members as the cornerstones of a strengthened and united community which would most certainly be forced to mount a desperate defense in the very near future.

All told, over half of the Jewish population of Paris was affiliated with Jewish organizations.[1] Like the varied population it served, Jewish organizational life in the 1930s was a patchwork quilt of competing identities and solutions to the "Jewish question." Most organizations were without structure and name, *groupuscules* of Jews from the same city in eastern Europe who met socially in neighborhood cafes. Others, such as the myriad of protest movements that blossomed in the uncertain climate of the 1930s, were ad hoc committees created in response to particular problems arising within the community and were disbanded within months after their founding. Many groups barely merited the title Jewish, serving merely as social and recreational alternatives for Jews barred from membership in general clubs. A number of organizations such as the Consistoire and the Fédération, however, managed to achieve prominence and respectability within and without the community. Tightly structured, transcending special interest, and openly Jewish in their concerns, they grew in time to become the quasi-official spokesmen of the major segments of the Paris Jewish population.

On the whole, native Jews did not look favorably on the maintenance of specifically Jewish organizations. For many, the stigma attached to Jewish identification could only hinder their attempts at integration into the larger French community. Assimilants, they viewed the proclamation of Jewish emancipation in 1791 as not only granting equal rights but also marking the end of the notion of a Jewish community and of particular Jewish institutions. Even those native Jews who continued to practice their faith could not easily reconcile the individualistic spirit which they associated with French life with the communal separateness represented by organizations such as the Consistoire de Paris. If Judaism were merely a question of personal belief having little effect upon one's participation in French society, many reasoned, why the necessity for an organization banding together Jews?

Leaders of the Consistoire de Paris were only too well aware of the dilemma facing native Jews. In its statements, the central religious body of the native community placed special emphasis upon its limited role. As a result of the laws of separation of 1905 and 1906, the *Association consistoriale israélite de Paris*, in its capacity as a member of the *Consistoire central israélite de France*, was reclassified as a religious association (*association cultuelle*) and was restricted in its activities to those matters pertaining to Jewish religious practice. No longer the directing body of Parisian Jewry, the Consistoire de Paris, so its leaders argued, had become merely one of many religious organizations in Paris, providing only those services necessary for the continuance of the faith.

Despite its protestations, the Consistoire de Paris never had more than 6,000 members in the 1930s, a figure that represented barely one-fourth of native families in the French capital.[2] Consistorial efforts to broaden its membership base were hindered by its traditional association with affluent Jews. The restriction of voting to the wealthy, typical of consistorial policy in the nineteenth century, had long since given way to open membership, but the high membership fee assured that recruitment would be mainly from the upper echelons of the Paris Jewish community. Although financial exigency and the necessity to compete with other Jewish organizations vying for dominance in the interwar years led to acceptance of a significant number of older immigrants into the religious body, the Consistoire in the 1930s continued to be controlled by wealthy Alsatian Jews.[3]

Of the many wealthy Jews who helped to forge Consistoire policy, special mention should be made of the Rothschilds. Throughout most of 125 years, the religious body had been led by a member of this banking family who often single-handedly assured its financial solvency and administrative efficiency. Alphonse de Rothschild, the eldest son of Jacob or James de Rothschild, who helped to establish the family's financial empire in Paris in the early nineteenth century, was president of the Consistoire central de France from 1871 to 1905. His brother Gustave was largely responsible for the creation of the Association consistoriale israélite de Paris in 1905 and served as president of that organization until his death in 1911. The third of James's sons, Edmond, was by far the most active Rothschild president of the religious body, not only responsible for the building of a number of important synagogues and *oratoires* in the capital to cater to newly arriving immigrants but also a major force in the establishment of Jewish settlements in Palestine in the first two decades of the twentieth century. Upon his death in 1934 he was succeeded by his son Robert who played a crucial role in the formation of Consistoire policy in the 1930s. Rothschild wives were also very active in consistorial functions, often serving as *patronesses* of charitable organizations and chairwomen of fund-raising drives. The "Rothschildization of French Judaism" was the way one Jewish writer described the role of the banking family in the French Jewish community of the mid-nineteenth century.[4] Almost one hundred years later, Rothschild influence within the native Jewish community of Paris remained undiminished.

Because of the elevated social position of many of its members, the Consistoire de Paris was generally viewed by French government leaders as the quasi-official spokesman for the Paris Jewish community. The dominant role of Paris Jewry in French Jewish life and the fact that the administrative and institutional structures of the Consistoire central and its Paris affiliate were closely intertwined (they shared the same office building on the rue de la Victoire, for example), meant that in many cases the Consistoire de Paris spoke for French Jewry as well. Cordial relations between the French government and the Consistoire de Paris had been established during World War I when Parisian rabbis delegated by the Consistoire central were asked to serve on government advisory boards along with priests and pastors in a gesture to the *union spirituelle* of France in its moment of crisis. Throughout the 1930s consistorial representatives were consulted by the various government agencies dealing with the refugee problem. Similarly, it was expected that Consistoire officials would frequently intervene with French political leaders on matters concerning the Jewish community. In the Paris community at large, Consistoire leaders spoke at meetings as representatives of Parisian Jewry, while consistorial synagogues hosted interfaith religious services. Although not an official organ of the Consistoire, *L'Univers israélite* was avidly read by Jew and non-Jew alike as a gauge of Jewish reactions to current events.[5]

Within the Paris community itself, the religious body maintained a complex network of institutions and organizations to serve the needs of both members and nonmembers. As an *association cultuelle*, it presided over the functioning of some twenty-two houses of worship including three synagogues erected before 1880, several *temples* servicing the religious needs of native Jews in the newer areas of settlement in the western portions of Paris, and a number of *oratoires* catering to recently arrived immigrants. In addition, the organization maintained a *beth din* or Jewish law court which relied upon Biblical and Talmudic law to pass judgment on religious matters such as marriage, divorce, and conversion. The Consistoire was also responsible for keeping a watchful eye on thirty-three kosher butchers in Paris and on the various kosher slaughterhouses established outside of Paris to serve the community. In an average year in the 1930s Consistoire rabbis officiated at some 800 funerals and 400 marriages, many of which involved Jews not affiliated with the religious body.[6] Although the Consistoire had no legal authority to compel Jews to follow the rulings of its various subsidiary organizations, the wide range of its religious activities alone attests to its position in the community as something more than an *association cultuelle*.

But the Consistoire's activities were not confined to community religious life. Aside from its political involvement with the French government, the religious body also played an active role in the cultural and social life of Paris Jews, which assured it of an influence that went beyond the limited number of practicing Jews. At its high point, the Consistoire in the 1930s ran forty-three schools with a combined enrollment of 1,300 students.[7] Other educational activities included the maintenance of three Jewish day schools, a rabbinical seminary, a school for young girls, two dormitories for

Jewish students, a vocational school, and various foundations granting scholarships to deserving native Jewish students.[8] A primitive
social service system was also provided by a number of loosely
affiliated mutual-aid societies whose main purpose was to secure
burial plots in Paris cemeteries for their members. Most social
service organizations affiliated with the Consistoire, however, were
charitable institutions run by members' wives and catered to the
needs of newer immigrants.[9] Although as much as 80 percent of the
Consistoire's budget was earmarked for aid to immigrants, the
association's purpose was not solely humanitarian. In most cases,
grants-in-aid carried with them a severe warning concerning the
"proper" attitudes that newly arrived Jews should have toward their
host country.[10]

Despite its varied activities, not all practicing native Jews in Paris
chose to affiliate with the Consistoire. The *Union libérale israélite*,
created at the end of the nineteenth century, recruited its members
from the richer and more assimilated Jews in the western sections of
Paris. Far less traditional than the Consistoire, it drew much of its
liturgy from the German Reform movement. At the other extreme
stood the *Communauté israélite de la stricte observance* which, as its
name implied, took a dim view of even the minor changes that the
Consistoire had instituted in its religious service. Largely composed
of Alsatian Jews, it carried on the religious practices of Ashkenazic
communities in Alsace and western Germany at the end of the
eighteenth century.

French Jewry, as much of western European Jewry, rejected the
notion of separate Jewish political organizations. As we shall see, its
definition of Jewish identity precluded any intermingling of Jewish
concerns with contemporary political questions in France. Though
natives were to be found in small numbers on both the extreme
Right and Left of the French political spectrum,[11] it appears that
most French Jews who affiliated with political parties were drawn
toward the *Parti radical-socialiste*. Its frequent appeals to the ideals
of the French Revolution and its moderate stands on social and
economic issues found ready acceptance among the largely bourgeois
native community which traced its origins to the proclamation of
Jewish emancipation issued on September 27, 1791.[12]

Nevertheless, the turmoil of the early 1930s in France led to the
creation of a number of native Jewish political organizations. By far
the most important was the *Ligue internationale contre l'antisémitisme* or LICA as it was generally called. Originally established in

February 1928, LICA was not actually a Jewish organization, but its activities in defense of Jews persecuted in eastern Europe assured it of a large Jewish following. The organization found particular support among French Jewish youth, who came in droves to its meetings to hear Bernard Lecache, LICA's fiery and youthful leader. Native youths were also attracted by the organization's emphasis on direct confrontation with anti-Semites, a policy which often led to scuffles between LICA supporters and Fascist bands on the streets of Paris. The militant nature of the organization's activity and its willingness to make alliances with left-wing groups against Fascism caused great concern among adult natives and led to the creation of a number of religiously oriented youth groups under the auspices of the Consistoire de Paris.[13]

The *Union patriotique des Français israélites* was an organization established in June 1934 in response to the outburst of antiforeigner feeling after the Stavisky Affair. Appealing largely to the assimilated Jews of Paris (many of its members were also members of the Union libérale israélite), the organization sought to dispel any notion that there was a "Jewish question" in France. Taking much of its rhetoric from groups like the *Croix de Feu*, the Union patriotique stressed national unity and patriotic devotion to France. Although the Consistoire expressed great interest in the organization when it was first created, the Union patriotique was largely discredited as a result of its decision banning immigrants from membership in December 1934. Even at its high point in the period before the victory of the Popular Front, the organization played a largely negative role in opposition to left-wing Jewish groups and never achieved a membership of more than 1,500.[14]

One of the main thrusts of the Union patriotique was its emphasis upon Jewish participation in the French army during World War I. The period of the 1920s saw the establishment of a number of veterans' organizations among both native and older eastern European elements. By the 1930s there were two organizations consisting solely of eastern Europeans who had volunteered upon their arrival in Paris, two for Alsatian and Sephardic Jews, one combining both native and immigrant veterans, one of Polish veterans, and one for veterans of various Allied armies.[15] In the 1920s most of these groups restricted their activities to social get-togethers, participation in patriotic parades and ceremonies, and social services for members and their families. With the rise of Nazism, however, veterans' organizations assumed a more political role as participants in the various Jewish protest actions organized by the community and in the mass demonstrations typical of the Popular Front era. The crowning achievement of these groups was the International Congress of Veterans of World War I held in Paris in 1935 and attracting delegates representing over 450,000 Jewish former combatants throughout the world.[16]

No survey of native organizations would be complete without mention of the *Alliance israélite universelle*. Created in the mid-nineteenth century in response to persecutions against Jews in North Africa and the Middle East, the Alliance's main interests generally lay beyond the borders of France. The development of the Jewish refugee problem in France in the 1930s, however, redirected its concern, and the decisions of the Alliance during this period had a great bearing on the native reaction to the Nazi threat. Similarly, Alliance leaders often represented Paris Jewry at the various international Jewish conferences held throughout the 1930s. By and large, membership in the Alliance and the Consistoire overlapped in the 1930s, and the two native organizations were generally in agreement on major issues.[17]

Jewish communal life in eastern Europe had centered around the synagogue. In the sheltered environment of the *shtetl*, religious beliefs and practices shaped every facet of life. It is not surprising, therefore, that the synagogue was one of the first institutions established by immigrants upon their arrival in Paris. As we have seen, the Consistoire had established storefront *oratoires* to serve the religious needs of newly arrived immigrants. With the exception of older Russian and Polish immigrants who saw membership in consistorial synagogues as an easy means of access to French society, however, most immigrants chose to set up their own houses of worship with a liturgy that reflected their own religious traditions. By the 1930s there were hundreds of little synagogues, or *shuls*, each carrying on the particular religious practices of the areas from which its members came.[18] In opposition to both the Consistoire and rival immigrant religious groups, each *shul* established its own *beth din*, *kashruth* commission, and religious school system. Although some attempts were made by the Consistoire to establish a federation of all Jewish religious groups in Paris, most of the traditional immigrant congregations were unwavering in their opposition, fearing eventual absorption by the native organization and the subsequent loss of the right to practice their particular religious traditions.

Another institution that was established by immigrants upon their arrival in Paris was the mutual-aid society or *landsmanshaft*. The first such society, *La Loi sacrée*, was created sometime in the first half of the nineteenth century by a small group of Polish Jews. Other groups followed in 1856, 1866, 1875, and 1880 although their activities were mainly limited to the arrangement of burials for deceased members. The influx of Russian immigrants at the end of the century led to a blossoming of new societies and a widening of their activity. No longer merely *khevre kadishn* (burial societies), these societies provided basic social services such as aid to the sick and unemployed, cultural programs, and legal advice. In 1920 most of the societies founded by early immigrants from eastern Europe were incorporated in the *Entr'aide fraternelle*, an organization created by the Consistoire de Paris to aid in the rapprochement between natives and early immigrants.[19]

The mutual-aid societies created by immigrants arriving from eastern Europe after World War I were similar to those founded by earlier immigrants. Like the latter, these groups provided social services to their members, including medical aid, charity, credit to those seeking to establish their own businesses, and funeral arrangements. Unlike older immigrants, however, eastern European Jews arriving after World War I generally refused to ally with the Consistoire. Unable to gain citizenship, and distrustful of native Jews, the newly arrived immigrant was forced to rely on his own mutual-aid society to provide those services which French society denied him or which he rejected outright in the name of Jewish separatism. Mutual-aid organizations thus functioned as all-encompassing institutions providing not only social services but also cultural, educational, and recreational activities for their members. Here an immigrant would see the familiar faces of former residents of his hometown or *landslayt* (hence the name *landsmanshaft*) and forget the many problems that he faced daily in confronting the strange and often hostile environment that was Paris. It was not surprising, therefore, that these societies attracted well over half of all eastern European Jews in Paris in the period before World War II.[20]

The variety of backgrounds of Jewish immigrants in Paris and the necessity that many felt to reestablish ties with the "Old Country" assured the rapid growth of *landsmanshaftn* and mutual-aid societies in the 1930s.[21] By 1939 there were said to be almost 200 such groups, each jealously guarding its independence against attempts at consolidation and unity. Nevertheless, in 1926 a loose federation of societies was constituted, the Fédération des sociétés juives de France, grouping together at various times between 50 and 90 societies.[22] Its goals as outlined by Fédération leaders in the 1930s were imaginative and far-reaching: "Coordinate the scattered efforts of groups and individuals; stimulate the adaptation of immigrant Jews to French life, while at the same time developing Jewish cultural activities; serve as the representative body of the immigrant Jewish population; and contribute to a closer collaboration with the great organizations of French and world Jewry."[23]

Despite its great hopes and influence in the Paris immigrant community—in the early thirties over 20,000 immigrant families were affiliated with its member societies—the Fédération's activity was hampered by the inactivity of its leaders, members themselves of various societies, who were unwilling to tamper with the atomized structure of the organization.[24] Fédération activities were also weakened by the unwillingness of individual societies to part with the sizable amounts of money they had collected from their members in the form of dues and contributions. Lacking funds, the Fédération thus remained a loose conglomeration of societies, much prized by those seeking to reshape the Jewish community yet unable to act independently in an efficient and coordinated manner.

Although severely restricted by its decentralized structure, the Fédération nevertheless managed to carry on an extensive program of cultural and educational activity within the immigrant community. Aside from the local services of individual societies, the organization maintained a number of charitable works catering to the entire immigrant population. In 1935 alone the total budget for this activity approached 3,000,000 francs, almost twice that of the Consistoire.[25] The Fédération also ran the largest immigrant library in Paris in the 1930s with an impressive collection of Yiddish, French, Hebrew, Russian, Polish, and German books. Its so-called Popular University, the first of its kind in Paris, offered a grab bag of courses to the Yiddish-speaking community ranging from Jewish History and Yiddish Literature to General Health Problems and French. In 1934 the Fédération created its own school system with 300 students. As opposed to the Consistoire-supported schools that were largely religiously oriented, the Fédération's schools emphasized Yiddish culture and Jewish history. The organization also ran discussion groups, concerts, social clubs, and sports programs in alliance with its affiliate societies.[26]

Many of the eastern European immigrants who came to Paris in the late twenties and early thirties were disdainful of the Fédération and its network of mutual-aid societies. Expelled from their homelands because of political activity, they had no sympathy for what they regarded as outworn remnants of eastern Europe. Often Marxian in orientation, they viewed the *landsmanshaftn* as charitable organizations foisted upon new immigrants by older bourgeois immigrants. Impelled by a desire to create a culturally and politically active immigrant community, they rebelled against what they considered the fragmentation of Jewish life and the apathy of Jewish society leaders.[27]

It was not surprising, therefore, that immigrant militants immediately set about to create their own organizations. The first groups established in the 1920s were known as *patronatn*, or relief societies, and concerned themselves almost exclusively with the fate of Jewish political prisoners in eastern Europe. Banding together into an association known as the *Royte Hilf* (*Secours rouge*, or Red Help), *patronatn* members were motivated by a desire to retain ties with Jewish political movements in their homelands. Few thought that their stay in Paris was anything more than a temporary respite from the revolutionary struggle in eastern Europe. As hopes of returning to their homelands dimmed, however, their attention turned inward toward the cultural, political, and social problems of immigrants in Paris.

The change was signified by the slogan "Mit ponim tsu Frankraykh" ("Let us turn our attention to France") adopted by left-wing immigrant groups in 1934. Attempting to compete with the Fédération, the newer organizations placed special emphasis upon wooing workers and petit-bourgeois elements of the immigrant community. Continual stress was placed upon the need to counter "bourgeois" attempts to dull "Jewish working-class consciousness." *Landsmanshaftn*, left-wing immigrants argued, were tools of the *patrons* in the "Jewish" trades who, in their capacity as presidents of societies, used their power to lash out at workers and artisan members. In contrast to older societies which "took pity" on new immigrants and talked about "doing them favors," the new mutual-aid groups were said to offer "constructive" financial assistance divorced from charitable and philanthropic paternalism.[28] Newer societies were also lauded as not discriminating according to national or local origin.

By 1938 left-wing immigrants had succeeded in establishing a separate school system with about 400 students, a Popular University with instruction in the history of the Jewish labor movement, a library specializing in Yiddish translations of Marxist classics, a choir whose repertoire consisted of Yiddish translations of revolutionary songs, and cultural discussion groups on Jewish revolutionary consciousness.[29] Of particular interest in the drive to create a revolutionary Jewish culture in Paris was the *Parizer Yidisher Arbeter Teyater* (Yiddish Working-class Theater) or PYAT established in 1934. PYAT was created by militants to counter what they regarded as "bourgeois trash" on the Paris Yiddish stage. In contrast to the escapist fare of Jewish capitalists, the theater imported famous directors of the Polish Yiddish theater to stage "revolutionary" plays and Yiddish classics with social significance.[30] As we shall see, newer immigrant organizations also spearheaded protest campaigns, calling for a firm response to anti-Semitism while denouncing religious and *klal-yisroeldike* doctrines espoused by nonpolitical elements within the Jewish community.

The timidity of *landsmanshaftn* in the face of Nazi persecution abroad and xenophobia in France led many immigrants, both old and new, to join the new organizations. The rapid growth of these groups culminated in the creation of the *Farband fun Yidishe Gezelshaftn (Union des sociétés juives)* in 1938, an umbrella organization seeking to counter the influence of the Fédération. Most of the societies that joined the Farband were not left-wing but instead were committed to a more active role for the immigrant community than that envisioned by the Fédération. In many cases they were older societies that had been "infiltrated" and eventually taken over by younger, more militant elements. Other societies joining the Farband did so only to participate in one or two activities sponsored by the organization. Although never as large as the Fédération, the left-wing organization and its affiliates were to play an active role in the painful reconstruction of the immigrant Jewish community after World War II.[31]

Another result of the influx of the new immigrants was the growth of Jewish political movements. Most older immigrants, coming from small communities in eastern Europe, tended to shy away from political activity in Paris. Even those among the Russian immigrant population who had been active in anti-Tsarist movements generally cooled their revolutionary ardor when confronted with the economic opportunities that Paris offered them.[32] New immigrants, on the other hand, arrived in the wake of an economic crisis. Trained in the various revolutionary movements in Poland, Hungary, and Rumania, they now sought to establish a Jewish revolutionary milieu in Paris.

By far the most influential of the "political" immigrants were the Communists. In 1923 militants fleeing from political trials and imprisonment in Poland succeeded in creating the first specifically Jewish Communist organization in Paris. In the late twenties they were joined by immigrants who had originally come from eastern Europe and Palestine and who had joined the Parti communiste français when they first arrived to work in the mines and factories of the Nord. By the early thirties immigrant Communists had established their own mutual-aid societies, youth groups, athletic teams, dramatic companies, and cultural committees. In late 1933 a daily Yiddish newspaper, the *Naie Presse*, was founded to service the rapidly growing politically militant Jewish population in Paris.[33]

Although nominally independent, most of the groups fell under the influence of the "Jewish subsection" of the Parti communiste français. Originally created to care for the needs of left-wing immigrants unfamiliar with the French language, the Yiddish-speaking section of the party was a major force in Jewish life in the 1930s. The actual number of card-carrying immigrant Communists was small, no more than 300.[34] The strength of immigrant Communist organizations lay rather in their energetic activity—they were prime movers in the creation of the Jewish Popular Front, for example—in a period when larger and more influential immigrant organizations remained apathetic.

There was no specifically Jewish section within the SFIO (French Socialist Party). Nevertheless, the party did find support among older immigrants, many of whom had been active in social-democratic movements in eastern Europe. The SFIO also maintained loose contacts with a number of Jewish socialist groups within the community, including the French section of the Zionist *Poalé-Sion Hitachdouth* (*Parti socialiste juif unifié*), the forerunner of the present-day Mapai Party in Israel, and the *Medem-Farband*, the Paris branch of the Bundist movement. In addition the party took an active interest in the plight of Jewish refugees in the 1930s through its participation in the *Centre de liaison des comités pour le statut des immigrés*, a broad-based group involving most of the major immigrant organizations in Paris, as well as through the creation of a *comité du droit d'asile* within its syndicalist central, the *Confédération générale du travail* (CGT).[35] In general, however, the SFIO failed to win over more militant elements within the eastern European community who tended to associate socialism with reformism or, even worse, with the reactionary policies of Poland's Marshal Pilsudski.

By far the most active socialist movement within the immigrant community itself was that of the Bundists. The first Bundist organization in Paris was founded in 1900 by Polish and Russian political refugees. Although various satellite groups were established in subsequent years to cater to the needs of its members, the Bundist organization in Paris remained largely a willing servant of the movement's central headquarters in Warsaw.[36] Staunch believers in the viability of world revolution, the Bundists made few attempts to ally with the largely reformist French socialists.[37] Nor did they take an active part in the various Jewish unity movements in Paris in the 1930s. To ally with Jewish "bourgeois" elements, they argued, would be to betray the interests of the Jewish working class whose only hope lay with the international proletariat. Relatively isolated from left-wing circles both within and without the immigrant Jewish community, Bundists faced great difficulties in adapting to French life. Small in number, the Bundists nevertheless played an important role in the Paris immigrant community as a sectarian gadfly to the Jewish Communists.[38]

The actual number of Zionists among immigrants in Paris in the 1930s is unknown.[39] Zionist ideals were often intertwined with the religious beliefs of traditional Jews, but their basis lay in a messianic impulse rather than in a search for a political solution to the plight of Jews. Nevertheless, by the 1930s there existed a large number of Zionist movements in Paris. Highly sectarian, they ran the gamut from Revisionists, with their emphasis upon Jewish militarism, to the Poalé-Sion Hitachdouth, the strongest of all the groups, which argued for the creation of a socialist Jewish State in Palestine.[40] In between stood the General Zionists, a nondescript group that attracted nonpolitical elements, and *Mizrahi*, a group supported by natives and older immigrants fearful of left-wing activity and committed to the reconstruction of a Jewish homeland "within the stricture of the laws and institutions of our ancient Torah."[41] Despite (or maybe because of) the plethora of organizations, Zionist ideas had little influence upon immigrants in Paris in the prewar period. Most immigrants saw their future in France and refused to place their hopes on what seemed to be a utopian dream.

Despite the conditions in the "Jewish" trades that militated against organized activity, Jewish trade unions were to be found in Paris as early as the turn of the century. Under Bundist leadership, the Jewish trade-union movement grew and by 1914 included most of the Jewish hatters, tailors, bakers, bottlemakers, shoemakers, and waiters in Paris.[42] The failure of the *Parizer Yidisher Arbeter Farband* (Paris Jewish Worker Federation) in 1921, however—a failure stemming in part from internal dissension over whether to join the burgeoning Communist movement in France—led many militant immigrants to leave Jewish unions. Those who remained directed their unions into the *Confédération générale du travail*, the non-Communist federation of trade unions. The majority, however, joined general unions affiliated with the then newly created and Communist-inspired *Confédération générale du travail unitaire*.[43]

The influx became so great in certain unions that CGTU organizations with large immigrant memberships were forced to create separate Yiddish-language sections. These sections were not independent units—the CGTU and the Parti communiste français opposed the notion of separate Jewish unions—but rather intermediary groups between the union leadership and newly arrived immigrants who did not understand French. [44] Aside from day-to-day information dispensed to all union members, the language sections were also responsible for the integration of Jewish immigrants into the French working-class movement, a task that implied the eventual elimination of Yiddish-speaking sections.[45]

Jewish membership in Paris trade unions varied greatly throughout the prewar period. The fact that many immigrants were engaged in seasonal work, the large number of home-laborers in the "Jewish" trades, the preponderance of women among Jewish workers, the limitations placed by the French government upon the employment of aliens—all helped to keep the number of unionized immigrants at a relatively low level.[46] Jewish trade-union leaders thought they saw a turning point after the strikes of June 1936. The militant activity of workers in the "Jewish" trades brought Jewish membership in trade unions to its highest level in the prewar period, over 12,000 with 6,000 to 8,000 alone in the clothing trades. Within a few months, however, membership had returned to the pre–June level of 2,500, or about 3 percent of the immigrant Jewish working force in Paris.[47]

One of the main reasons for the relatively small Jewish membership in labor unions was the failure to organize *façonniers* and artisans. Although numerous overtures were made by Jewish sections of trade unions to artisan elements in the clothing and textile trades, the continual conflicts between workers and *façonniers* destroyed any hopes for an organizational rapprochement between the two groups.[48] Many *façonniers* and artisans were also wary of alliances with workers because of what they regarded as their unique situation in the "Jewish" trades. Neither workers nor *patrons*, they felt that their only hope lay in the creation of separate professional organizations to defend their own interests.[49] In this they were supported by older immigrants within the Fédération who feared the politization of artisans and *façonniers* as a result of membership in labor unions.

All in all, there were ten separate organizations of artisans and home-laborers in Paris in the 1930s. As with Jewish working-class groups, membership remained relatively small, although the participation of Jewish artisans in the strikes of June 1936 temporarily increased the number of affiliates.[50] Caught between *patron* and worker, the Jewish artisan could not rely on the larger and more powerful managerial and working-class organizations to defend his interest. Forced to fend for themselves, Jewish artisan organizations remained powerless to counter the onslaught of antiforeigner legislation passed in France in the decade before World War II.

There were many mutual-aid societies in Paris geared specifically to immigrant merchants and peddlers. Attempts to consolidate them into a strong federation, however, proved unsuccessful. Most *petits commerçants* viewed the establishment of a federation as a form of unionization. Unions were a working-class concern, it was argued, and thus demeaning to the "independent" elements in the community.[51] Besides, the formation of such organizations would inevitably lead to involvement with "political extremists," anathema to older immigrants seeking to gain acceptance among Frenchmen.

Nevertheless, some newer immigrants, forced to become peddlers because they could find no other work, succeeded in founding a Communist-oriented federation in the 1930s. Unable to join French merchant organizations because of antiforeigner sentiment,[52] older immigrants in turn were led to organize their own federation affiliated with the Fédération des sociétés juives de France. A tenuous union was created between the two federations in 1934, but internal bickering kept the "unified" organization weak and divided. Immigrant merchants thus were forced to fall back on the scattered and generally ineffective societies that they had originally created.[53]

The organizational structure of the Paris Jewish community in the 1930s was one of confusion, duplication, and atomization. In part the fault lay with Jewish organization leaders, fearful of absorption by larger organizations and jealously guarding their fragile independence. In part it lay with the barriers erected by the various groups against the "others" who differed in national origin, political belief, or social standing.

Beyond the pettiness of society leaders and the dogmatism of militants, however, lay a far more divisive factor. In order to coordinate the activities of Jewish organizations, it was necessary that there be common agreement on just what constituted a specific "Jewish" action. The conflicting and often contradictory attitudes in the community toward the nature of Jewish identification, brought sharply into focus by the events of the 1930s, spelled doom for any hopes of a truly cohesive organizational structure among Paris Jews.

Notes

1. Zosa Szajkowski in his work, "Dos Yidishe Gezelshaftlikhe Leybn in Pariz tsum yor 1939," p. 217, claims that 48,000 Jewish families were members of Jewish organizations in the 1930s, a figure he arrives at by adding together the members of mutual-aid societies, the Consistoire de Paris, and Jewish youth organizations. Unfortunately, Szajkowski's method is not completely valid. For one thing, he has not considered the possibility that some Jews may have belonged to more than one organization. Nor does he seem to recognize that membership in mutual-aid societies and Jewish youth groups included a small but significant number of Jews living outside of Paris. One may question, finally, whether one can consider members of Jewish youth groups as heads of families as Szajkowski seems to do.

2. For a detailed study of consistorial membership, see the article by William Oualid in *L'Univers israélite*, December 9, 1932, and the minutes of the *Assemblée générale ordinaire* of the Association consistoriale israélite de Paris (Paris: Sécrétariat générale, 1933, 1934, 1935).

3. For a discussion of membership fees, see the archives of the ACIP, B132, Lettres reçues, 1935, Affaires administratives: Propagande cultuelle.

An interesting insight into the haut-bourgeois character of consistorial membership is provided by a letter to the religious body written in 1935. In the letter an irate member claimed that the doors to the rue de la Victoire synagogue were blocked on the High Holydays by the chauffeurs of wealthy congregants who stood around smoking cigarettes and talking. (Letter dated January 4, 1935, in the archives of the ACIP, B131, Lettres reçues, 1935, Divers.)

Roblin claims that in the 1930s three-quarters of the members of the Consistoire were of Alsatian origin (p. 138). A reading of the minutes of the various committees of the organization as well as a careful study of the membership lists of the various synagogues in Paris reveals that by the 1930s there were a number of Sephardic and older eastern European immigrants who had achieved positions of authority.

4. Alexandre Weill, cited in *Histoire des juifs en France*, p. 370.

5. For a discussion of the Consistoire de Paris' relations with *L'Univers israélite*, see the archives of the ACIP, AA21 and AA23, Conseil d'administration, 1929–35, 1936–38, meetings held May 22, 1934, March 16, 1937, October 21, 1937, and May 3, 1938. After five years of fruitless discussion, it was finally agreed that the Consistoire would subsidize the paper in return for a certain number of pages each issue for its

announcements and some editorial control over the articles. In actuality, most of the writers for *L'Univers israélite* were loyal members of the Consistoire.

6. Roblin, pp. 139-40; A. Alperin, "Yidishe Gezelshaftn un institutsies in Pariz in 1939," in *Yidn in Frankraykh*, ed. A. Tcherikover, vol. 2 (New York: YIVO, 1942), pp. 249-50.

7. Archives of the ACIP, B127, Lettres reçues, 1933, Affaires religieuses, p. 6 of a report on "L'Instruction religieuse à Paris."

8. Pierre Lazareff, "Les Oeuvres de bienfaisance et d'éducation," in *La Question juive vue par vingt-six éminentes personalités* (Paris: EIF, 1934), p. 143.

9. Probably the most important charitable organization run by the Consistoire was the *Comité de bienfaisance israélite de Paris.* Created in 1809, its activities in the 1930s included medical care, subventions to students, payment of rents, the care of infants and the elderly, and the maintenance of a credit union. The Comité was run mainly by wealthy native women who as *dames patronesses* were each designated to care for four or five needy families. For more information on the Comité, see Lazareff, "Les Oeuvres de bienfaisance," pp. 141-42.

10. One of the prime targets for patriotic propaganda was the largely immigrant student body of the native-run *Ecole de travail.* As far as I could determine from my reading, students were required to sign a pledge that they would serve in the French army upon graduation from the school (see especially *L'Univers israélite*, December 22, 1933). Upon graduating, they were often given a stern warning not to become involved in political activity. One speaker at the school graduation in January 1937 concluded his remarks by saying: "Young workers, you are entering into troubled waters where a dangerous ferment reigns. Your responsibility is to ignore it, following your own road, working to the best of your ability while recognizing that your future depends upon your will and your integrity rather than upon lists of work grievances. It is in the workshop and not in political marches that I want to see former students of the Ecole de travail" (cited in *L'Univers israélite*, January 15, 1937).

11. There were a few native Jews in the Parti communiste français, but their ties with the Jewish community were practically nonexistent. The statement by André Wurmser, a native Communist, that "the first obligation of a Jew is to strive to eliminate his identity as a Jew" was typical of their attitudes toward Jewish identity (cited in Pierre Aubery, *Milieux juifs de la France contemporaine à travers les écrivains* [Paris: Plon, 1957], p. 299).

Jews could also be found in right-wing groups such as the *Action française* and Jacques Doriot's *Parti populaire français.* For a fascinating example of the attitudes of one such Jew, see René Groos, *Enquête sur le problème juif* (Paris: Nouvelle Librairie Nationale, 192?).

12. Typical of the Parti radical-socialiste's appeal to native Jews was a statement condemning Nazism issued soon after Hitler's accession to power. The statement began with the following historical note: "The Parti radical-socialiste, loyal to the essential ideals of France and of the Republic, recalls that the Revolution, by the decree of September 27, 1791, abolished all discriminatory legislation against Jews" (cited in *Paix et Droit*, March 1933, p. 8). For a discussion of some prominent Jewish members of the party, see *Hebdo-Pariz*, July 12, 1935.

13. The three most important native Jewish youth groups were the *Union universelle de la jeunesse juive*, created in 1921 and claiming 2,000 members in the 1930s; the *Eclaireurs israélites de France*, a scouting group organized in 1923 which also had 2,000 members; and *Chema Israël*, a discussion group centering on matters of Jewish

interest. The Union universelle often assumed independent positions which conflicted with Consistoire policy. Its leadership contained a sizable number of militant sons and daughters of older immigrants. The other two groups remained largely under Consistoire influence and emphasized moral behavior and Jewish ritual in conscious opposition to the more politically oriented activities of organizations like LICA.

For information on the Union universelle, see the columns devoted to youth in *Le Journal juif* and *Samedi* during this period. For information on the Eclaireurs, see the article on Jewish scouts in the *Bulletin du Centre de documentation et de vigilance*, June 3, 1937, and the organization's own periodical, *L'Eclaireur israélite de France*. For a typical discussion at a Chema Israël meeting, see the article "Le Judaïsme, est-il subversif?" in *L'Univers israélite*, January 15, 1937.

14. A major source for information on the Union patriotique is their bulletin, of which only scattered issues remain in the YIVO Library. For other sources of information, see the articles in *Chalom*, July–August 1934, and *L'Univers israélite*, May 11, 1934, December 28, 1934, March 27, 1936, and January 22, 1937.

15. Szajkowski, "Dos Yidishe Gezelshaftlikhe Leybn," p. 226.

16. Discussions with M. Taumann, secretary of the *Association des anciens combattants engagés—Volontaires juifs: 1914-1918*, on June 14, 1970.

For a contemporary view of the congress, see *Archives israélites*, June 20, 1935.

17. The Alliance also maintained the most important Jewish library in Paris during this period. The library remains today one of the largest repositories of Jewish documents in the world and was an invaluable source for many of the works I used in the preparation of the study.

18. For a detailed examination of the more important immigrant religious congregations, see Szajkowski, "Dos Yidishe Gezelshaftlikhe Leybn," p. 217.

19. For information on the Entr'aide fraternelle, see *L'Univers israélite*, December 1, 1933, and January 18, 1935.

20. The column reserved for announcements by mutual-aid societies published daily in *Pariser Haint* is a major source for information on the activities of these organizations. The announcements published on November 14, 1936, a date picked at random, reflect the wide range of activity: the *Zhelichover Landslayt* announced a general meeting in a cafe; the *Brest-Litovsk* society noted that there was to be a general meeting to discuss preparations for their annual ball, the creation of a health clinic, and the plight of Jews in Poland; the *Fraynd fun Minsk-Makovietsk* had a poetry recital; and the *Verayn fun Poylishe Yidn* announced a discussion on "Illness in the Family."

For a complete list of mutual-aid societies in the period, see *Almanach juif, 1931*, pp. 84-95.

21. Technically, there was a difference between *landsmanshaftn* and mutual-aid societies. The former concerned themselves solely with former residents of a specific city or town in eastern Europe; the latter did not restrict their membership to those with a common birthplace. Both, however, performed similar functions and provided similar services to their members. In this sense the two terms can be used interchangeably.

22. For a list of the members of the Fédération in 1935, a good year for the organization, see the Fédération's *Rapport moral et financier: Exercise 1935-1936* (Paris: ICC, 1936), pp. 32-34.

23. Ibid., p. 6.

24. There were two presidents of the Fédération during the period under study.

Israel Jefroykin came to Paris in 1920 after being active in the *Yidishe Folkspartei* in his native Lithuania. His involvement in various international Jewish relief efforts in the 1920s catapulted him to a position of prominence in the immigrant community. Marc Jarblum was born in Warsaw but moved to Paris in 1907. Leader of the *Poalé-Sion Hitachdouth,* he was instrumental in giving the Fédération a strongly Zionist stamp after his accession to the presidency in 1936. Despite good intentions, neither was able to break the control which the various *landsmenshaftn* exerted on the central organization.

25. *Rapport morale et financier,* p. 9.

26. For more information on the cultural and educational activity of the Fédération, see the organization's *Rapport de l'activité pour l'année 1934* (Paris: Imprimerie Polyglotte N. L. Danzig, 1935).

27. Left-wing immigrants often argued that the leaders of the Fédération were either *patrons* or owners of shops servicing (and thus exploiting) the immigrant population. In fact, Israel Jefroykin and Marc Jarblum, the two presidents of the organization in the 1930s, were a travel agent and a lawyer, respectively, while M. Judcovici, the vice-president, was a *patron* in the leather trades.

The difference between old and new societies was summed up by the president of the Brisker society in the following manner: "As opposed to many other societies, the Brisker society began its activity, not with death [graves] but with life, expressing the natural law that death comes after life and that the demands of life are greater, stronger, and more urgent than the demands of dying" (cited in "Der Veg fun di gezelshaftn," in *Tsen yor Farband fun yidishe gezelshaftn* (Paris: Farband fun Yidishe gezelshaftn, 1948), p. 98.

28. See, for example, Y. Lerman, *Far der Fartaydikung fun unzer folk* (Paris, 1938), pp. 33–34.

29. For a full discussion of the cultural activities of the newer societies, see the speech by Y. Lerman at the Yiddish Culture Congress held in Paris in September 1937, cited in *Naie Presse,* September 20, 1937, and the article by Lerman in *Naie Presse,* January 30, 1938.

The emphasis upon building Jewish working-class consciousness among immigrants is exemplified in the song "We are Workers' Children," taught to the students of the afternoon schools and sung by the workers' choir. The lyrics read in part as follows:

> We are workers' children
> Our father is on strike
> Our father is on strike
> Mother is comforted
> Come boil a pot of soup.
>
> We go barefoot
> Naked and ragged
> Naked and ragged
> And police shoot workers in the streets.
>
> . . . .
>
> I say to Father: You know
> That when I am older

That when I am older
I will be a great hero
A Soldier, a Communist.
(*Naie Presse*, July 10, 1935.)

30. The role of PYAT was described by one collaborator in the following manner: "The theater is a forum where a portrait of their [the Jewish masses'] needs, the tragedy of their lack of rights, protests against oppressors, and their struggle for bread, justice, and freedom can be reflected in a highly artistic form" (*Naie Presse*, September 12, 1935).

For a history of the theater, see the article on B. Tshubinsky in *Naie Presse*, February 14, 1936.

31. According to Alfred Grant, a prominent left-wing organizer in the Jewish community in the 1930s, there were seventy societies in attendance at the first meeting of the Farband (Alfred Grant, "Fun Keygenzaytiker Hilf," in *Tsen yor Farband fun Yidishe gezelshaftn*, p. 20).

For a complete list of member societies, see "Der Veg fun di gezelshaftn," pp. 87–151.

32. In his novel *La Double Tare*, Elie Eberlin describes the political attitudes of a group of Russian Jewish diamond merchants in Paris. Speaking of Russia, he notes cynically: "But there, the Jewish merchants and salesmen had to concern themselves with politics whether they liked it or not, because government oppression kept them on their toes. . . . In Paris, it's not the same; these pearl and diamond merchants are not bothered by the authorities, thus enabling them to live in a condition of gross materialism" (Paris: Editions SNIE, 1935), pp. 94–95.

Jacques Bielinky, a Russian immigrant and an important member of the Consistoire, explained the transition of a "Red Jew" in Paris in the following manner: "He arrives in Paris with 50 francs in his pocket and settles in on the rue de l'Hôtel de Ville. By dint of hard work and perseverance, he climbs the social ladder to end up in a comfortable apartment on the avenue Kléber" (cited in a report on Jews of the Etoile area found at YIVO in the Bielinky Archives, untitled folder).

33. It is difficult to piece together a biographical sketch of a typical immigrant militant in Paris in the 1930s. A study of the biographies of over seventy Jewish trade union leaders killed during World War II, contained in Yidisher Intersindikaler Komisie, *In Kamf far frayhayt* (Paris: OJFSNAJ, 1948), pp. 128–77, reveals that the typical militant was born in Poland of an artisan family. Though often receiving an intensive religious training in his youth, he generally rejected it at an early age and entered into revolutionary trade-union activity. Expelled from Poland in his early twenties, he came to France either to study or to work in the mines of the Nord. The economic crisis of the early thirties led him into the "Jewish" trades, where his trade-union background propelled him into a position of leadership. More often than not, he was also a member of the Jewish subsection of the Parti communiste français.

34. Discussions with W. Carol, August 4, 1970. A brochure issued in 1930 by the *Main d'oeuvre étrangère* (MOE), the central organization of the party's language sections, noted that there were only 100 Jewish immigrants in the party (*L'Importance de la M.O.E. et les diverses immigrations: Bulletin spécial d'informations de la section centrale de la M.O.E.* [Paris: Parti communiste français, 1930], p. 81).

35. For a discussion of the SFIO's activities to aid Jewish refugees, see the article by Magdeline Paz in *Le Populaire*, May 26, 1936.

36. In an article published in 1947 in *Unzer Tsayt* (Our Times), a Bundist

publication, Raphael Riba, a leading Bundist in Paris in the 1930s, attempted to differentiate beween two periods in the movement's activity in the capital: the period before 1932, when Bundists were mainly concerned with helping fellow Bundists in eastern Europe; and the period after 1932, when members of the newly formed *Yidisher Sotsialistisher Farband in Frankraykh* turned their attention to problems within the Paris Jewish community (Raphael Riba, "Yidisher Sotsialistisher Farband 'Bund' in Frankraykh," *Unzer Tsayt*, November–December 1947, pp. 159–61).

A reading of the movement's paper, *Unzer Stime*, which began publication in 1936, however, reveals that interest continued to center mainly on political events in Poland.

37. According to *Naie Presse* (August 15, 1934), a biased source, the Bundists did not get in contact with the SFIO until 1932. *Le Populaire*, the SFIO's daily newspaper, did publish occasional articles about the Bund's activities in Paris. See, for example, the article commemorating the first anniversary of the *Yidisher Sotsialistisher Farband in Frankraykh*, published on April 8, 1933.

38. As Hillel Kempinsky, presently the archivist of the Bund in New York, noted in his discussions with me in December 1970: "It was hard to be a Bundist outside of Poland." The largest and most successful Bundist organization in Paris, the *Arbeter Ring* (Workmen's Circle), had only about 500 members in the 1930s (Szajkowski, "Dos Yidishe Gezelshaftlikhe Leybn," p. 212). All in all, the number of Bundist activists in Paris during this period probably numbered no more than 1,500 to 2,000.

39. The only overall figure of Zionists I could find in my research was contained in an article in *Naie Presse* published on October 16, 1934. In the article the writer claimed that there were 6,000 Zionists in France in 1919.

In the Paris elections to the World Zionist Congress of 1933, there were 1,326 votes cast: 242 for the General Zionists, 450 for the Poalé-Sion Hitachdouth, 77 for the Radicals (?), 491 for the Revisionists, and 69 for a splinter Revisionist group (*L'Univers israélite*, August 11, 1933). The elections of 1937 saw 1,855 votes cast: 745 for the Labor coalition, 538 for the General Zionists, 271 for Mizrahi, 199 for the Party of the Jewish State (Revisionist), and 102 for the Sephardim (*L'Univers israélite*, July 30, 1937). The figures indicate only the relative strength of the various movements. The vast majority of Zionist sympathizers in France did not belong or contribute to any movement and thus could not vote and only a minority of those granted voting rights actually cast their ballots.

40. The Poalé-Sion Hitachdouth maintained its own newspaper in Paris, the *Naye Zeit* (New Time), which is a major source of information on the movement. Similarly, the Revisionists issued a bulletin in French, the *Bulletin de presse sioniste-revisioniste*. The major source for information on Zionist activity in France, however, is *La Terre retrouvée*, run by a group of native and older immigrant Jews.

41. Cited in *Affirmation*, July 7, 1939. *L'Univers israélite*, in its issue dated October 26, 1934, relates an anecdote which reflects the factionalism of immigrant Zionist movements in Paris. A police agent reported to his chief that he had just arrested six Revisionists, four Jewish Statists, five Poalé-Sionistes, three Mizrachists, and two General Zionists. "Where are they?" the chief asks. "Outside," the agent replies. "Unguarded?" the chief wonders. "It's not necessary," the agent answers. "They're guarding each other."

42. For a detailed study of the Jewish working-class movement in Paris before World War I, see S. Fridman (Zosa Szajkowski), *Etyudn tsu der geshikhte fun ayngevanderter yidishn yishuv in Frankraykh* (Paris: Fridman, 1936).

43. According to W. Carol and Y. Lerman, two former immigrant Communists that I interviewed, most militants looked with disfavor upon the CGT because of its reformist posture and what was regarded as its less than sympathetic attitude toward immigrants. See also Grant, p. 13.

For a general discussion of Jewish trade-union activity within the CGTU, see Yidisher Intersindikaler Komisie, *In Kamf far frayhayt*, pp. 33–54.

44. A statement by the *section centrale* of the MOE issued in 1930 summed up the dangers which the Communist leadership saw in the creation of national language sections: "If strong national language sections exist in the Paris region, it is because their uncontrolled activity [remains] unchecked by union leadership, which has not sufficiently responded to their autonomist tendencies and is not concerned enough with the particular grievances of immigrants (the Jewish section in textiles, for example).... [Such activity] can easily be directed toward a dangerous nationalism that might lead them into isolated actions destined in most cases to certain failure" (cited in *L'Importance de la M.O.E.*, p. 81).

45. The Yiddish-language sections of the CGTU, as was the Jewish subsection of the Parti communiste français, were only a part of the network of foreign-language sections maintained by the two organizations in the period before World War II. The Yiddish-language sections in each union were joined together in a central *Comité intersyndical*, which in turn was part of a larger *comité* representing all of the language sections in the CGTU. Similarly, the Jewish subsection was one section of the Main d'oeuvre étrangère (MOE) (later renamed the *Main d'oeuvre immigrée* (MOI) because of the bad connotations connected with the word *étrangère*), which represented some fifteen language sections in the party's *Comité central*.

46. Another factor that kept Jewish union membership low was the continual battle between Bundists and Jewish Communists within unions themselves. The former attacked Communist union leaders for betraying the specific interests of Jewish workers and for attempting to destroy freedom of expression within the unions. Communists, in turn, claimed that Bundists were spreading dissension among workers by shaking confidence in union leaders. For the opposing views, see *Unzer Stime*, March 10, 1939, and *Naie Presse*, March 14, 1939.

47. For figures on immigrant membership during this period, see *Naie Presse*, November 27, 1936, July 30, 1939; Szajkowski, "Dos Yidishe Gezelshaftlikhe Leybn," p. 236; and Yidisher Intersindikaler Komisie, *In Kamf far frayhayt*, p. 48.

48. One of the main stumbling blocks was the unions' insistence upon differentiating between *façonniers*, who did not employ any workers, and *entrepreneurs*, who did, the former being regarded as acceptable allies of the working-class, the latter as merely another type of *patron*. Artisans, of course, would brook no separation in their ranks. For a discussion of the unions' view, see *Naie Presse*, December 10, 1934.

49. For an insight into the Jewish artisan's mentality and particularly his attitude toward participation in labor unions, see the articles in *Pariser Haint*, October 22, 1935, and July 6, 1936.

50. Szajkowski places the membership of the ten organizations before June 1936 at 2,476 and after June 1936 at 4,253, an increase of 72 percent. As with Jewish trade unions, membership declined to pre-June levels within months after settlement of the strikes (Szajkowski, "Dos Yidishe Gezelshaftlikhe Leybn," p. 236).

51. An article by Y. Goldberg, secretary of the central organization of Jewish

merchants, small dealers, peddlers, and grocers in France, published in 1938, reflects the particular mentality of *petits commerçants*. Citing the "historic role of the middle classes" in France, Goldberg went on to explain why the role and size of the Jewish merchant populace in the Jewish community was as large as that of the middle classes in French society (*Hantverker Vort*, June 1938, p. 5).

52. For an example of such sentiments, see the discussions of the *Congrès national des marchands français* in *Naie Presse*, February 18, 1937.

53. For information on the two Jewish merchant federations, see *Pariser Haint*, December 25, 1933, and *Naie Presse*, November 29, 1934, and December 14, 1934.

4 The Nature of
Jewish Identification

The question "What is a Jew?" has perplexed Jews in all ages. Ironically, Jewish emancipation in the nineteenth century, far from eliminating the question as its supporters had hoped, only made it more intense. Faced with the possibility of assimilating, the modern Jew was suddenly confronted with the dilemma of a dual identity. Committed to both the past traditions of the Jewish people and the future hopes of the nation which had recently granted him full citizenship, the emancipated Jew searched desperately for a self-defined present which would synthesize his conflicting loyalties.

The painful process of demarcating the boundaries of their loyalties and commitments often led Jews to the most contradictory self-definitions. While some saw Jewry as a nation scattered among other nations and in continual search for its homeland, others defined Jews as a spiritual community bound only by the religious tenets of the Jewish faith. While some spoke of a civilization united by a common history and culture, others denied a separate Jewish identity, arguing that the notion of a "Jew" was an artificial construct imposed by historical circumstance and perpetuated by self-delusion.

All of these definitions had their proponents and detractors within the Paris Jewish community in the 1930s. Concern with Jewish identity was heightened by the confrontation between natives and immigrants. Heirs to the first modern act of emancipation, native Jews seemed comfortable with an identity that scarcely differentiated them from their fellow countrymen. The existence of a large immigrant population in their midst, however, made them sensitive to the often antithetical pulls of Jewish and French commitment. Immigrants, in turn, intensely and viscerally Jewish, were forced to confront for the first time a society that offered them an alternative identity. The relative economic and social success of native Jewry, reflective of their integration into French society, disturbed and intrigued many immigrants with its implication that

Jewish identity was a matter of personal choice, to be accepted or rejected as one saw fit.

The rapid rise of Nazism in the 1930s gave added urgency to the question What is a Jew. Here was an ideology that defined Jews in "scientific" racialistic terms. No allowance was made for those who wished to disassociate themselves from other Jews. Those natives and immigrants who previously had boasted of their liberation from Jewish ties now were forced to reexamine their positions. Those who continued to maintain a Jewish identity were led to reassert it more strongly in defiance of the Nazi threat.

Native Jewish identification was shaped by a particular view of the past which saw the French Revolution as the cardinal event in modern Jewish history. For natives, Jewish life in Europe before 1789 was characterized by parochial nationalism and religious obscurantism. Persecuted by the larger society around them because of differing religious and cultural traditions, Jews were forced to isolate themselves into small, tightly structured communities. In time, however, what had previously been defended as a necessary evil now became in the eyes of many Jews a positive good. Thus, the pariah nature of Jewish life was transformed through Jewish tradition into an affirmation of national exclusivism, an all encompassing ideology that placed emphasis upon the necessity of Jews to separate themselves from non-Jews. Jewish communities became states within states—politically, culturally, and economically independent units totally impervious to the winds of change sweeping across Europe in the period before the French Revolution. The rigidity of the Jewish position led only to increased hostility on the part of non-Jews and an unwillingness to accept Jews as equal members of society. The result was a still greater isolation of Jewish communities. At the outbreak of the French Revolution, the Jewish communities of Europe presented a picture of ossification and decay.[1]

The advent of the French Revolution, natives argued, enabled Jews in France at least to liberate themselves from their constraining past. While Jews of eastern Europe continued to suffer persecution, the proclamation of emancipation in 1791 granted French Jews, for the first time in modern history, full rights and privileges as citizens of the new French nation.[2] No longer forced to isolate himself in ghetto-like communities, the French Jew was now free to commingle with non-Jews on an equal basis. The opportunities provided by the new society meant a gradual wearing away of parochial national traditions and a growing acceptance of the new *patrie*. By the twentieth century, the French Jew, according to a leading Consistoire member of the 1930s, "has become so intermingled with them [the French] that he cannot conceive of living outside their midst." [3]

In reality, of course, the path of Jewish emancipation in France was far from smooth. As Arthur Hertzberg has pointed out in his work, *The French Enlightenment and the Jews* (New York, Columbia University Press, 1968), even the most avid non-Jewish supporters of emancipation were not devoid of anti-Semitic sentiments. Men like the Abbé Gregoire, the most vocal proponent of Jewish emancipation in 1791, continued to hold to the notion of the Jews as an alien element in society, although he did admit that they might be reformed through education. Despite the abbé's qualification, it was not difficult for many Frenchmen in the early nineteenth century and later during the Dreyfus Affair to regard the maintenance of a separate identity by Jews, however limited, as a sign that they were either incapable of reform or that they simply refused to assimilate into French society. Jews were also burdened by the stereotype of a Jewish nationhood which seemed to conflict with the cherished French Revolutionary ideals of individualism and loyalty to the *patrie*. French Jews in the nineteenth and twentieth centuries thus often found themselves accepted as individuals yet secretly despised as members of an alien people. A final element hindering full Jewish assimilation was the gap between legal emancipation and social acceptance. By the middle of the nineteenth century there were no legal barriers preventing Jews from partaking in French public life, yet Jews continued to be restricted in social relationships. The phenomenon of "a ghetto without Judaism" in which emancipated Jews rarely left the company of fellow Jews was in part a result of this lack of social acceptance. [4]

All this was largely ignored by French Jews in the 1930s. Imbued with the myth of Jewish emancipation, natives proved quite willing to reject "outworn" religious and cultural traditions for the sake of integration into French life. Firm believers in the progressive ideas and lofty sentiments of 1789, French Jews could not but be embarrassed by the continued maintenance of the "limited culture" that had served as the foundation of ghetto life before the French Revolution. Nor could they accept the strictures of Jewish communal life, dismissing all immigrant proposals to establish a *kehilah* (community) among Paris Jewry as a reflection of the "mentalité arrièrée" of eastern European Jews unwilling to accept the benefits

of emancipation. Those Jews who steadfastly insisted upon maintaining a traditional way of life seemed strangely out of place in
post-Revolutionary France. No longer the sages of the Jewish
community, they were now merely anachronisms, "the survivors of
an era which is happily dead and buried," as one native rabbi
described them in 1930.[5]

The native interpretation of the Jewish response to emancipation
seemed to leave few traditional beliefs unscathed. Indeed, the high
percentage of mixed marriages and conversions among French Jews
in the nineteenth and twentieth centuries shows that the process of
assimilation had progressed at an alarming rate.[6] The continual
decline in Consistoire membership in the 1930s and the poor
attendance at religious services also attest to the falling away of
religious belief among natives.[7] Yet not all French Jews who
accepted the benefits that French society granted them were led to
reject their religious traditions. What remained after allowances to
"progressive ideas" was, as we have seen, a surprisingly pious belief
in Judaism.

French Jews were aided in their reconciliation of religious practice
and "enlightened" behavior by the willingness of the Consistoire to
institute reforms in its ritual. Already in the nineteenth century, the
native religious body had introduced French prayers into the
Sabbath and holiday liturgy and had reinterpreted all references to
sacrifices, Jewish chosenness, and a physical return to Zion to make
them palatable to its "enlightened" membership. At the same time,
the largely Alsatian rabbinate adopted the German pastor's robe
worn during religious services and welcomed organ music and choirs
as a means of maintaining decorum during prayer. Consistoire
synagogues also were often used to hold patriotic ceremonies
honoring French war dead, while Sabbath morning sermons dealt as
much with loyalty to the nation as with the weekly Torah portion.
The spirit of reform that pervaded rabbinic circles in France in the
nineteenth and twentieth centuries explains in large part why, unlike
Germany, France never saw the growth of an important Jewish
Reform movement.[8]

For those who continued to practice their faith, Jewry could no
longer be viewed as a peoplehood. The French Revolution had
decreed, in the famous words of Stanislaus Clermont de Tonnerre,
that "one must refuse everything to the Jews as a nation, but one
must give them everything as individuals."[9] Judaism thus was to be
a private affair, restricted to the home and to the house of worship

and having no influence upon the behavior of Jews in their daily contacts with non-Jews. The separation of Church and State in 1905, in establishing the boundaries of the *cultuel* and the *laic* in French society, only solidified this attitude. French Jews henceforth referred to themselves as *Français israélites* or *Français de la loi mosaique*, the term *juif* (Jew) being used only to denote "less cultivated" coreligionists who continued to assert a distinctive Jewish peoplehood.[10] As a prominent member of the native religious community noted in 1938:

> You will never be asked whether you are first a Jew or a Frenchman.... One can understand such mistaken notions on the part of people who have suffered greatly ...; but with us, our private lives, our ideals, our beliefs do not depend upon the permission of others. Each one of us has the freedom to believe according to his personal faith, his particular tastes, his education. The nation, a clever alchemist, knows how to form a marvelous amalgam of these disparate races, of these mixtures, in its crucible and to extract from it, as from a magic beaker, a new being, regenerated, alive, vibrant, breathing faith and patriotism.[11]

The association of French ideals with Jewish belief was a major component of the native Jewish religious experience. The ethical tenets of Judaism as espoused by the Biblical prophets were said to have reached their ultimate fruition in the ideals of the French Revolution and in the democratic sentiments pervading French life. Time and time again, rabbis preaching sermons juxtaposed the basic beliefs of Judaism with the ideals of *la patrie*. Thus the proclamation of Jewish emancipation of 1791 was "like a new exodus from Egypt," the Declaration of the Rights of Man "comparable to the Ten Commandments," the victory of France and its allies in World War I as the victory of justice as preached by the prophets, and so on.[12] Rabbis exhorted their congregants to be good Frenchmen and thus by extension good Jews, thereby reinforcing the native's conviction that there could be no conflict between loyalty to the nation and adherence to Judaism.[13] When conflicts arose between the two loyalties, it was generally the Jewish commitment that suffered.[14]

The distinctiveness of the French Jewish experience and the denial of a Jewish peoplehood led natives to disassociate themselves from other Jews. Even native talk of a "spiritual community" of all Jews was not seriously believed by those who looked upon eastern

European religious traditions as, at best, "a joyous mish-mash of ideas."[15] Immigrants, in the native view, were exaggerated stereotypes of Jewish life before 1789. Unexposed to French culture, their backwardness was reflected not only in their bizarre religious practices but also in the boorishness and brashness that characterized their behavior in Paris. Throughout the 1930s French Jewish journals published articles and letters from "concerned" natives denouncing the activities of immigrants and demanding that the Consistoire intervene with newly arrived Jews to inculcate good manners. Immigrants were accused, among other things, of drinking tea "in a country where wine or beer is preferred," of being late for appointments, of ignoring local mores and defying government authorities, and of organizing noisy demonstrations and making trouble in the streets.[16] The conditions for acceptance into the native Jewish community were, in the words of William Oualid, "the eradication of all social and ideological differences" that separated immigrants from their French coreligionists.[17]

Behind the petty complaints lay a more fundamental difference separating immigrants and natives. For the native Jew, the eastern European immigrant lived a too "visible" Jewish existence. His brashness reflected not only bad manners but also the assertion of a Jewish identity that went far beyond the native's limited religious definition. The vocal expressions of Jewish solidarity by immigrants alarmed the native, for he feared that the intervention of the "Jewish question" in Paris would upset the delicate balance between Jewish religious practice and integration into French life that he had so carefully preserved.

Indeed, native Jewry's emphasis upon personal religious belief was severely shaken by the events of the 1930s. The uncertainty over the future of Jewry led many natives, and particularly native youth, to search for alternative Jewish identities. In part the search stemmed from the pressing need to organize a strong Jewish defense against anti-Semitism. In part it reflected the human longing for community in a period of despair and confusion. A Judaism defined merely as private belief seemed to offer little direction to individuals seeking to act collectively and assertively to solve the "Jewish question."[18]

The search for a new Jewish identity among French Jews found its reflection in the growth of youth-oriented political movements. The involvement of young native Jews in organizations such as LICA implied a Jewish commitment based upon the understanding that one could not escape one's Jewish identity.[19] To many of these French Jewish youth the behavior of native religionists smacked of timidity and even self-hatred. The elaborate explanations that native Jews furnished to justify their assimilation into French life seemed hypocritical and ultimately self-defeating. The only solution was to face the bitter reality that, as one young native explained, "you are kikes, you are Jews."[20] Once this fact was understood, Jews would rally to defend themselves against anti-Semites.

The small but active Zionist youth movement among natives and children of older immigrants was another reflection of the militantly defensive attitude taken by some French Jews in the face of Nazism. The Zionists based their Jewish identification on much the same ground as the political militants. The German experience and the rapid spread of anti-Semitism had put an end to the age-old debate between nationalists and proponents of assimilation. As the editors of *Affirmation*, a militantly Zionist journal published in 1939, stated: "The Jewish people, even if they wanted to, presently find it impossible to commit national suicide."[21] The growth of anti-Semitic movements within France itself showed that political and social equality was not enough to solve the Jewish problem and that, in and of itself, assimilation could not guarantee the security of the Jewish people.[22] The "Jewish question," so feared by French Jews, did indeed exist, native Zionists argued, and it could only be solved through the establishment of a Jewish homeland.[23]

The combination of dissent within its own ranks and the ever-worsening plight of Jews in Europe forced native religious Jews to reevaluate their attitudes. At first, Consistoire leaders moved quickly to stave off further alienation among its youth. *Chema Israël*, a debating group, was created to act as a public forum for discussions of Jewish concern, although more often than not meetings degenerated into propaganda sessions for renewed religious commitment.[24] A special chaplain's post for youth was established to bring wayward natives back into the fold.[25] Novel methods of Jewish education were devised to attract blase youth.[26] The dogged adherence of native Jewish leaders to a limited religious outlook, however, deprived them of much influence.

Far more important was the Consistoire's assessment of Zionism. As we have seen, natives by and large rejected the notion of a Jewish peoplehood.[27] As part of his acceptance into French society, the Jew was obliged to throw off everything that made him a pariah or retarded his development. The integration of Jews into French society did not mean total assimilation, however; natives did not wish to abandon their religious faith. Instead, they viewed their integration, in the words of Raoul Raymond Lambert, the editor of *L'Univers israélite*, as "a progressive adaptation, an acceptance of the obligations imposed by the social milieu, by the national collectivity that welcomes and in the end admits [them] without legal discrimination." [28]

The influx of stateless immigrants to France in the 1930s, however, forced natives to take a second look at the Jewish national question. Already in the early thirties, French Jewish leaders were beginning to speak of Zionism as a viable alternative for those Jews who were not fortunate enough to live in a democratic nation. [29] By 1937, with the growth of optimism over the possibility of the creation of a Jewish homeland, natives were talking of the settlement of eastern and central European refugees in Palestine.

The new attitude toward Zionism was best expressed in a sermon delivered by Rabbi Kaplan at the rue de la Victoire synagogue on April 2, 1937. [30] The idea of the return to Zion as a means of ending the oppression of Jews, Kaplan noted, was a continual theme in Jewish liturgy and Jewish history. In time, however, another solution had presented itself: emancipation, the granting of full civic rights to Jews. But the example of the French Revolution was not followed by other nations. The continued oppression of Jews culminating in Nazi barbarism meant that Jews in many countries continued to view the Holy Land as a place of refuge. "The resurrection of Palestine," Kaplan concluded, thus became "the great miracle of our time."

Yet despite the possibility of settlement that a Jewish homeland offered persecuted Jews, Kaplan continued, French Jews continued to look upon Palestine with great skepticism. Zionism seemed incompatible with the native's attachment to France, with his fidelity to spiritual values, and with his commonsensical understanding of the limited possibilities of development that Palestine offered. The patriotism of French Zionists, however, was unquestioned. Obviously, Kaplan pointed out, "It would never occur to them [Frenchmen] that we are Zionists to the point of renouncing French nationality in order to reclaim Jewish nationality." Indeed, French Jews had a patriotic obligation to take an interest in Palestine in order to assure continued French presence in the Middle East. [31] Similarly, if Zionist leaders were opposed to religious values, it was only because native Jewry had not taken an active part in the movement. French Jews should now assume the responsibility of creating "a spiritual renaissance" in the Zionist movement so that those Jews who were contemplating settlement in Palestine would be immersed in "the spirit of the Torah." Finally, Kaplan argued, although the possibilities of development and absorption of Jews in Palestine were limited, native Jews were not to become Cassandras but instead were to hope for what minimal successes could be achieved.

Although much of native involvement in Zionist movements stemmed from a fear of their domination by political and anti-religious elements, the commitment to a national Jewish solution remained an important part of native thought in the 1930s. Of course, this commitment applied only to those less fortunate Jews who were not permitted to integrate themselves into the larger societies in which they found themselves. The long discussions on Zionism in native journals generally included a disclaimer that French Jews had little interest in personally participating in the establishment of a Jewish homeland. Instead, French Jews were said to have a messianic mission in the Diaspora as the exponents of the ethical teachings of the Biblical prophets. At most, a Jewish State established on a religious foundation would help to revive interest in Judaism among assimilated Jews.[32] The religious thrust of the natives' argument meant that in the end native Jews refused to go beyond the narrow limitations imposed by their particular view of the French Jewish experience.

By and large, religious Jews arriving from eastern Europe were shocked by the natives' attitude toward Judaism. Imbued with a vision of Jewish life that revolved around a tightly structured community, they were appalled by the degree to which native Jews had accepted and indeed assimilated into French life. Often victims themselves of anti-Semitism and thus continually forced to define themselves against the outside world, they could not understand the natives' continual allusion to the distinctiveness of the French Jewish experience. Nor could they accept the adoption of "goyish" or non-Jewish practices and the rejection of much of traditional belief in the name of some ephemeral idea of emancipation. As Israel Jefroykin, one of the presidents of the Fédération in the 1930s, noted, French Jewry seemed to immigrants to be like "a mental Androgenes, neither this nor that—possibly a mixture of dormant Jewish tradition and superficial European civilization."[33]

The immigrant's religious commitment stemmed from centuries of isolation. The long and tragic history of persecutions and pogroms had created a hard core of belief among Jews of eastern Europe that had enabled them to survive despite adverse conditions. Tampering with these beliefs, whether for the sake of "progress" or acceptance by the outside world, traditional Jews argued, would have the most disastrous results. Orthodox immigrants remained unimpressed by native arguments about the differences between an "enlightened" French government and "backward" eastern European regimes. The lesson of German Jewry had shown that even in the most "enlightened" countries it was suicidal to lower one's defenses.[34]

But the maintenance of strict adherence to Judaism among immigrants did not stem only from a refusal to participate in non-Jewish society. Religious belief for the practicing immigrant was a total commitment which aided him in coping with all problems, whether mundane or spiritual. There was no separation of duties into secular and religious realms as espoused by French Jewry. To do so, it was argued, would be to reduce Judaism to a catechism, a lifeless set of doctrines having little influence on daily life. Far from an outworn doctrine, traditional Judaism had shown a remarkable resiliency and adaptability in the face of the myriad of problems that had beset Jewry throughout its history. There was no reason to believe that it could not survive the French experience.[35]

In actuality, of course, religious beliefs differed widely among traditional immigrants. National origin was by far the most important factor in shaping religious practice, although Jews from the same country often differed among themselves according to particular rituals native to specific cities or *shtetlakh*. The numerous *shuls* that grew up in Paris in the period between the two world wars attested to the zealousness with which immigrants guarded their own religious practices, however little they differed from other Jews.[36] By the 1930s the French capital was dotted with small religious communities, microcosms of eastern European *shtetlakh* transported to western Europe.[27]

Despite the plethora of *shuls*, the immigrant's life in Paris did not favor the continuation of religious belief and practice. Exposed to new ideas and ideologies, many immigrants were led to reject religion as outdated and irrational. Still others found religious practice to be a major obstacle in their attempts to establish social relations with Frenchmen.[38] Those that persisted in Jewish practice were also betrayed by their economic conditions. Poorly paid, they could not afford to buy the more expensive kosher meats required by

Jewish law. Nor could they observe the Sabbath, since many businesses in the clothing and textile trades remained open on Saturday. Even home-laborers who ostensibly controlled their own work schedule were forced to work the entire week in order to earn a subsistence income.

Yet in spite of the many obstacles, a sizable proportion of the immigrant population continued to practice their faith, if only in a partial sense. Although Sabbath services were poorly attended, immigrants flocked to the *shuls* on the High Holidays.[39] The buying power of most immigrants was curtailed sharply by their worsening economic condition, yet merchants did thriving business during the holiday seasons. The religiously oriented Yiddish daily *Pariser Haint* continued to outsell the Yiddish Communist paper throughout the 1930s. Even the Belleville area, the center of left-wing activity among immigrants, maintained a number of synagogues and kosher butchers.[40]

One of the most interesting measures of the religiosity of immigrants was the viciousness with which left-wing elements in the community attacked Judaism and religious leaders. In the period before the rise of the Popular Front, the pages of *Naie Presse* abounded in anticlerical propaganda. Religious leaders were depicted as exploiters and parasites, thriving on the naiveté of the Jewish masses.[41] Judaism, Communists and Bundists argued in good Marxist form, was the "opiate of the Jewish people," a series of myths and deceptions used by rich Jews to obfuscate class consciousness and thus create a passive acceptance of bourgeois exploitation among the mass of Jews.[42] In moments of desperation, left-wing immigrants even accused religious leaders of engaging in alliances with anti-Semites to further their own selfish ends.

The rise of Nazism and the need for an active Jewish response forced Communists at least to take another look at the mass of practicing immigrants in Paris. The fact that a large number of Jewish artisans and workers continued to practice Judaism despite the protestations of their political and trade-union leaders also led left-wing immigrants to reevaluate their anticlerical position.[43] Beginning in September 1936 a series of articles were published in *Naie Presse* calling specifically on religious Jews to band together against Nazism and anti-Semitism. Gone were the articles condemning reactionary clerics and parasitical sextons. In their place one read of blessings made in synagogues in support of Léon Blum (a "blow against Hitler," the writer noted) and of a funeral of a young Jewish Communist at which both the *kadish*, the traditional hymn for the dead, and the *Internationale* were sung.[44]

Bundists and other sectarians were quick to point out the opportunism of the Communists' change of heart. In article after article in *Unzer Stime*, Bundists attacked Communist attempts to woo religious immigrants. The Communists' acceptance of alliances with "clerico-reactionary" organizations, they maintained, represented a betrayal of the interests of the Jewish working class and a complete reversal of previous positions held by Communist leaders. The goal of the "progressive" forces in the Jewish community was not to further myths and deceptions among the Jewish masses but to destroy them and to replace them with rational and relevant ideas.[45]

It was certainly true, as the Bundists maintained, that Communist overtures to religious Jews stemmed in part from political opportunism, specifically the desire to widen their influence over the immigrant community. Yet beyond the Communists' political machinations lay a beginning attempt to redefine traditional beliefs in modern-day terms. One of the most interesting examples of this attempt can be seen in the changing attitudes of left-wing immigrants to the Passover holiday. In the period before the Popular Front, each Passover season was greeted in the pages of *Naie Presse* with scathing articles denouncing the holiday and its elaborate ritual observance as a sham perpetrated by bourgeois Jews upon the well-meaning but naïve Jewish masses. The Exodus story, trumpeted by religious leaders as the liberation of the Jewish people, was revealed in the left-wing press as a complete myth and its ideal of freedom nothing but a hidden form of enslavement to religious dogma.[46] In 1938, however, in the wake of increased persecution of Jews in central Europe and pessimism sweeping over the Paris immigrant community, Communists began to call upon Jews to look to their holidays for inner strength. In an article published in *Naie Presse* on April 16, 1938, for example, a Communist writer spoke of Passover as a festival of freedom. Although debunking much of the Biblical story, he concluded that the history of the Exodus could well give Jews in Fascist-controlled lands hope for eventual liberation. To be sure, none of the articles could be interpreted as a return to traditional Judaism. Yet the continual references made to religious beliefs and practices showed that many immigrant Communists were dissatisfied with a pat anticlerical posture in the face of anti-Semitism.[47]

For many immigrants, religion was only one part of *yidishkayt*, a concept that can be defined roughly as the compendium of eastern European *shtetl* culture. It was not necessary to accept all of the accoutrements of the *shtetl* to partake in *yidishkayt*. Of more importance was the weltanschauung that lay behind the cultural patterns—the "Jewish soul"— born through centuries of daily life in the ghetto and alive wherever Jews maintained their ties with eastern European culture. No matter what the attractions of other cultures that Jews encountered in their travels in the Diaspora, *yidishkayt* could never be erased completely from the immigrant's psyche. As a writer in *Pariser Haint* noted in talking of *yidishkayt*: "Its spinning wheel has woven a cloth that no other wheel can unravel."[48]

The medium of transmitting *yidishkayt* was the Yiddish language. Originating in central Europe and developed in the daily contacts among Jews in eastern Europe, Yiddish was said to be part of popular folklore, untranslatable into other languages, and uninteresting to anyone not steeped in *yidishkayt*. To know Yiddish, therefore, was to experience the "Jewish soul." No wonder that the writer of the article cited above stated: "Frenchmen can never understand [Yiddish] and never want to know it." It followed that for Jews to forsake Yiddish would mean the destruction of a vital link between eastern European culture and Jews scattered throughout the world.[49]

For left-wing immigrants the idea of *yidishkayt* smacked of a return to the ghetto. What was needed, they argued, was not a wholesale acceptance of the eastern European cultural heritage in the form of some mystical "Jewish soul" but rather a selective application of its more "progressive" elements to the new community that immigrants were creating in Paris. Vehemently opposed to assimilation, left-wing immigrants were equally opposed to nostalgic longings for a past that could never return.[50]

The problem of choosing exactly what was "progressive" in *yidishkayt* proved a ticklish one for left-wing immigrants. All agreed that Yiddish was to be maintained as the distinctive language of the Jewish masses, but there was great confusion over exactly what its role was to be. The very same intellectuals who argued in the pages of *Naie Presse* against the idea of Yiddish as an end in itself saw no contradiction in writing picayune articles detailing the "progressive" manner of spelling Yiddish words.[51] Similarly, although committed to the view that literature should reflect the modern-day problems of the Jewish masses, many left-wing immigrants could not bear to part with the Yiddish classics. The result was a desperate and often ludicrous attempt to reinterpret the works of Sholem Aleichem, Mendele Mokher Seforim, Y. L. Peretz, and other classical writers as works of "socialist realism" reflecting the plight of the Jewish masses.[52]

Despite valiant attempts, left-wing efforts to borrow selectively from *yidishkayt* were doomed to failure. Although most were adamant in their rejection of traditional religion, many Communists, as we have seen, had begun to reevaluate their anticlerical statements by the late thirties. Those that did not attempt a reevaluation remained unwillingly tied to the religious ethos through their adherence to Yiddish. Thus, for example, while Communists and Bundists alike judiciously avoided the use of the word *Judaism* (except to refer derogatorily to the beliefs of native Jewry) and defined *yid* (Jew) as someone who spoke Yiddish, they could not avoid religiously derived words like *shabos* (Saturday) and *yuntav* (holiday). Nor could they eliminate the many expressions taken from Biblical and Talmudic sources. At times of great despair in the immigrant community, one could even find traces of the "Jewish soul" among left-wing elements.[53] Nor was it uncommon to find them defending the values of *shtetl* life against the onslaught of modern popular culture.[54] In the end, the cloth of *yidishkayt* spoken of by the writer in *Pariser Haint* proved too well woven for left-wing immigrants to separate its fibers.

Although Zionism had little influence among Paris immigrants in the prewar period, the idea of a Jewish people or *klal yisroel* was an important part of *yidishkayt*. The Jews were a people, immigrants argued, not because of a common land but rather because of a common history and culture. Jewish history attested to the past existence of a nation in the Land of Israel. When the Jews were forced to flee into exile, the national unit broke up into many small communities scattered throughout the world. In eastern Europe persecution had led Jews to create a strong communal life where the laws of Judaism took the place of state and government. In cities like Paris, where Jews were relatively free to do as they wished, the community was said to be badly fragmented. Yet despite differing views on the nature of Jewish identity and the physical distance separating one community from another, there existed a bond of all Jews that transcended particularities of place and time. It was this bond of an ongoing Jewish people or community, the traditional saying went, that made all Jews responsible for one another.[55]

In actual fact, of course, most immigrants were not completely honest in their espousal of *klal yisroel*. *Yidishkayt* was based upon the culture of the *shtetl*. It thus was as alien to Alsatian and Sephardic Jews, the former only dimly recalling their ghetto past, the latter never having experienced it, as it was to non-Jews. In the end, the notion of a Jewish community for immigrants came to be defined negatively as a community separate from native elements. Even among immigrants, however, there were sharp differentiations made along the lines of geographical origin and Yiddish dialect.

At first, left-wing immigrants attacked both Zionists and *klal-yisroeldikes* for their notions of a distinct Jewish people. For them, Jews could not be a nation as long as capitalist society separated humanity into opposing classes. The idea of *klal yisroel* was particularly reprehensible since it talked of the unity of bourgeois exploiter and oppressed worker in the name of some illusory people lacking territory, common language, and government. As long as capitalist society existed, left-wing immigrants maintained, Jews would be divided objectively along class lines, although subjectively prey to the irrational ties of religion and a religiously oriented culture. With the coming of revolution, however, Jews would be free to develop a "true" culture. Only then would they be able to call themselves a nation. The experience of Birobidjan, the short-lived Jewish republic in the Soviet Union, was pointed to as an example of Jewish national liberation through the victory of socialism.[56]

The emphasis that left-wing Jews placed upon revolution as the precondition for the development of a "true" Jewish culture led them to downplay interest in Jewish cultural life in the period before the Popular Front. Where cultural matters were discussed, interest centered more on the evils of *shtetl* life transferred to Paris than on alternative cultural patterns. True, immigrant Communists often spoke of a "revolutionary Jewish working-class culture" and the need to become acquainted with the life and ideas of the Jewish laboring masses. Yet the Jewish working class was never defined as a separate entity; "revolutionary Jewish working-class culture" was merely the application of universal patterns of working-class life to a Jewish milieu. Jewish workers thus were urged to study their history less as a reflection of a distinctive cultural heritage than as a pragmatic necessity in order to prepare for the impending world revolution.[57] Similarly, Jewish Communists demanded that workers' children become proficient in Yiddish so that they would be better able to communicate with their parents and thus grow to understand the nature of the class struggle in the Jewish community.[58]

The clear-cut Marxian analysis of the notion of a Jewish people belied an ambiguity in left-wing immigrants' minds. Although seemingly bound to a theory of class conflict, writers in *Naie Presse* often spoke of the "glorious traditions of the Jewish people" and of "Jewish liberation" from persecution and oppression.[59] Words like *tradition*, *culture*, and *people* were bandied about in left-wing discussions of Jewish life, especially in the period after the rise of the Popular Front, but were never clearly defined. Y. Lerman, a leading Jewish Communist in the 1930s, reflected this vagueness in a speech he gave before the Yiddish Culture Congress in 1937. After stating that the "Jewish culture" that immigrants were creating in Paris was only part of the "larger Jewish culture," he called for the conservation of "the best of *Jewish tradition*—the tradition of the struggle for freedom represented by the Maccabees and the Bar-Kochbas; the struggle for truth represented by the Spinozas, Mendelsohn, and Marx; the ability to penetrate the *soul of a people* represented by Yiddish classical writers such as Mendele, Sholem Aleichem, Peretz, etc." [italics added].[60]

Once again the answer lies with a change of heart and attitude that was clearly noticeable in left-wing Jewish ideology in Paris in the 1930s. Political immigrants arriving in the capital between the two world wars were shocked to find a Jewish cultural life that bore a striking resemblance to the repressive atmosphere that they thought they had left behind in the eastern European *shtetl*. It was not surprising, therefore, that left-wing polemics in Paris merely took up where polemics in eastern Europe had left off. The enemies were the same—religion, *klal-yisroeldike* ideas, *yidishkayt*. Only the battle-ground had changed. The rigidity of the Communist tactic of class against class, which made little allowance for the specific conditions existing in different countries, and the fact that many left-wing immigrants did not view Paris as a place of permanent settlement only reinforced the left-wing Jewish view.

By 1935 left-wing Jewish ideology had undergone a remarkable transformation. In part this stemmed from a change in the Communist "line," which now preached a more liberal attitude toward the non–working-class masses. Jewish Communists now felt free to devote their attention to the thousands of petit bourgeois and artisan elements that made up the bulk of the Jewish community in Paris. A more important factor was the recognition by left-wing Jewish immigrants that their future lay not in the revolution in eastern Europe but in the development of the Paris Jewish community and its alliance with forces of revolutionary change in France.

The redirection of left-wing concerns toward the problems of the Jewish community in Paris brought with it a clear-cut espousal of the necessity for a new Jewish culture. Significantly, Jewish culture was no longer viewed as class-bound. Jewish workers were now said to be only the "best bearers of modern Jewish culture in France" and not the subject of the culture itself, a redefinition that implied that all Jews could participate in the new cultural patterns that were in the process of forming.[61] If some of the more dogmatic immigrants continued to speak of a Jewish proletarian culture,[62] most left-wing immigrants looked to a cultural life that would reflect the problems and hopes of the immigrant community in Paris as a whole.

But what exactly did a modern Jewish culture entail? As we have already seen, left-wing immigrants placed great emphasis upon the selective application of so-called "progressive" aspects of *shtetl* life to modern-day problems. Similarly, Lerman's speech before the Yiddish Culture Congress in 1937 reflected the concern with "the best of Jewish tradition," that is, with those events and figures in Jewish history that could provide examples to Jews faced with persecution and oppression in the 1930s. If these attempts were not always successful (and the speech by Lerman certainly reflects the confusions that grew out of these attempts), it was only because such a reassessment had never really been attempted before. When one considers that the reassessment was spearheaded by left-wing elements heretofore caught up in an ideology that had no room for notions of a specific Jewish culture or a Jewish peoplehood, one sees how difficult a task it was.

Although left-wing immigrants took a particularly active interest in the question of a modern Jewish culture in Paris—they were responsible for the convocation of the International Yiddish Culture Congress in Paris in 1937, for example—it would be wrong to assume that the other immigrants were not equally concerned with the problem. Unlike militants who tended to link Jewish culture with the struggle against Fascism, nonpolitical elements saw the development of a Jewish cultural life in Paris less as a momentary response to conditions around them than as part of a great ongoing tradition.[63] Cultural patterns were to develop naturally from the daily experiences of eastern European Jews in Paris. The end result was not really a "new" culture, as left-wing immigrants argued, but rather a synthesis arising from the interaction between eastern European culture and the cultural life of western Europe.[64] There was thus no need to weed out that which was "reactionary" in *yidishkayt*. Jewish history had shown how Jews in strange lands adapted themselves to their new environment. Those aspects of *shtetl* life that were not applicable to life in Paris would merely drop away from disuse. This was not to say that nonpolitical immigrants did not fear assimilation. They had only to look at native Jewry to see where a lax attitude might lead. Yet immigrants felt that as long as they could build a strong community with effective educational and cultural institutions, there was nothing to fear.

It is difficult to gauge the reaction of the average immigrant to these developments. It is clear that already in the early thirties, there were signs of cultural change in response to problems encountered by immigrants in Paris. At first, accretions were minor and often unintentional. French words began to seep into the vocabulary of Yiddish-speaking immigrants. Thus, for example, the words *façonnier* and *marchand* replaced *alayn arbeter* and *klaynhandler*, respectively, in discussions of the "Jewish" trades. Similarly, French phrases such as *Merci* and *Il n'y a pas de quoi* began to be used with more frequency in immigrant conversations. Business contacts between immigrants and Frenchmen led to the creation of hybrid phrases like *a la gelt*, that is, working for a percentage without a fixed salary, and *makht attention*.[65]

Aside from the unconscious accretions reflected in the introduction of French words into Yiddish, there were other signs of a growing accommodation of immigrant Jews to French life. Thus immigrants flocked to the courses in French language and literature offered by the various popular universities.[66] Similarly, studies of the reading habits of immigrants conducted by Jewish libraries in Paris revealed that although books by Yiddish writers continued to be in greatest demand, there was also increasing interest in French writers such as Henri Barbusse, Romain Rolland, and André Malraux.[67] One might also point to the decrease in the number of nostalgic articles in the Yiddish papers dealing with eastern Europe and their replacement by long and detailed analyses of life in Paris.[68]

Equally significant was the appearance of a number of fictional pieces in Yiddish newspapers dealing specifically with immigrant life in Paris. In most cases, these *feuilletons* or serials were written to propagandize a particular point of view and had little literary merit.[69] Yiddish writers in Paris produced few serious works on the Jewish community before World War II.[70] Keenly interested in contributing to the new culture, they nevertheless felt uneasy writing about a community that was only in the process of becoming. The "Old World" was settled and fixed, one writer noted in an article in *Pariser Haint*; life in Paris, on the other hand, seemed "formless, splintered, and subject to blind fate."[71]

None of these developments, however, sheds light on the question of the immigrant's receptivity to the notion of a modern Jewish culture. At most, they provide an insight into immigrant accultura- tion, certainly a necessary condition for the growth of a distinctive Jewish culture in Paris. The fact is that there was preciously little in Paris in the 1930s that could actually be called a newly developed Jewish cultural pattern. The concept of a modern Jewish culture was a topic of much discussion in the Yiddish dailies and certainly did not go unnoticed by immigrants. Yet most Jews thought of it, if they thought of it at all, only in terms of some future development. It should also be noted, as pointed out to me by all of the individuals that I interviewed who had been active in the Paris community in the 1930s, that the necessity for Jews to react quickly to events in the 1930s gave them little time to ponder the problems involved in the creation of a new culture.[72] One may therefore venture the guess that although the life of the average immigrant was changing to fit the new environment of Paris in the 1930s, he was only dimly aware of it and certainly not in any structured sense of the creation of a modern Jewish culture.

Notes

1. For native discussions in the 1930s of French Jewish history, see, for example, Bauer and the speech by Philippe Erlanger, a member of the *Comité central* of the Alliance israélite universelle, at a meeting of Chema Israël and cited in *L'Univers israélite*, December 31, 1937.

2. In actual fact, it was not until the fall of the Bourbons in 1830 and the accession of Louis Philippe to power that the last restriction on Jewish rights was eliminated.

3. William Oualid, in an article in *La Revue juive de Génève* (June 1934), p. 361. Oualid is one of the more interesting French Jewish leaders in the period. An Algerian Jew, he showed a rare sensitivity to the plight of eastern European Jews in Paris and was one of the most ardent supporters of a rapprochement between the native and immigrant communities. A professor at the Faculté de Droit of the Sorbonne, and a close friend of Léon Blum, he often made *démarches* to government leaders on behalf of refugees. Because of his rather tolerant views, and in his capacity as secretary of the *Section administrative* of the Consistoire de Paris, he was often delegated to act as the organization's representative at functions sponsored by the immigrant community.

4. For a discussion of the "ghetto without Judaism" phenomenon as it applies to French Jewry, see Pierre Aubery, p. 29.

5. Bauer, p. 3.

6. For discussions of conversations among native Jews, see Ruppin, *The Jews in the Modern World*, p. 323; and Joseph Bonsirven, "Chronique du Judaïsme français," *Etudes*, January 5, 1933, pp. 64–83.

7. Consistoire membership increased from 4,144 in 1930 to 7,114 in 1932. From 1932 on, however, membership was in continual decline. At the same time, bar mitzvahs and religious marriages declined sharply in the 1930s, although the decline in both cases was in part attributable to the devastating effect of World War I on the French male population. (Figures taken from the Consistoire's *Assemblée générale ordinaire, 1935*, pp. 27–28.)

8. In his book on the Paris Jewish community during the Dreyfus Affair, Marrus cites Rabbi Simon Debré, who in an article in the *Jewish Quarterly Review* in April 1891 suggested two other reasons why a Reform movement was never strong in France. First, there was the general indifference of most French Jews to religious matters; thus, few natives had strong enough religious convictions to sustain a modernization movement. Second, there were few Orthodox Jews in France and thus few defenders of a strict religious tradition. The lack of a visible foe weakened the chances for an effective counterattack of reform. (Cited in Marrus, pp. 63–64.)

9. Cited in Hertzberg, p. 360.

10. For a fictionalized account of the difference between the two terms, see Edmond Cahen, *Juif, non! . . . Israélite* (Paris: Librairie de France, 1930).

An article in *L'Univers israélite* on October 20, 1933, cited an anecdote that was very popular among native Jews. It was easy to differentiate among Jews, the story went. A *juif* was someone who earned less than 300,000 francs a year; an *israélite* earned more than that; a *français d'origine sémitique* earned above 1,000,000; and a Christian earned above 10,000,000!

11. Speech by Dr. Ulmann at a ceremony at the Notre Dame de Nazareth synagogue cited in *L'Univers israélite*, July 8, 1938.

12. Passover sermon by Rabbi Jacob Kaplan cited in *L'Univers israélite*, April 15, 1937; article on youth in *L'Univers israélite*, July 14, 1939; speech by Rabbi Champagne at the Tournelles synagogue on the anniversary of the armistice ending World War I, cited in *L'Univers israélite*, November 19, 1937.

13. See, for example, the collection of sermons by Rabbi Jacob Kaplan, officiating rabbi at the rue de la Victoire synagogue in the 1930s and now Chief Rabbi of France, titled *Les Temps d'épreuves* (Paris: Editions de Minuit, 1952).

14. See, for example, the fascinating debate sponsored by Chema Israël on religious versus secular schools and cited in *L'Univers israélite*, January 21, 1938. While the director of a Consistoire-supported parochial school argued for the maintenance of Jewish day schools, a leading member of the Consistoire central denounced religious schools as particularist and divisive, arguing that Jews had a mission to mingle with non-Jews.

The exaggerated patiotism of some French Jews often blinded them to potential conflicts between the two loyalties. A highly revealing article published in *L'Univers israélite* on January 31, 1936, showed that natives could not understand the obstinacy of a Seventh Day Adventist in refusing to participate in military drills on Saturday, a religious prohibition that was also observed by orthodox Jews. The writer's conclusion was that the individual was probably mentally unbalanced!

15. Raoul-Raymond Lambert in *L'Univers israélite*, April 8, 1938.

16. For some examples of complaints, see the articles by Rabbi David Bermann in *Chalom* (March 1934) and Joseph Milbauer in *L'Univers israélite* (January 26, 1934).

Even *Samedi*, a journal run by older immigrants, although generally sympathetic to the newer immigrants' plight, criticized the latter for seeing anti-Semitism everywhere, speaking more than one language at a time, and always wanting to know who was Jewish and who was not (*Samedi*, April 24, 1937).

17. Quoted in an interview with Oualid published in *Le Temps*, November 30, 1933.

Rabbi David Bermann summarized the native's position when he stated that the French Jew "views and senses matters in a manner more like his Christian compatriots than his foreign coreligionists" (cited in *Archives israélites*, April 11, 1935).

There was a marked difference in native attitudes toward German Jewish refugees, whose history closely resembled their own. Jacques Bielinky, in his article "Les Victimes de l'Hitlérisme à Paris," published in *Menorah*, March–April 1933, p. 20, found German Jews arriving in Paris to be quiet, well dressed, polite, patient, and most importantly, inconspicuous.

18. One observer, writing in *Kadimah*, a journal published in Strasbourg, described the search for Jewish identity on the part of young natives in the following manner: "Jewish youth, reaching adolescence or born during the war, never having known, or having received Jewish culture from their parents, had to create a Jewish identity for themselves which, though not new, was intensely personal. Two factors influenced them: Zionism and anti-Semitism. They are not elements which constitute a religious revival, but pushed hard enough, they might become so. In the previous century, Jews divorced from religion remained attached to Israel through philanthropy. That seems to have been replaced today by the sense of ethnic Jewish identity" (Meyerkey in *Kadimah*, October 1933, p. 4).

19. The attitudes of young native militants toward their own Jewish identity was summed up by Lecache in an article he wrote for *Droit de vivre*, LICA's newspaper, on December 14, 1935. The article concluded with the following personal testament: "Like the most ardent of my friends, I believed in civilization and in the primacy of certain spiritual and moral values over the exigencies of base politics.... [At the same time], too many emotions, a too active sensibility, a too pronounced concern for the plight of a people whom I was surprised to discover I loved despite its many faults, instilled within me the soul of an underdog."

20. *Affirmation*, January 27, 1939.

21. *Affirmation*, January 20, 1939.

22. *La Terre retrouvée*, September 25, 1934.

23. A typical case of a young native caught up in Zionism in the 1930s was that of Juliette Stern. In an article published in *La Terre retrouvée* on June 25, 1935, she explained how she was led to Zionism by observing German Jewish refugees in Paris. Suddenly, she noted, "I felt attached to this collectivity by distant fibers I thought long broken." Taking a trip to Palestine in the early thirties, she was deeply moved and returned to Paris a committed Zionist. Concluding her personal statement, she explained, "I am at peace. My love for France will never diminish, but Palestine has an equal place in my heart."

For another personal statement, see the article by Dr. Léon Filderman in *La Terre retrouvée*, March 1, 1937.

24. Some of the topics discussed were "Judaism is social justice but not collectivism," "The Judaism is universalism without the *Internationale*," and "Is Judaism subversive?"

25. The rabbi eventually appointed to the position of youth chaplain, Mayer Jaïs,

was later to become Chief Rabbi of Paris. For information on the appointment, see the archives of the ACIP, AA23, Conseil d'administration, 1936–38, meeting of January 11, 1938.

26. By far the most imaginative program devised was a car rally where contestants were required to answer questions such as: "Identify two great French writers born of a Jewish mother, one of whom is associated with famous attempts, the other with a voluminous pursuit of unrecoverable treasure," and "Identify the person within the Paris Jewish community who has the same profession as his father, father-in-law, grandfather, and brother-in-law."

27. Such sentiments were also to be found among older immigrants affiliated with the Consistoire. Jacques Bielinky, a Russian immigrant and a frequent contributor to native Jewish publications, echoed the feelings of both native and older immigrant Jews when he noted in 1933 that "if Judaism lacks the two essential conditions for nationhood, a land and a state apparatus, it more than makes up for these lacunae with its 'spiritual territory of Israel' and with its code of ethics, which is also spiritual. Judaism, tied to its immortal past, has no need for Zionism in order to affirm its national consciousness" (*Kadimah*, April 1933, pp. 12–14).

28. *L'Univers israélite*, March 19, 1937. As editor-in-chief of *L'Univers israélite* until 1938, Lambert acted as the semiofficial spokesman of the Consistoire. His articles unerringly mirrored the opinions of the religious body, and his statements were often used by natives and immigrants in their arguments for and against the Consistoire. A major figure in the *Union générale des israélites français*, an organization established by French Jews during the war to deal with the Vichy government, he was deported in 1943 and met his death in a Nazi concentration camp.

29. See, for example, the article in *L'Univers israélite*, February 17, 1933.

30. The sermon is reproduced in Kaplan's collection of sermons, *Les Temps d'épreuves*, pp. 53–63.

31. This theme was taken up by no less a personality than Léon Blum in an article titled "Can One Be Both a Jew and a Frenchman?" published in *Pariser Haint* on May 11, 1936.

32. See, for example, the appeal by French rabbis to vote Mizrahi in the elections to the World Zionist Congress held in 1939, reproduced in *L'Univers israélite*, July 6, 1939. Among other things, Mizrahi was alleged to fight "religious ignorance and political demagoguery ... apathy toward the great moral and spiritual values of the Torah, materialist and atheistic doctrines, and the class struggle that weakens the Yishuv's ability to resist."

33. *Hebdo-Pariz*, April 12, 1935.

34. For an excellent discussion of the dilemma of the assimilationist in the face of Nazism, see the article by Dr. A. Gunzbourg in *Pariser Haint*, March 11, 1934.

35. For a discussion of "integral" or orthodox Judaism by an immigrant rabbi, see *L'Univers israélite*, March 4, 1938. For an insight into the activities of an "Old World" rabbi in Paris, see the obituary notice for Rabbi Herzog of the "Pletzl" in *Yidishe Presse Revue*, October 12, 1934.

36. The Consistoire attempted to establish *oratoires* to cater to immigrants of all origins but met with little success. In a report written to the Consistoire, the native rabbi of one *oratoire* explained his difficulties in ministering to immigrants. Among other things, the rabbi noted, there were continual conflicts between Hassidic and Mithnagdic members of the congregation. (Hassidism was a movement originating in

eastern Europe in the early eighteenth century that rebelled against the rigidity of much of Jewish law and sought instead to reemphasize the joy and personal emotionalism involved in religious worship. Mithnagdim, literally "opponents," sought a more strict interpretation of Jewish law and practice.) Similarly, some of the congregants insisted on spitting on the floor during one of the prayers, an allusion to the sign of contempt displayed by some orthodox Jews during a portion of the service to those nations who did not recognize God. Others, the rabbi went on, demanded the right to walk up and down the aisles during the services. Still others wanted sermons to be given in Yiddish. (Archives of the ACIP, B129, Lettres reçues, 1934, Affaires religieuses, letter from the rabbi of the *oratoire* on the avenue Sécrétan, dated January 7, 1935.)

37. Attempts to unite the various communities met with failure. For more information on these attempts, see the archives of the ACIP, AA21, Conseil d'administration, 1929–35, meeting of March 20, 1934; and B130, Lettres reçues, 1934, procès-verbaux de Section administrative et financière, meeting of March 12, 1934.

38. Social pressure often led immigrants to partake in non-Jewish holidays. A writer in *Pariser Haint* on January 3, 1936, summed up the traditional immigrant's attitude toward Christmas and New Year's in the following manner: "They certainly know that the two holidays are alien to the Jewish spirit, and from a Jewish standpoint they will have nothing to do with them. Yet they celebrate them automatically because the entire life of the city is structured so that one is forced to celebrate them."

Similarly, a writer in *Naie Presse* on December 23, 1937, noted that Christmas gift-giving had been adopted by many Jewish working-class parents.

39. Jacques Bielinky, in an article on immigrant *shuls*, claimed that there were about 50,000 congregants at High Holyday services in October 1935 (*L'Univers israélite*, October 18, 1935).

40. For a report on the Belleville synagogues, see the archives of the ACIP, B130, Lettres reçues, 1934, Auditions de groupements de banlieue et de la péripherie.

41. See, for example, the series of articles on the "Rabbi of Montmartre" in *Naie Presse*, April 1934.

42. As one writer noted in an article in *Naie Presse* on April 16, 1935, "The struggle to open the eyes of the Jewish working class to religious superstition, to tear them away from the clutches of clerics, also involves the struggle to weaken the influence of the bourgeoisie over artisans and to win them over to the working-class movement."

43. On August 28, 1934, for example, a writer in *Naie Presse* grudgingly admitted that 80 percent of the congregants of "Pletzl" *shuls* were workers or artisans.

44. *Naie Presse*, September 17, 1936.

45. See, for example, the article in *Unzer Stime*, March 14, 1936. Communists often responded to these attacks with quotes from Marx and Lenin to justify their downplaying of anticlerical propaganda. See, for example, the article by F. Korn in *Naie Presse*, September 26, 1936.

46. See, for example, *Naie Presse*, March 21, 1934, and April 8, 1935.

47. There appear to have been a number of immigrant Communists who continued to practice their religious tradition. A sympathetic article by A. Kremer in *Pariser Haint* (November 3, 1936) noted that there were many Jewish Communist parents who hired private tutors or *melamdim* to train their children for bar mitzvah.

Even Bundists could not escape the pull of tradition. David Einhorn, a Bundist militant in Paris, developed a rather involved thesis in the 1930s that sought to ally traditional Judaism with socialist internationalism. Although Einhorn certainly did not reflect the views of the majority of Bundist sympathizers, his ideas did find numerous reflections in articles published in *Unzer Stime*. For an examination of his ideas, see *Unzer Stime*, May 16, 1936. For a typical article that makes reference to Jewish tradition, see *Unzer Stime*, February 22, 1936.

48. *Pariser Haint*, January 20, 1933.

49. According to Roblin, 80 percent of all foreign-born Jews and 50 percent of all native-born Jews in Paris in the 1930s spoke Yiddish. All in all, 65 percent of the Jewish community spoke the language (p. 91). According to statistics presented at the Jewish Pavillion of the International Exposition held in Paris in 1937, there were 100,000 Yiddish-speaking Jews in the French capital (cited in *Naie Presse*, August 15, 1937).

In some areas of the city, Yiddish-speaking immigrants made up as much as 90 percent of the total population. See the report by Rabbi Eisenstadt, an early Russian immigrant assigned by the Consistoire to immigrant congregations, in the archives of the ACIP, B127, Lettres reçues, 1933, Affaires administratives, Administration des temples: Julien LaCroix.

50. The attitude of Jewish militants toward eastern European Jewish culture was summed up by a member of PYAT, the Yiddish working-class theater in Paris, who after viewing the adaptation of a play written by a German Communist and staged by the theater, announced triumphantly: "We have taken off our *kapotes* [the long black coats worn by traditional Jews in eastern Europe]." (Cited in *Naie Presse*, February 4, 1938.)

51. For the articles on Yiddish spelling, see *Naie Presse*, August 29, 1935, and June–July 1937.

52. A writer identified only as "M," for example, talked of Mendele's use of Yiddish to "crush the ghetto walls of religious decay and backwardness, of decrees and rules by kosher-meat tax collectors and Don Quixotes of ignorance ... [thus helping to pave the way for Jews to] build factories, collective farms, cities, and an independent republic [in the Soviet Union]" (*Naie Presse*, January 11, 1936).

For other analyses of Yiddish classical writers, see *Naie Presse*, April 18, 1935, December 14, 1935, and May 16, 1936.

PYAT was wracked with bitter debate over the question of what plays to present to its audience. Some members, like David Licht, a prominent director of the Polish Yiddish theater, argued for the presentation of Yiddish classics that embodied the rich tradition common to all Jews. Others, like Baruch Winogura, the culture critic for *Naie Presse*, took a more dogmatic stand and called for the presentation of original pieces reflecting the revolutionary potential of the Jewish working class in Paris. The debate was still unresolved when PYAT was dissolved in 1939. For Licht's attitude, see *Naie Presse*, May 7, 1937; for Winogura's position, see *Naie Presse*, June 4, 1937.

53. An article published in *Naie Presse* on January 30, 1938, for example, noted that "Jewish sorrows are as old as the world." Referring to the tragedies that befell Jews in 1937, the writer remarked that "we had the impression that just about the same thing happened in 1936, 1935, and, who knows, maybe in 1235 and even earlier."

54. Jewish Communists were particularly incensed by what they regarded as trash and sensationalism on the Yiddish stage. Thus, a reviewer of a "modern" Yiddish film noted in an article in *Naie Presse* on January 4, 1938, that "this is not one of

those cheap Yiddish films that must be 'exotic' to the audience and must appeal to their instincts through cheap songs. This is a modern film, full of original Yiddish folklore from the Polish-Jewish *shtetl* . . . from the old country."

55. For a typical example of the *klal-yisroeldike* position, see *Pariser Haint*, October 21, 1934. Zionists tended to go one step further in their arguments about Jewish peoplehood, pointing to the League of Nations' recognition of Jews in eastern Europe as a "national minority."

56. See, for example, *Naie Presse*, April 15, 1934, and December 18, 1935.

Much of Communist rhetoric about Birobidjan stemmed from the desire to counter Zionist propaganda. In personal discussions, W. Carol, a Communist militant in Paris in the 1930s, admitted that immigrant Communists had no real interest in personally participating in the Birobidjan experiment or in applying the notion of a Jewish national region to France after the revolution. Their main concern was to work for the revolution; they thought little of its long-range effect upon Jews.

57. See, for example, the article by Baruch Winogura in *Naie Presse* on February 17, 1934.

58. The Jewish Communists' attitude toward the education of working-class children was best reflected in the deliberations of the Educational Committee of the *Kultur-rat*, the central cultural organ of the left-wing immigrant community. In an article published in *Naie Presse* on March 23, 1934, the committee expressed its concern over working-class children's lack of understanding of their parents' plight in the following terms: "Where are the thousands of eight- and ten-year-old children of Jewish working-class parents? What does a mother say when there is no bread in the house? How does a father explain why the future is so uncertain? What do thousands of mothers and fathers think about their children's future, when they see them being taught by the enemy daily or, at best, by a person not caught up in the struggle of modern life, untainted from childhood? How is it possible in today's world that working-class adults hand their children over to their enemies?"

59. For some examples, see *Naie Presse*, January 1, 1937, and September 17, 1937.

50. Cited in *Naie Presse*, January 17, 1937.

61. See, for example, Lerman in *Naie Presse*, September 3, 1937.

Bundists recognized the *klal-yisroeldike* nature of the Communists' position. See, for example, the article in *Unzer Stime*, August 25, 1938.

62. See, for example, the article by Baruch Winogura in *Naie Presse*, April 14, 1939. In the article Winogura argued that Jewish "proletarian" literature had three main goals: to establish the central role of the Jewish worker in literature; to make literature "ideologically responsible"; and to aid in the struggle against reactionary forces in Jewish culture. Despite his rather sectarian view, Winogura recognized that the "times call for a more general approach to appeal to all social groups."

Communists like Winogura were obviously a source of great embarrassment for the movement in the late thirties. The militants I interviewed refused to speak about him in any detail, arguing that he was something of an "oddball" who had never been able to accommodate himself to the "freer" atmosphere of Paris life. Nevertheless, the fact that he was able to continue publishing in *Naie Presse* right up until the outbreak of World War II seems to show that at least some immigrant Communists continued to hold to a dogmatic view of Jewish life in Paris throughout the 1930s.

63. A. Alperin, the editor of *Pariser Haint* and a leading opponent of left-wing elements in the Jewish community, reflected the difference between the two views when he spoke of "those who pull the golden chain of Yiddish works from the ancient

treasures down until today and who forge our national future on the basis of our past; and those who place emphasis upon the present and for whom the holy words of the past are only a question of party politics" (*Pariser Haint*, September 24, 1937).

64. Immigrants were insistent on the fact that they did not wish to recreate the ghetto in Paris. As Vevyorke noted in an article published in *Pariser Haint* on January 9, 1938: "Modern Jewish culture demands that we partake of the culture in which we live."

65. For a discussion of the blending of French and Yiddish words, see the article by Nisan Frank in *Pariser Haint*, March 11, 1938, and the article "Frantzoyzer Verter inem Parizer Yidish," by M. Levinski, in *Yidn in Frankraykh*, 2:193–204.

66. Arnold Mandel, in his novel *Les Temps incertains*, pp. 32–33, described his experiences as a private tutor of French for immigrant Jews in Belleville. Although extremely interested in learning the language, he noted, immigrants proved troublesome students. Lessons frequently degenerated into debates, his students always demanding why one had to speak in a certain way. Totally frustrated on one occasion, Mandel wrote that he told an immigrant that if he did not pay attention, he would have to teach Yiddish to his concierge. The immigrant, a religious Jew, replied that the concierge would know Yiddish when the Messiah came. Quite so, Mandel retorted, and it would not be until then that the immigrant would know French!

For details on French courses at the popular universities, see the Fédération's *Rapport de l'activité pour l'année 1934*, p. 11; and *Naie Presse*, January 14, 1937.

67. For a study of the reading habits of immigrants frequenting the library run by the Fédération, see *Pariser Haint*, November 13, 1935; for immigrants frequenting libraries run by left-wing elements, see *Naie Presse*, January 18, 1936, and June 17, 1937.

Not surprisingly, those frequenting the left-wing libraries tended to read more books relating to the Communist movement than those attending the Fédération library. Both readerships, however, preferred Yiddish classical writers above any others.

68. The change in content in at least two of the three Yiddish dailies published in Paris in the 1930s also stemmed from the change in editorial staffs. Both *Pariser Haint* and *Unzer Stime* were subsidiaries of larger newspapers based in Warsaw. Their editorial staffs, at least in the beginning, tended to be hand-picked journalists sent to Paris from the Polish capital. As a result, both newspapers depended to a great extent upon news releases and articles coming from Poland. The situation began to change in the mid-thirties when immigrants residing in Paris and committed to the future of the Paris Jewish community attained positions of authority on the newspapers. *Naie Presse*, although independent throughout its existence, nevertheless reflected the desire of many of its writers in the early thirties to return to eastern Europe as soon as it was politically feasible. The redirection of immigrant Communist concerns in the mid-thirties found its reflection in the increasing number of articles on French life.

69. Many of these *feuilletons* dealt with the plight of the *façonnier*, a subject of great concern to both left-wing and nonpolitical immigrants. Other topics included the immigrant wife, Jewish *clochards*, and life in the "Pletzl." For two representative *feuilletons*, see *Parizer glikn* (Paris Fortunes) by Nisan Frank and *Mizrakh un maarev* (East and West) by V. Vevyorke, both published in *Pariser Haint* in late 1936 and early 1937.

70. The only novel on Paris life written in the 1930s was Shlomo Kornblum's *Rue*

de Belleville, published in Warsaw in 1935-36. The work was sharply criticized by Paris intellectuals because of the writer's unfamiliarity with the immigrant community in Paris. See, especially, Vevyorke's criticism in *Pariser Haint*, April 5, 1938.

The first novel on Paris immigrants published in the capital was B. Schlewin's *Yidn fun Belleville* (Jews of Belleville). Although not published until 1948, one can find its origins in a number of short stories written by Schlewin and published in *Naie Presse* in the 1930s.

71. V. Vevyorke in *Pariser Haint*, January 8, 1937.

72. All of the immigrants I interviewed stressed the uncertainty of their situation in the 1930s. Most of them were only in their twenties during the period and were more concerned with finding employment, dodging *gendarmes* searching for "illegal" immigrants, and establishing social relationships than with thinking about their roles in the cultural life of the Paris Jewish community. The fact that these immigrants, both nonpolitical and political, were able to lay the foundations for a distinctive immigrant culture in Paris in the face of the many obstacles they encountered is a testament to their idealism and youthful energy.

5   The Jewish Question
and the Jewish Response,
1933-37: Natives

In his work *Peut-on être juif aujourd'hui?* Roger Ikor
argues that there are fundamental differences among Jews in their
reactions to anti-Semitism. For Jews living in concentrated areas
and relatively unassimilated into the larger society, anti-Semitism
represents an external threat that can be dealt with through a
strengthening of the Jewish community from within. For more
assimilated Jews, however, anti-Semitism arises within the milieu in
which they live. No longer accepted as equal members in society,
they are now viewed as aliens who must be extirpated from the non-
Jewish community. Separated or at best only weakly tied to other
Jews, they do not know where to turn for aid.[1]

Ikor's differentiation may well be applied to native and immigrant
Jews in Paris in the 1930s. Integrated into French society in much
the same manner as their coreligionists in Germany had been
integrated into German society, native Jews were profoundly shaken
by the rise of Nazism in Europe. Bound together only by religious
ties and distrustful of eastern European Jews in Paris, they frowned
upon the idea of a specific Jewish response to anti-Semitism.
Instead, they placed uncertain faith in the humanitarianism of the
French government while cautioning fellow Jews not to arouse anti-
Semitism among their fellow Frenchmen. Immigrants, on the other
hand, had only recently left a milieu where Jewish identity was
traditionally defined against the outside society. They thus sensed
the danger of anti-Semitism more quickly than native Jews. Generally unconcerned with the image that they presented to Frenchmen,
they moved rapidly if not always effectively to mount a Jewish
protest. The contrast between the two groups can best be seen in the
differing reactions to the "Jewish question" raised in the 1930s and
in the attempts to formulate an appropriate response to the threat it
posed.

The present chapter will deal with the native community; the
following chapter with eastern European immigrants. Both chapters

will be concerned almost exclusively with the period between 1933 and 1937, beginning with the accession of Hitler to power and ending with the fall of the Blum government. It is in this period that one finds the most intense activity in the Paris Jewish community. The rise of Nazism, the growth of xenophobic feeling in France, the influx of German Jewish refugees, the victory of the Popular Front—all were instrumental in shaping the attitudes of native and immigrant Jews in Paris. By 1938 a basic pattern of attitudes and responses could be discerned which would change only slightly in the last two years before the outbreak of war.

Native Jews greeted the accession of Adolph Hitler to power in Germany in January 1933 with only mild consternation. If a few more prescient French Jews feared an upsurge of anti-Semitism in Germany as a result of the Nazi victory, most natives dismissed Hitler's anti-Jewish statements as merely propaganda designed to sway the German masses.[2] As late as November 1934, French Jews, reading accounts of a ball sponsored by the native philanthropic society *Pour nos enfants*, could laugh along with participants who saw Hitler depicted as a bumbling fool continually forgetting to put on his pants.[3] One could even find individuals in the native community who, although denouncing the brutality of totalitarian goverments, were favorably impressed by their sense of discipline and their ability to mold youth.[4]

The mood began to change only as Hitler's racial theories became known. This was not the largely religious anti-Semitism, the conflict between *goy* and *yid*, that even the most assimilated Jews had known in their own lives. Nazism was something horribly new and differ-ent:—a theory that rested not on the actions and beliefs of Jews but on their immutable biological and racial traits, a theory that sought to tackle the "Jewish question" in its entirety and to solve it once and for all. The large influx into Paris of German Jewish refugees, heretofore regarded as the most successfully assimilated of all Jews in Europe, provided telling proof of the new nature of anti-Semitism.

Yet if French Jews were only too well aware of the effects of Nazi anti-Semitism, few understood its raison d'être. Most discussions of Nazism in native journals merely begged the question by arguing that Nazism was totally irrational and thus, by implication, could never be fully explained. Germans were described as men "un-swayed by reason" who sought a scapegoat for their ills in the Jew.[5] Natives also spoke of the use of anti-Semitism by power-hungry leaders to lull the German masses into passively accepting Nazi hegemony.[6] Leaders of native organizations proved singularly unsuccessful in explaining the Nazi phenomenon to the mass of French Jews. Their rigidly religious outlook only led them to the conclusion, voiced by Rabbi Kaplan in a sermon given at the rue de la Victoire synagogue, that Jews were being punished by God for their rejection of Judaism.[7]

Far more significant was the complete lack of discussion of the role of the Jew in the creation of Nazi anti-Semitism. With only a few exceptions,[8] most articles in native journals saw the Jew as a convenient scapegoat or as just one more victim in the never-ending history of Jew hatred. Limited by their own narrow definition of Jewish identity, they were convinced that Nazi anti-Semitism was merely another manifestation of Christian hatred for Jew. The fact that most German Jews were complete assimilants seemed to have no effect upon native consciousness. As late as July 1939, Raoul-Raymond Lambert could write in *L'Univers israélite* that Jews were being thrown out of their countries for committing the crime "of remaining faithful to the religion of Abraham and of Jacob, of attempting to pray according to their own conscience, of living according to their faith, acting according to the divine commandments which in the past enabled them to build a house of peace open to all men of good will."[9]

Native Jews faced a far more pressing problem when they turned their attention to anti-Semitic movements in France. On the one hand their unwavering belief in the French democratic spirit led them to reject the idea that anti-Semitism could ever become a major force in the country. Anti-Jewish groups appeared to be aberrations, bands of cranks and demented men recruited from the Paris *demi-monde* who remained on the fringe of society. The pseudoserious nature of groups like the *Camelots de roi*, the elaborate rituals, the ornate uniforms, the exaggerated oratory were explained away as empty spectacles that in the words of one writer in *L'Univers israélite* resembled nothing so much as "a prison court-yard."[10]

Behind the self-assured tone of natives, however, lay very real fears of the growth of anti-Semitism in France. Even in the early thirties, before French anti-Semitic groups had adopted the militant tone and racial theories of Nazism, native Jews followed the attacks of men like Charles Maurras and Léon Daudet with great interest and concern. Not only were the newspapers of anti-Semitic groups read with great care, but the accusations they contained, no matter how absurd, were answered in meticulous detail. In articles and public statements, French Jewish leaders announced that Jews were neither millionaires nor Communists, neither financiers nor revolutionaries, and gave detailed analyses to prove their contentions.[11] There were even those among the native Jewish community who readily admitted that the attacks of anti-Semites were at least partially justified and were necessary correctives to a laxness in behavior on the part of Jews.[12]

Despite their concern, French Jews refused to believe that anti-Semitism was endemic in France. The espousal of racism by certain anti-Semitic groups in the country in the mid-thirties only reinforced native assurances that Jewish hatred had never been a potent force in France, for now anti-Jewish incidents in Paris could be explained as Nazi provocations and anti-Semitic groups could be identified as tools of the German government whose purpose was to weaken the unity of the French nation. Native Jews thus could convince themselves that anti-Semitism was in fact an external threat to the ideals of liberty and progress that formed the basis of French society.[13] In this peculiar logic which all but ignored the outbreak of anti-Semitism during the Dreyfus Affair, it followed that to oppose anti-Semitism was to save France from her mortal enemies.[14]

The argument that anti-Semitism in France was merely a German import answered the question of where such ideas came from but left unresolved the all important question of why they arose. The failure of native Jewry to recognize that Nazism and movements borrowing from it, unlike previous forms of anti-Semitism, were directed against both "ghettoized" and assimilated Jews led them to reject any notion of their own involvement in the rise of anti-Semitism in France. In the twisted logic of many French Jews, their exemplary conduct as French citizens, much like the conduct of their German coreligionists, shielded them from attacks by xenophobic elements. Instead, they sought an answer in the activities and behavior of eastern European immigrants in Paris.

As we have seen, French Jews regarded the boorishness and brashness of immigrants as repugnant to the French spirit. The tendency of immigrants to partake in noisy demonstrations and political meetings seemed to French Jews an affront to the host country that had freely welcomed them. With the rise of xenophobic feeling in France in the mid-1930s, these traits came to be viewed as endangering the future of the French Jewish community as well. No longer merely reflections of a "backward mentality," immigrant behavior was now said to be the major cause of anti-Semitic feeling in France.

The native position was bluntly stated by Robert de Rothschild, the president of the Consistoire de Paris, in speeches he prepared for the organization's General Assembly held on May 27, 1934, and May 26, 1935.[15] In essence, Rothschild argued that immigrants who "arrive among us with their memories and habits of Poland, Rumania, and elsewhere" retarded the assimilation process and helped create xenophobic feeling among Frenchmen. Equally dangerous was the tendency of immigrants to involve themselves in French politics, and particularly in left-wing activity.[16] The acceptance of immigrants into France, Rothschild stated, did not give them the right to discuss the policies of a country that offered them a place of refuge. Obviously taken up by his own rhetoric, the president of the Consistoire concluded the speech given in 1935 with a statement that he originally had included in his draft but had then deleted because he thought it too controversial to air publicly: "If they are not happy here, let them leave. They are guests whom we have warmly received, but they should not go about rocking the boat."[17]

The overriding fear of the association of Judaism with Bolshevism was the major factor that shaped French Jewish attitudes toward the question of the appropriate response to anti-Semitism. Consistoire leaders continually railed against the tendency of immigrants to align the attack upon anti-Semitism with the struggle against Fascism. Such activity, they argued, distorted the essentially humanitarian issue of the persecution of Jews which would normally receive the support of all Frenchmen regardless of political persuasion. In its place, immigrants had substituted a political issue that was not only irrelevant but was also bitterly opposed by honest and sincere conservative Frenchmen.[18] The natives' position did not actually imply that Jews could not participate in political activity. It merely demanded that they participate as Frenchmen and not as Jews seeking a solution to the "Jewish question."[19] Immigrant involvement in radical politics had disturbed the natives' careful synthesis of personal religious belief and active participation in French society. For the first time, natives were forced to recognize that there might indeed be a divergence between French interests and Jewish concerns.

The natives' position against Jewish political activity logically should have extended to the activity of their own organizations. Indeed, Consistoire leaders argued throughout the 1930s that the religious organization was forbidden by the Laws of Separation from participating in secular activity of any kind.[20] Yet an examination of the statements and actions of Consistoire leaders in the period between 1934 and 1936 reveals that, far from a disinterested observer, the religious organization was often closely aligned with a number of right-wing movements in France.

The relationships between the Consistoire and French right-wing movements have their origins in the aftermath of the riots of February 6, 1934. Although natives did not seriously believe that the storming of the Chamber of Deputies by right-wing bands had been motivated by anti-Semitism, they feared the latent antiforeigner feeling evident among the rioters.[21] French Jews were also disturbed by the participation of many immigrants in the various left-wing demonstrations organized after February 6 to counter the "Fascist menace."[22] Similar flirtations with radical politics in Germany were in large part responsible for the rise of Nazism and its association of Judaism with revolutionism. There was certainly a need to oppose anti-Semitism, natives argued, but the cause could not be won by alliances with groups pledged to overthrow French society.[23]

For the leaders of the Consistoire, the struggle against anti-Semitism could best be waged by the return to the *union sacrée* of World War I, when Frenchmen put aside their petty squabbles to affirm their unity behind the national war effort. The call for national unity had two definite advantages from the native point of view. On the one hand, it would divert attention from the political and economic ills of France which lay at the source of xenophobic feeling in the country. In this sense, it would also block further polarization of French society between Left and Right, already evident in the months after February 6. On the other hand, it would provide French Jews with an opportunity to display their patriotism, sorely questioned in the face of immigrant involvement in left-wing activity and of the Stavisky Affair.

In 1932 the Consistoire had conducted a memorial service in the Notre Dame de Nazareth synagogue to honor French soldiers of all faiths who had died in World War I. In 1933 a decidedly political tone was introduced into the ceremony when 500 members of the *Croix de feu*, a right-wing veterans' organization, led by their president, Colonel Casimir de La Rocque, paraded down the aisles of the rue de la Victoire synagogue in a display of national unity.[24] The ceremony was to be repeated in 1934, 1935, and 1936 and would include, besides the Croix de feu, members of the *Union national des anciens combattants,* whose secretary, Georges Lebecq, had been an active participant in the February 6 demonstrations; the *Union patriotique des français israélites,* the Jewish patriotic organization; and the *Jeunesses patriotes,* a nationalistic youth group founded by Pierre Taittinger, which was later dissolved under the Popular Front.[25] Also in attendance were prominent clergymen, representatives of the Ministry of War and of the government, and important Consistoire members. At most meetings Rabbi Kaplan, as Chief Rabbi of the rue de la Victoire synagogue, would give a speech emphasizing the loyalty of French Jews to *la patrie.* Natives made no attempt to disguise their real intentions in promoting such ceremonies. As Meyerkey, a native journalist writing in *L'Univers israélite,* noted after the 1934 ceremony: "This ceremony of the *union sacrée* was a complete success. It is hoped that it will contribute to the abatement [of hatred] so necessary at this time."[26]

Consistorial involvement with right-wing groups went beyond religious ceremonies. On at least two occasions, Rabbi Kaplan was delegated by the Chief Rabbi of Paris to speak at Croix de feu meetings. No longer concerned with merely countering the image of the Jew as foreigner, Kaplan praised the activities of the organization and acclaimed La Rocque as a "heroic leader." Citing the need for a spiritual revival in France to restore its moral prestige after the events of February 1934, he lauded the Croix de feu for its profound attachment to the ideals of France. Concluding his remarks at one of the meetings, he noted that although "not having the honor of being a member of your association, I still regard myself as one of you."[27]

Kaplan's public avowal of support for the Croix de feu occasioned bitter debate among Consistoire members. Leaders of the organization were led eventually in 1937 to forbid any future participation of rabbis in outside functions without the express consent of the Consistoire itself.[28] What bothered most members, however, was not consistorial involvement in political affairs but rather Kaplan's indiscretion in failing to consult with Consistoire leaders before making his statement.[29]

For some French Jews, participation in patriotic organizations was only a partial answer to the problem of anti-Semitism in France. What was needed, they argued, was the establishment of a distinctively Jewish patriotic organization that would counter the image of the Jew as left-wing agitator. The Union patriotique des français israélites, created in June 1934, sought to oppose anti-Semitism through an emphasis upon Jews as loyal citizens of France.[30] Led by Edmond Bloch, a veteran member of extreme right-wing groups in Paris, the organization stressed the role of French Jews in World War I. The solidarity of the trenches, exemplified in the story of Rabbi Abraham Bloch, who was killed while giving a crucifix to a dying soldier, had dissipated in the internal bickering and political strife that characterized French life after the war. Jews, in particular, had lost their faith in *la patrie* and, under the influence of groups like LICA, had sought to ally themselves with divisive forces. The influx of immigrants who, in the words of the founding declaration of the Union patriotique, "want to participate in our internal politics by introducing doctrines which, contrary to their statements, have nothing at all to do with the Jewish religion," only fed the flames of anti-Semitism, itself a reflection of the profound faction-alism in French life.[32] A generation of Frenchmen, both Christians and Jews, alienated from spiritual values, seemed hopelessly lost in an atmosphere of distrust and disloyalty. Now faced with the twin enemies of Bolshevism and Nazism, whose barbaric practices threat-ened French civilization, Frenchmen seemed powerless to react.[33]

The only solution, members of the Union patriotique argued, was for Frenchmen to band together in a "total union of hearts and minds." Jews had a special obligation toward France because it was the first nation, in the words of Bloch, "to have made us equal with all others."[34] Recognizing clearly that there was a growing divergence between French and Jewish interests, the leader of the organization argued that Jews had to continue to show their gratitude by openly proclaiming their loyalty to the nation before their loyalty to Jews and by opposing all elements in the Jewish community who made "open alliance with revolutionaries, thereby arousing the hostility of all French nationalist elements."[35] Only by doing so could they win back the trust of Frenchmen.

The creation of a Jewish patriotic organization was warmly received by Consistoire leaders. Robert de Rothschild, in his speech before the General Assembly of the organization in March 1934, actually suggested a name for the new organization and welcomed its participation in activities of the Paris Jewish community.[36] At subsequent sessions of the assembly, supporters of the Union patriotique pledged their readiness to follow the dictates of the Consistoire and voiced the hope that the religious body would take an active interest in the organization's growth and expansion.[37] The question remained dormant until June 1934 when, under pressure from some of its members, the Consistoire agreed to enter into discussions with the patriotic organization. The result of these meetings was a compromise. Although the Consistoire refused to support the Union patriotique openly, lest it be accused of supporting a political organization, it agreed to allow the patriotic group to send letters to the Consistoire membership to solicit new members and financial aid.[38] Members of the Union patriotique were less than jubilant over the Consistoire's decision. For the Consistoire it represented a happy if somewhat questionable solution to the problem of the organization's involvement in political affairs.

The creation of a Jewish patriotic organization with overt ties to right-wing organizations showed that there were many natives who felt a strong attachment to right-wing ideology. For the majority of French Jews, however, support of organizations such as the Croix de feu was predicated on a sincere but naïve belief that only movements for national unity could preserve the democratic and liberal ideals of France to which Jews owed their emancipation. If Consistoire leaders often mouthed right-wing slogans about the threat to French civilization from "Fascist paganism and Bolshevik materialism," they usually combined such rhetoric with appeals for a day when all men would live together in peace and brotherhood.[39]

Indeed, natives walked a tightrope in their attempts to dispel notions of an alliance between Jewish interests and the interests of the Left. The fear of the association between Judaism and Bolshevism led them to emphasize their strong opposition to the Soviet Union. At the same time, they had to be careful lest they fall into line with the more extreme anticommunist sentiments of the far Right which saw the salvation of Western civilization in Hitler's Germany. The result was a concerted effort on the part of French Jewish spokesmen to find a middle path that would emphasize their opposition to all forms of totalitarianism while at the same time defending the ideals of the French Republic.

Problems came to a head in 1936, however, when the Consistoire again asked La Rocque and the Croix de feu to participate in the annual memorial service at the rue de la Victoire synagogue. Two events had occurred in the months before the ceremony that cast doubts on the attachment of the right-wing organization to the ideals of the French Republic. First, there was the refusal of La Rocque to disassociate himself from Croix de feu leaders in Constantine, Algeria, who openly preached hatred of Jews among the Arab population. La Rocque showed a similar unwillingness to disavow the statement by Xavier Vallat, a prominent right-wing deputy and a member of the Croix de feu, attacking Léon Blum, the new premier, as a tactless and stupid Jew. Secondly, there was the demand by the newly elected Popular Front for the dissolution of all patriotic leagues as a threat to a democratic France. How could the Consistoire continue to maintain alliances with the Croix de feu, many natives asked, when it was publicly proclaimed an enemy of the ideals which French Jews held so dear? Would not the religious organization's decision to hold the ceremony be viewed as a political act and thus contrary to the Consistoire's own espousal of political noninvolvement?[40]

The Consistoire's weak attempt to justify its decision to hold the ceremony did little to mollify dissension within its own ranks.[41] The ceremony itself, held on June 14, 1936, was accompanied by massive protests outside the synagogue and bitter diatribes in both the native and immigrant Jewish press. In the months following the ceremony, a number of prominent members resigned in protest against the Consistoire's action.[42] The religious organization seemed to have had its own misgivings after the service. In an article published in *L'Univers israélite* five days after the ceremony, Lambert unconvincingly argued that the Consistoire had made a commitment to the Croix de feu months before the victory of the Popular Front and felt that it could not renege on its agreement. It is significant, however, that the service of June 14, 1936, was the last of its kind conducted by Consistoire rabbis in the period before the outbreak of World War II. Though the religious organization continued to hold patriotic ceremonies up until 1939, it expressly banned participation by any groups that had been declared illegal under the Popular Front.

Despite its break with French right-wing movements, the Consistoire continued to maintain warm relations with the Union patriotique des français israélites. The two organizations saw eye to eye on the question of the outcome of the crucial elections of April–May 1936. Although the Consistoire never openly advocated the election of any specific candidates, its continual emphasis upon the need to destroy the myth of a "Jewish political bloc" was a clear warning to Paris Jews to think carefully before voting to the Left.[43] Consistoire leaders also seem to have given their blessing to Edmond Bloch, the president of the Union patriotique and a candidate in the "Pletzl" area.[44] There is also strong reason to believe that an important member of the Consistoire central personally visited Léon Blum after his victory and urged him to retire in order to prevent the outbreak of

anti-Semitism.[45] In all events, it was obvious from the articles published in *L'Univers israélite* after Blum's victory that the Consistoire
was less than enthusiastic with the prospect of having a Jew as
premier of France.[46] Nor was it surprising that the journal published
a declaration of the Union patriotique expressing disapproval of the
government coalition because some of its members were alleged to
be collaborating with the Comintern.[47]

The Consistoire was never to break openly with the Union
patriotique. Nevertheless, the latter's increasing association with
known anti-Semites and its decision banning all foreign Jews from
membership disappointed many natives who had previously welcomed the patriotic organization as a counterforce to the increasing
influence of groups like LICA.[48] By 1938 there was only minimal
contact between the two organizations. Although the Union
patriotique survived until the outbreak of war, it was never to regain
the influence it had while under the sympathetic eye of the
Consistoire.

The Consistoire had initiated its contacts with right-wing groups
because it feared the association of the "Jewish question" with
left-wing politics. Yet the demand for a strong Jewish stand against
anti-Semitism was not limited to left-wing immigrants. Concerned
natives and immigrants affiliated with the Fédération des sociétés
juives de France argued with equal fervor for a specific Jewish
response to the threat of Nazism. The Consistoire, as the self-
proclaimed spokesman of the Paris Jewish community, could not
ignore these demands. Not only did it fear losing the support of
natives disenchanted with its activities, but it also risked alienating
religious immigrants who might be sympathetic to joining the
organization.

As we have seen, French Jews generally opposed demonstrations
organized to protest the persecution of Jews in central Europe. The
irresponsibility displayed by immigrant leaders at protest meetings,
and their alienation from French life, natives argued, led them to
make impossible demands upon the French government and to
attack precisely those forces who could be of greatest help to Jews.
The involvement of natives in protest actions, it was further argued,
would only result in the besmirching of the reputation of the only
element in the Jewish community that was respected by the French
government and by Frenchmen in general. Few natives understood
the important role that the Consistoire could play in assuming the
leadership of a Jewish campaign against Nazism.[49] Instead, French
Jews spoke of quiet diplomacy carried on by Jewish "notables" and

urged both natives and immigrants to make themselves as inconspicuous as possible.[50]

The emphasis upon the invisibility of the Jewish community led
Consistoire leaders to reject other forms of Jewish protest. Thus, the
idea of a boycott of German goods was dismissed as irresponsible
and giving credence to the belief that Jews were seeking to control
the world's economy.[51] Similarly, French Jews responded to the
attempts by LICA to defend Jewish quarters from attacks by anti-
Semitic bands with calls for calm and with assurances that, in the
words of one observer in *L'Univers israélite,* "it would be folly and
an impossibility for any group to organize a pogrom in this quarter
where eight out of ten inhabitants are Jews."[52] In still another
instance, the murder in February 1936 of the leader of the Swiss
Nazi party by David Frankfurter, a Polish Jewish youth who had
seen his family sent off to a concentration camp, aroused great
sympathy among immigrants in Paris and triggered off a number of
large demonstrations. In contrast, Arnold Mandel, a young writer
expressing the views of the Consistoire, called Frankfurter's act "the
banal act of a desperate man" and voiced the hope that "a day will
come when he will be pardoned and forgotten."[53] Consistoire
leaders even shied away from religious ceremonies that might be
construed as a Jewish protest against Nazi persecution. It was not
until 1937 that the religious organization allowed specific prayers to
be recited in synagogues in support of persecuted Jews.[54]

Nor would natives countenance Jewish protest on the international
level. In June 1933 both the Consistoire and the Alliance israélite
universelle received letters from the *Comité français pour le Congrès
mondial juif de 1934* inviting them to send delegates to a prepa-
ratory congress that was to be held the following year.[55] The request
was to be repeated in 1936 and 1938 without any success.

A study of the debates in the *conseil d'administration* of the
Consistoire and the executive of the Alliance sheds light on the major
attitudes of French Jews toward the question of a Jewish response.
One position, maintained by a small group of natives led by William
Oualid, called for a flexible attitude. The mere fact that immigrants
in Paris had rallied to the cause of the congress, they argued, should
have been reason enough for native organizations to take a serious
look at the possibilities that a World Jewish Congress offered. The
organizers of the French committee for the congress were immigrants having only tangential contact with the Paris Jewish community, and thus the decisions they made would not reflect French
Jewish opinion. It thus was the obligation of the Consistoire to

become involved in the World Jewish Congress if only to assure that the interests of French Jewry were defended. The participation of the religious body, these natives concluded, could only enhance its position as the true representative of the Paris Jewish community.[56]

The opponents of participation offered varying arguments. Some rebelled against any action that involved only Jews, a position that carried the Consistoire's opposition to Jewish protest to its logical extreme.[57] Others voiced concern over the election procedure for the congress, arguing that new immigrants by their sheer numbers would outvote the established Paris Jewish community.[58] Still others pointed to the failure of a number of large Jewish communities around the world to choose representatives, thereby assuring that the congress would remain in the hands of political or Zionist elements whose goals were said to be inimicable to the interests of French Jewry.[59] Finally, there were those who fell back on the time-worn argument that the Consistoire was forbidden by French law from participating in any secular activity.

In their arguments, both supporters and opponents looked to the Alliance, the international representative of French Jewry, for the final decision. The statement issued by the organization in 1933 in response to the original letter from the Comité français summarized the native position.[60] The Alliance, the statement began, recognized the tragic situation of Jews in central and eastern Europe and was ready to participate in all appropriate activities in the name of Jewish solidarity. It was necessary, however, to distinguish between philanthropic, economic, and moral action, which could be undertaken on the international plane without raising any objection or criticism, and political action, which had to take into account the variety of Jewish communities and their situations. After a discussion of the differences between assimilated Jewish communities of western Europe and eastern European communities which were generally considered to be linguistic, ethnic, and religious minorities with special status, the statement concluded that no Jewish congress could generalize either action. It followed, therefore, that each community should act separately in conjunction with their government or with the League of Nations. Any other agreement would meet with strong opposition on the part of French Jewry, since they could not consider themselves as belonging legally or politically to any nation other than the French nation without going against the oath of allegiance and loyalty pledged by their forefathers.

The Alliance's position followed logically from the native's definition of his own Jewish identity. Tied to France by tradition and culture, he could not accept any notion of a loyalty beyond the borders of the nation. Defining himself as a Frenchman of the Jewish religion, he saw no reason to transcend the normal channels of protest and public expression available to all Frenchmen. If he grudgingly admitted the need for Jewish solidarity in certain cases, he was careful to point out the distinctiveness of the French Jewish past, which separated him from other coreligionists.

Although there was general opposition on the part of natives to participation in specific Jewish action both on the national and international levels, they could not avoid the problem of the German Jewish refugees.[61] At first, natives welcomed German Jews fleeing from Nazism. After all, many reasoned, German Jews were largely assimilated, cultured, wealthy, and skilled—a welcome change from the mass of eastern European immigrants who offended native sensibilities daily. The sad spectacle of assimilated Jews reduced to poverty and expelled from a country to which they had been completely loyal undoubtedly moved many natives to act on their behalf.[62]

The creation of the *Comité central d'assistance aux émigrants juifs* in April 1933 marked the first attempt by Paris natives to coordinate their aid programs for refugees. In June, in response to the large influx of German Jews, the Comité united with a number of immigrant-run groups to form the *Comité national français de secours aux refugiés allemands, victimes de l'antisémitisme*. In December, the Comité national was officially recognized as the French representative on the Advisory Committee of the League of Nation's High Commission for German Refugees.[63] From the beginning, however, it was clear that the organizers of the Comité national had more than humanitarian interests on their minds. The rather involved title of the committee represented a concerted effort by its members to avoid overt mention of Jews. In its first public statement, the group made clear what its goals were to be.[64] The Comité had been established, the statement read, because there was needless duplication among the many organizations formed to aid Jewish refugees. In particular, organizers denounced the daily *démarches* to government authorities by representatives of immigrant groups each claiming to speak in the name of Jewish refugees.[65] Not only did such intercessions fragment the aid program, but they also annoyed government officials whose assistance was vital for the success of the effort. The creation of a committee led by French Jews, "who are the only ones qualified to deal with the authorities on matters of asylum, aid, housing, and hospitalization" for refugees, would put an end to the harrassment of government leaders.

The activities of the relief organizations reflected two main fears that plagued French Jews: immigrant involvement in French affairs in a period of rising xenophobia, and the alienation of French government officials. As expected, the Comité national was run exclusively by prominent native Jewish and non-Jewish leaders in Paris, immigrants having been excluded from all positions of authority.[66] No action was undertaken without careful consultation with government officials and particularly with the Minister of Interior. Officially recognized by the French government as the sole Jewish representative body on the refugee problem, the Comité national took great pains to plead the government's cause before the Paris Jewish community. Thus it continually argued that France was merely a way-station in the refugee's journey to other countries or in his repatriation to Germany.[67] For those refugees who insisted on remaining in France, the Comité national urged settlement in areas like Corsica and the Midi, where unemployment was relatively low. Cognizant of the high percentage of professionals in the German refugee population, the organization was quick to point out that "only a few intellectuals whose talents are deemed particularly valuable" to the nation would be allowed to remain.[68]

In the period between the creation of the Comité national in June 1933 and its dissolution in July 1935, relations between native Jews and German refugees deteriorated rapidly. The accession of Hitler to power had sent not only German Jews but also so-called *Ostjuden*, Jews who had come to Germany from Poland after World War I, fleeing to France. Eastern European in dress, mannerism, language, and religious practice, the latter had many of the same characteristics of the immigrant population already the majority among Jews in Paris. Attempts by older immigrants within the Consistoire to defend eastern European refugees met with little sympathy among frightened natives.[69] Hostility was also evident in the attitudes of French Jews toward native German Jews. Despite their rhetoric about welcoming their German coreligionists with open arms, French Jews never made serious attempts to integrate German refugees into the Paris community. Contact between French and German Jews was restricted almost exclusively to discussions between French Jewish officials of relief organizations and German refugees seeking aid—a situation which did not lend itself to the creation of friendly social relationships between the two groups. Most German Jews, for their part, never seriously considered remaining in France. They regarded Paris a poor replacement for Berlin, at best a temporary asylum until the excesses of Nazism had been tempered by the realities of governing the German state. Those that thought of remaining in the French capital shunned religious organizations like the Consistoire and instead set up their own groups, not unlike immigrant *landsmanshaftn*, to maintain contact with their homeland. French Jews regarded this conscious separation as a sign of cliquishness and a refusal to intermingle with their "inferior" coreligionists in Paris.[70] They were also incensed by the unwillingness of more wealthy German Jews to help less fortunate refugees. The increased tension between Germany and France, as well as the rise in antiforeigner feeling following the Stavisky Affair, only further exacerbated relations between the two groups.[71]

By 1935 the activities of the Comité national had come almost to a complete standstill. Money was conspicuously lacking, since many natives, having originally supported the relief effort, now opposed it as futile and contrary to the interests of France.[72] The organization was also stymied by its reliance upon the French government which, because of internal economic difficulties, made it almost impossible for refugees to remain in the country. To add to the Comité national's problems, the increased restrictions placed upon aliens in France were coupled with an ever-increasing emigration of Jews from Germany.[73] Even leaders of the relief organization were beginning to question whether the refugee problem could ever be solved.[74]

The dissolution of the Comité national was announced in late July 1935. In its final declaration, the organization pointed to the economic crisis and political disturbances as the major causes for its demise.[75] Although continuing to maintain a small legal-aid office and credit union facility, the Comité national urged German Jewish refugees to emigrate to new countries. From 1935 until the outbreak of the war, native leaders were to argue for an international solution to the refugee problem. The accession of the Popular Front to power provided a brief interlude in which natives again looked to the French government to accept refugees into France and its possessions.[76] The fall of the Blum government in June 1937, however, brought more stringent legislation against aliens. The following year saw the creation of a *Comité de coordination d'aide et de coopération*, whose main purpose was to collect funds to aid recently arrived Jewish refugees from Austria. By November 1938, however, Julien

Weill, the Chief Rabbi of Paris, was declaring openly that a solution to the refugee problem depended more on Great Britain and the United States than on France, which "from all evidence can accept no more new immigrants."[77]

As we have seen, much of French Jewry's criticism of a specific Jewish response to anti-Semitism stemmed from its fear of alienating French government officials. The activities of the Comité national showed that even when natives were forced to partake in such action, they did so only with the express consent of the French government. Indebted to France for their emancipation, native Jews could well believe that its leaders would continue to champion their rights as equal citizens. If at times government officials seemed to be less than understanding of the Jewish plight, it was only because they were said to have strayed from those ideals that made France, in the words of J. H. Dreyfuss, Chief Rabbi of France in the early 1930s, "a light to the nations." What was needed, Dreyfuss argued, echoing the sentiments of French Jewry, was a return to reason, "to more humane sentiments, more in keeping with the ideals of the great nation which they [government leaders] represent."[78]

The natives' reliance upon government officials did not preclude an active involvement in the plight of persecuted Jews. As the central religious body of Paris Jewry, the Consistoire maintained direct contact with various government agencies. The close social ties between native leaders and government officials assured the organization of a sympathetic ear in French government circles. With the rise of Nazism in Germany and its anti-Semitic reflections in France, these contacts were widened to include officials in the Ministry of Foreign Affairs. Too often accused of merely passively accepting the fate of Jews in central and eastern Europe, native leaders in the 1930s were in fact continually urging government officials to act to aid Jews in other countries and advising them on the refugee problem in France.[79] As Dreyfuss's statement showed, however, this activity was viewed less as a special plea for Jews than as a call to French leaders to return to the ideals of 1789.

In its first editorial after the accession of Hitler to power, *L'Univers israélite* spelled out the attitude native Jewry was to maintain throughout the 1930s despite the vicissitudes of French foreign policy.[80] In essence, natives argued that France's policy toward Nazi Germany could never be in conflict with its unwavering loyalty to the ideals of humanitarianism. In the early thirties, French Jews found little difficulty justifying their point of view. Despite growing xenophobic feeling among its citizenry, France remained willing to accept refugees fleeing from Germany. The close working relationship between native leaders and government officials seemed to reflect a basic sympathy on the part of the French government to the plight of Jews. Natives could even point to aspects of French foreign policy that showed that the government was seeking to isolate Germany from the rest of Europe.[81] If French leaders continued to speak of accommodation with Hitler, natives argued, they were only carrying on the policy of peaceful coexistence as espoused by Aristide Briand.[82]

The policy of relying on the good will of the French government could only be maintained as long as it was believed that there was essential agreement between the national interests of France and the interests of European Jewry. By the mid-thirties, however, the belief seemed to be severely shaken. The failure of British statesmen to actively oppose Hitler's occupation of the Rhineland in 1936, the impotence of the League of Nations, the stalemated negotiations surrounding the formation of the Stresa Front—all led France to seek its own modus vivendi with Germany. No longer based upon notions of peaceful coexistence, governmental policy was motivated by a frantic desire to avoid war at all costs. Within France itself, the beneficent policy of accepting refugees had long been replaced by a view of France as at best a temporary place of refuge which could not and would not allow refugees to remain in the country for extended periods of time.

Native Jews were suddenly confronted with what appeared to be major divergencies between the interests of France and the interests of European Jewry. The changes in French foreign policy meant that to oppose accommodation with Germany in the name of humanitarianism would be to argue for war. Similarly, to request a more open policy toward refugees in France would be to ignore the economic crisis in the country. In responding to these dilemmas, French Jews made clear which interests they regarded as more crucial. Thus, for example, in an article opposing native involvement in the World Jewish Congress which was to be held in Geneva in 1935, Lambert noted that the congress was being held at the same time that Pierre Laval was signing a pact with Hitler on the limitation of airplane production in the two countries. In arguing that the congress implied an international commitment beyond the nation, he stated bluntly that "as a French citizen ... I cannot logically vote for war in Geneva and for peace in Paris."[83] By 1937 Lambert would argue that despite persecutions in Germany, French Jews would be "the last ones to demand that our country adopt a policy of hatred."[84] By the time the Munich Pact was signed in September 1938, the conflict between Jewish concerns and French national interest had been clearly resolved by native Jews. Chief Rabbi Weill echoed the sentiments of most natives when he noted in November 1938: "No one is more sympathetic than I am to the misery and pain of the 600,000 German Jews. But nothing seems more precious and necessary to me than the maintenance of peace on earth."[85]

Throughout the 1930s the policies of the established native community had come under increasing attack from more militant French Jews. Even within the Consistoire itself there were men like Oualid who argued for a more flexible attitude toward the question of a specific Jewish response. Oualid's arguments were taken up and expanded by the sons and daughters of natives and older immigrants who rebelled against the unwillingness of their parents to openly avow their commitment to fellow Jews. Banding together around movements like the *Union universelle de la jeunesse juive*, some now called for a distinct "Jewish policy" which did not take into account the interests of France.

The argument for a "Jewish policy" was outlined by Wladimir Rabinovitch, a young Zionist activist, in the pages of *Chalom* in 1933.[86] The need for a "Jewish policy," Rabinovitch argued, stemmed from the fact that Jews were a cultural minority and not merely a religious grouping. Nazis recognized this fact; hence their singling out the Jews as an enemy of the German nation. As soon as Jews recognized that they were a distinct people, Rabinovitch stated, they would understand that they had "the right to think and act as Jews in political matters within the context of the national life of the country in which we live. When we start thinking this way, then we will have *our own* policy for peace, and *our own* policy for economic growth."

Rabinovitch was unequivocal in his conviction that Jewish policy need not agree with French foreign policy. He was particularly resentful of native attempts to intermingle French ideals with Jewish ideals.[87] Jews should stop worrying about the problem of reconciliation between France and Germany, Rabinovitch argued, and begin worrying about the plight of Jews. If there was a conflict between the concerns of France and the concerns of Jews, it was the latter to which Jews had to devote their attention. As he stated: "Jews must struggle against Hitler's anti-Semitism, even if Hitler is or will become the ally of France."

Although the idea of a "Jewish policy" found great support among native militants,[88] there were many who refused to accept the notion implied in Rabinovitch's argument that Jews would find no allies in their struggle against anti-Semitism. In particular, militants looked to the French left-wing movements for aid. Even within the Consistoire, there were those who questioned the organization's support of right-wing movements under the guise of political neutrality. The resignation of a number of prominent members after the Croix de feu ceremony in 1936 has already been mentioned. Other members went further and argued that the Consistoire should actively support the Popular Front, since it was common knowledge that left-wing movements were more sympathetic to the Jewish plight than were movements on the Right.[89]

By far the most active native supporters of left-wing movements were to be found in LICA. Lecache's organization was one of the first groups in the Paris Jewish community to organize a protest against Nazi persecution of the Jews.[90] Throughout the 1930s LICA was the most militant of all Jewish groups in the struggle against anti-Semitism both in central Europe and in France itself. Denouncing the cautious proposals of Consistoire leaders as "the policy of working in silence," its supporters called instead for direct confrontation with anti-Semitic bands and the public picketing of businesses that continued to deal with Nazi Germany.[91]

The increasing involvement of LICA with left-wing movements, however, caused a profound split in its membership. Members like Fernand Corcos, who was also active in the Consistoire, argued that as a Jewish organization, LICA's main responsibility was to unite the Jewish community and not to engage in "irrelevant" struggles against Fascism. Militants like Lecache countered that the plight of Jews was intimately tied up with struggle against dictatorships.[92]

By 1935 the organization had clearly aligned itself with the movement for a Popular Front, calling upon its members "to work among the democratic organizations of the nation for the strengthening of ties between parties and philosophies, for the victory of popular aspirations."[93] With the victory of the Popular Front in 1936, LICA devoted most of its energy to supporting "progressive" programs, the plight of Jews now relegated to only one aspect of the struggle against Fascism. The gradual transformation of the organization from a movement to counter anti-Semitism (as its name implied) to one of many movements fighting to preserve the Popular Front culminated in Lecache's admission in December 1937 that LICA was no longer a Jewish organization but rather a movement struggling against all forms of oppression created by racism.[94]

Despite Lecache's statement, LICA remained the most stalwart defender of Jewish rights within the native community in Paris. Although Lecache eventually denied its specific Jewish orientation, LICA was in fact to play a role in the attempts at unification of the Paris Jewish community in the two years directly before the outbreak of war. In choosing to ally Jewish action with the struggle against Fascism, the organization reflected the belief of many natives that anti-Semitism would never be erased without the elimination of those regimes that fostered it. The decision of its members to support the activities of left-wing movements in France followed logically from that choice.

In his memoirs on the Dreyfus Affair, Léon Blum argued that the reaction of French Jews to anti-Semitism in the 1930s was much the same as that of their fathers forty years before. Speaking of both the Dreyfus Affair and Fascism, he noted that natives "believed that anti-Semitic agitation could be deterred by their cowardly neutrality. They secretly cursed those among them, who in exposing . . . [their cowardice], created public resentment." In his judgment, they failed to understand "that no precaution, no pretense would fool the enemy and that they would soon become the victims of triumphant anti-Dreyfusism or Fascism."[95]

Although Blum's analysis may well have applied to native attitudes during the Dreyfus Affair, and Marrus' recent work seems to bear out at least some of his contentions, his analogy to the 1930s is far too simplistic. The reaction of most natives to Nazism and to anti-Semitism in the formative years between 1933 and 1937 reflects the faithful adherence of French Jewry to the ideals of liberalism. In essence, this meant a belief in the rationality of men and in the dream of emancipation as formulated during the French Revolution. Translated into day to day activity, it implied the willingness of native leaders to argue with anti-Semites on their own grounds in the conviction that the latter would sooner or later realize the irrationality of their position. Similarly, it meant a reliance on the beneficence of French government leaders who, as guardians of French liberalism, could only be sympathetic to the plight of an oppressed people.

The tragedy of French Jewry was that it remained true to its liberal heritage in a period when most Frenchmen were seriously questioning if not rejecting the liberal view. Tied to a belief in the panacea of emancipation, natives were blind to the profound anti-emancipation thrust inherent in both the German and French forms of racialism. While French Jews pondered over how anti-Semitism could arise in a country which had so willingly assimilated Jews, anti-Semites borrowing freely from Nazi theory attacked European democracies for allowing assimilated Jews to destroy their nation's racial purity. While natives sought to bury the "Jewish question" in appeals to humanitarian sentiments, anti-Semites were exposing the "insidious" influence that Jews exerted in countries which had placed humanitarianism before interests of state.

Natives showed a similar ignorance of the political winds of change sweeping across France. Imbued with a faith in the politics of compromise, they were helpless to react to the polarization of French society on the Left and Right. When eventually forced to choose, their fear of the association of Judaism with Bolshevism led them into the arms of right-wing forces whose calls for national unity were mistaken by natives as an appeal to the French democratic tradition. Beyond the petty quarrels of political parties, they looked to the French government as a stabilizing influence which they hoped would approach the "Jewish question" from a moral and not a political point of view. Morality, however, meant little to a government which saw itself torn between war and peace.

By 1937 the natives' liberal beliefs had all but been shattered by the events following the accession of Hitler to power. It remained for the Munich crisis to destroy the final remnants of that belief. As we shall see, however, the fervor with which natives had clung to the liberal view left them with few alternatives in the last year of peace but to pray that somehow men would return to reason and common sense.

Notes

1. Roger Ikor, *Peut-on être juif aujourd'hui?* (Paris: Editions Bernard Grasset, 1968), pp. 162–63.

2. See, for example, the article in *Archives israélites*, January 12, 1933.

Alliance leaders seemed to have a keener insight into the nature of Nazi anti-Semitism. In the February 1933 issue of *Paix et Droit*, the organ of the Alliance, Alfred Berl, the chief editorialist, described how the extermination of Judaism in all its forms was viewed by Nazi theoreticians as the first step in the extirpation of communism and liberalism, the major ideological rivals of the Third Reich. Berl noted, however, that he did not expect any violence against German Jewry since Hitler feared the reaction of the "civilized West."

3. For an account of the ball, see *Le Journal juif*, November 23, 1934.

4. See, for example, the article entitled "Exemples à suivre," in *L'Univers israélite*, September 1, 1933. In the article, the author, Fernand Lévy-Wogue, a member of one of the most distinguished Jewish families in Paris, commented favorably on totalitarian youth groups as movements to emulate in the intellectual and physical education of Jewish youth in Paris.

5. See, for example, the article by A. Mitzri in *Samedi*, April 11, 1936.

6. See, for example, the article by J. Tchernoff, an early Russian immigrant, in *Samedi*, June 19, 1938.

7. Kaplan concluded his sermon on September 21, 1933, with the following words: "The Eternal allowed the Children of Israel to weather the cape of the Middle Ages in order to reach the age of the French Revolution. An era of liberty was finally granted the descendants of the Patriarchs. What hymns of praise our fathers offered to heaven! In less than 150 years, what has this deference to God become? Ingratitude. While Jews grew to earn respect, the Jewish religion lost its vitality. 'You will be a people of priests and a holy nation,' the Eternal said. An opportunity was offered Israel to fulfill its magnificent divine mission among men. Instead, it has neglected the obligations imposed by its religious fate, increasingly alienating itself from the worship of God, gladly paying this price which no one has demanded in order to sit at the banquet of life" (Jacob Kaplan, *Les Temps d'épreuves*, pp. 28-29).

8. One noteworthy exception was an article by Jacob Fromer in *L'Univers israélite*, December 21, 1934. In the article, Fromer argued that Jews were hated throughout history because their view of the world differed from that of other peoples.

9. *L'Univers israélite*, July 21, 1939. Similar sentiments were expressed by the Consistoire central after the passage of the Nuremberg Laws in Germany in September 1935. In denouncing the Nazi regime, the central organ of French Jewry stated in its public communique issued in October 1935: "In persecuting the sons of Israel, whose religious genius gave the world the example of worshiping one God, German racism manifests its hatred of all religions, of all moral values that aspire to bring men together in a common ideal of peace, justice, and love" (cited in *Paix et Droit*, October 1935, p. 3).

10. *L'Univers israélite*, December 29, 1933.

11. There is an extensive collection of clippings from various anti-Semitic newspapers in folder *L*, Juifs d'Allemagne, in the archives of the ACIP. For examples of answers by Jewish leaders see especially the articles by Edmond Cahen, the native novelist, in *L'Univers israélite* (May 10, 1935) and by Henri Prague, the editor of *Archives israélites*, in his journal on November 30, 1933.

12. In an article in *Samedi*, generally regarded as a journal of young militants, on February 26, 1938, for example, Pierre Loewel criticized a fellow Jewish writer's attack on Louis Ferdinand Céline's viciously anti-Semitic work, *Bagatelles pour un massacre*. Loewel argued that Jews should approach any criticism of themselves with an open mind. He concluded that each Jew should make his life an argument against anti-Semitism.

13. See, for example, the article in *Samedi*, May 28, 1938. In taking this position, natives sought to avoid the troublesome problem of the existence of anti-Semitic movements in France before 1935. Robert Loewel in an article published in *L'Univers israélite* on November 10, 1933, admitted that anti-Semitism did exist in

France in the nineteenth century but that its doctrines were taken up and implemented in Nazi Germany and then reimported to France!

14. The issue of *L'Univers israélite* dated July 19, 1935, was devoted almost entirely
to the death of Alfred Dreyfus and to the Dreyfus Affair, yet most articles dealt with
the Dreyfusards' spirit of republicanism and liberalism. Dreyfus, himself, was seen as
only incidentally Jewish.

15. Rothschild's speech at the 1934 meeting is contained in the Consistoire's
Assemblée générale ordinaire, 1934, pp. 14–15. His speech given at the 1935
Assemblée générale was actually a toned-down version of the original draft.
Nevertheless, it occasioned a near scandal in the Jewish community. Immigrants were
so véhement in their protests that the Consistoire, in an article by Lambert in
L'Univers israélite on June 14, 1935, was forced to mollify some of Rothschild's
accusations. The original draft of the speech, complete with emendations, can be
found in the archives of the ACIP, B132, Lettres reçues, 1935, Affaires administratives: Assemblée générale.

16. A line crossed out of the draft of the 1935 speech stated: "Internationalism is
an admirable thing when it is a question of charity, but from the political point of
view, and in particular from a Jewish point of view, it is extremely dangerous."

Other participants at the two meetings were less subtle in their condemnations. A
certain M. Israel openly declared at the 1935 meeting that Léon Blum and the Jewish
Communists were responsible for anti-Semitism in France.

17. Archives of the ACIP, B132, Lettres reçues, 1935, Affaires administratives:
Assemblée générale.

18. As an article in *L'Univers israélite* on June 1, 1934, stated in connection with
LICA's participation in the annual march to Pere Lachaise Cemetery to honor the
Communards: "The struggle against anti-Semitism has nothing to do with the desire
to 'celebrate the memory of the glorious men who died in the Commune,' and it
ill-serves Judaism to speak about it under the shadow of the red flag."

19. Natives made continual reference to the participation of Jews in all political
parties as a reflection of their integration into French society and as a counter to the
anti-Semitic charge that there was a left-wing Jewish political bloc. See, for example,
the cartoon in *L'Univers israélite*, April 15, 1935.

20. See, for example, the statement by Jacques Heilbronner, an influential member
of the Consistoire, contained in the archives of the ACIP, B127, Lettres reçues, 1933,
Affaires administratives: Assemblée générale. Heilbronner concluded that the Consistoire "is not permitted to either lead or participate in any political activity
whatsoever against Hitler's odious racist movement."

21. There were a number of Jews who participated in the demonstrations of
February 6, 1934. *Naie Presse* reproduced the proclamation of the PCF calling on its
members to march in the streets, and one may assume that at least a few immigrants
responded. In personal discussions, M. Taumann mentioned that he personally knew
of "misguided" Jews who participated in the demonstrations. Finally, there is a highly
interesting letter in the archives of the ACIP, B130, Lettres reçues, 1934, packet
addressed to Léon Blum, which relates the personal experiences of one Consistoire
member who proudly demonstrated in the streets for three hours along with "the
healthy elements of the nation."

L'Univers israélite reacted bitterly against the report issued by the Jewish Tele-
graphic Agency that Jewish shops were broken into during the evening of February 6.
"Who told them?" a writer noted in an article published on February 23. "It must

have been a Jew from Kiev, Cracow, or Jassy, who is used to making up stories to frighten Jews around the world."

22. Robert de Rothschild, in his speech before the Assemblée générale of the Consistore in May 1934, reflected native fears when he publicly questioned whether it was in the Jewish interest for LICA supporters to join the general strike of February 12, 1934, "marching at the head of the demonstrators crying: 'Down with this, down with that.' " (Consistoire de Paris, *Assemblée générale ordinaire, 1934*, p. 5.)

23. Alfred Berl summed up French Jewish attitudes toward immigrant involvement in left-wing activity in an article published on the first anniversary of the passage of the Nuremberg Laws. Addressing himself to immigrant Jews, he stated: "A sense of responsibility and self-interest should turn them away from extremist groups and programs which, through a 'vacation from legality,' seek the ruin of political institutions and of the social structure, thus endangering the very existence of our nation. From this standpoint, the Nuremberg events provide an important lesson for Jews. Hopefully, it will not be lost on them" (*Paix et Droit*, September 1936, p. 2).

24. For the correspondence between Albert Manuel, secretary-general of the Consistoire, and La Rocque, and the program of the ceremony, see the archives of the ACIP, B127, Lettres reçues, 1933, Affaires administratives: Administration des temples. In a letter dated May 25, 1933, Manuel wrote to La Rocque that "the Consistoire will give your ceremony as much publicity as possible, as it does for all important patriotic ceremonies."

25. For information on the participation of the various groups, see the archives of the ACIP, B132, Lettres reçues, 1935, Temples, Oratoires: Notre Dame de Nazareth.

26. *L'Univers israélite,* June 22, 1934. For a résumé of Kaplan's speech in 1935, see *L'Univers israélite,* June 7, 1935.

27. The speech was given before the women's section of the Croix de feu in March 1934 and is synopsized in *L'Univers israélite*, March 23, 1934, although Kaplan's pledge of affinity was purposely omitted. A more complete reproduction of the speech can be found in *Le Flambeau*, the organ of the Croix de feu, on April 1, 1934.

I could find no figures of Jewish membership in the right-wing organization. Most of the members, however, were recruited from the Union libérale. At least two prominent leaders of the organization's Paris section were Jews.

Kaplan, himself, never joined the Croix de feu, although he maintained close ties with veterans' groups throughout the 1930s, including the *Anciens combattants de Malagache* and the *Anciens combattants de la Bourse*. A recipient of the *Croix de guerre* in 1918 (and again in 1945) and assistant to the Chief Rabbi of France from 1933 to 1939, he was the logical choice of the Consistoire to officiate at patriotic ceremonies. For information on Kaplan's patriotic activities, see the archives of the ACIP, B132, Lettres reçues, 1935, Rabbinat.

28. Not surprisingly, the Consistoire did not bother to mention in its public statements concerning Kaplan's speech that it was the Chief Rabbi of Paris, at the behest of the Consistoire central, who had originally asked Kaplan to speak.

Albert Manuel expressed the view of the Consistoire when he stated at a meeting of the organization's *Comité d'administrative et financière* that Kaplan's presence at Croix de feu was "opportune" but that too much publicity would blow the incident out of all proportion and might shock some members of the organization. (Archives of the ACIP, B130. Lettres reçues, 1934. Procès-verbaux de Section administrative et financière, meeting of April 17, 1934.)

29. A notable exception was a letter sent to the Consistoire by Marius Kahn, a

member of the organization, which argued that the Croix de feu was a political organization and thus outside the concerns of the religious body. Kaplan's "panégyriques,' Kahn concluded, "lead one to fear that Rabbi Kaplan, who is so enthusiastic about their activity, might one day march at the head of the Croix de feu in an assault on the Palais Bourbon and the Ministry of the Interior." (Letter contained in the archives of the ACIP, B130, Lettres reçues, 1934, Consistoire: Section administrative et financière.)

30. According to the Union patriotique, membership had reached almost 1,500 by December 1934. (Union patriotique des français israélites, *Compte rendu de l'Assemblée générale du 19 décembre 1934* [Paris: Imprimerie Georges Lang, n.d.], p. 12.) A figure of 300 to 400 is given by Elie ben Gabriel in an article published in January 1935 in *Chalom*, p. 13. An examination of the membership of the *Conseil d'administration* published in the *Compte rendu*, p. 1, reveals that by and large, members were haut bourgeois natives.

31. The veracity of the story was continually questioned by natives opposed to the Union patriotique, and the latter spent much of its time searching for survivors of the war who could authenticate the incident. The Union patriotique eventually raised money to build a monument to Bloch at the site where he died.

32. Union patriotique, *Compte rendu, 1934*, p. 10.

33. Leaders of the Union patriotique seemed more concerned with the threat of Communism to France than the dangers of Nazi anti-Semitism. Stalin, for example, was described by Bloch as wanting "to chain the fate of France to that of Russia, to destroy our civilization by imposing his orientalism upon us." (*Bulletin de l'Union patriotique des français israélites*, December 1935, p. 1.)

34. Union patriotique, *Compte rendu, 1934*, p. 7.

35. Speech by M. Diamant-Berger at the constituent assembly of the Union patriotique, cited in *Chalom*, July–August 1934, p. 8.

36. The organization was originally called the *Ligue des israélites patriotiques*. Rothschild disliked the connotation, freely admitted by members of the new group, that some Jews were not patriotic. He therefore suggested switching the words *patriotiques* and *israélites* and calling the organization the *Ligue des patriotes israélites*.

37. See the statement by M. Lisbonne in *Chalom*, May 26, 1934, p. 13. Rothschild politely rejected the idea, stating that the Consistoire should be "above the melee."

38. A copy of the letter sent by the Union patriotique is contained in the archives of the ACIP, B131, Lettres reçues, 1935, Associations, oeuvres, sociétés: Sociétés diverses.

39. See, for example, the speech by Chief Rabbi Maurice Liber at a Union patriotique meeting held on March 16, 1936, and reproduced in *L'Univers israélite*, March 27, 1936.

40. For an example of such sentiments, see *Samedi*, July 4, 1936.

41. In an article published on June 12, 1936, Lambert reaffirmed the determination of the Consistoire to hold the ceremony. The Consistoire, "above all political parties," Lambert wrote, honored the request of the Croix de feu just as it would have honored the request of a group with an opposing viewpoint. Lambert's strong statement belied an uncertainty among Consistoire leaders as to the correctness of the action. For the first time, the religious organization admitted that there were groups with viewpoints opposed to that of the Croix de feu, thus implying that the latter was not a movement above parties but a political party itself. In the same article, Lambert

also expressed concern over the project presented by Darquier de Pellepoix, a municipal councilor and a Croix de feu militant, to create a special law for Jews in Paris restricting their economic activity and areas of settlement.

42. The protests were spearheaded by LICA, most immigrant groups refusing to involve themselves in the internal affairs of the native community. For accounts of the protests, see *L'Univers israélite*, June 19, 1936, and *Samedi*, June 20, 1936. For the reaction of the native press, see *Samedi*, June 27, 1936; for immigrant reaction, see *Pariser Haint*, July 1, 1936, and *Naie Presse*, June 15 and 28, 1936. For information on resignations, see *Samedi*, June 20, 1936.

43. In the only statement issued by a religious leader during the elections, Chief Rabbi Weill called upon Jews "to vote for serious, intelligent, and responsible candidates who are ardently attached to the greater interests of our country and state" (cited in *L'Univers israélite*, April 24, 1936).

44. In an article printed in *Droit de vivre* on May 16, 1936, LICA officials claimed that the secretary-general of the Consistoire "used his influence" in order to get Jewish residents in the "Pletzl" to vote for Bloch, but did not elaborate.

45. The exact nature of the *démarche* is unclear. In his pamphlet, *Léon Blum, juif et sioniste* (Paris: Editions de La Terre retrouvée, 1951), pp. 8–9, André Blumel claimed that a *démarche* was made in May 1936 by a childhood friend of Blum and "an important Jewish religious leader, an important personality in the Jewish community," who suggested that if Blum resigned as premier, he would receive an annual payment equal to that of a premier's salary for the rest of his life. Similarly, Jacques Bielinky, responding to a rumor in Jewish circles in 1936 that Chief Rabbi Liber had visited Blum before he took office, indirectly confirmed it by arguing that "such a visit, if it did indeed occur, is certainly not unconstitutional" (undated manuscript, "L'Antisémitisme en France," found in Bielinky Archives, Arts, actualités). My attempts to interview M. Blumel proved unsuccessful. In personal discussions, Roger Berg, editor-in-chief of *Journal des Communautés*, the organ of the Consistoire central, suggested that Blumel was probably referring to Chief Rabbi Julien Weill but personally doubted that the *démarche* had ever taken place.

Far more significant is the packet addressed: "Léon Blum, Demandes qui me furent faites vers le 6 février 1934" and signed by Israel Lévi, Chief Rabbi of France until 1935, contained in the archives of the ACIP, B130, Lettres reçues, 1934. The packet contains a grab bag of letters from Jews in Paris, most of which express concern over Xavier Vallat's attack upon Blum in Parliament in February 1934 and its effects upon the growth of anti-Semitism. A large number of letters denounce Blum as being responsible for anti-Semitism and demand that he stop all political activity. Others call for the Consistoire to publicly disassociate itself from Blum. There is no indication when and if Blum received the packet. It is undoubtedly true, however, that the Chief Rabbi was in communication with him to voice the concerns of the Jewish community over his actions. It is therefore not unreasonable to suggest that in 1936, Julien Weill, as Lévi's successor, may have asked Blum to resign.

46. In an article published on May 22, 1936, Lambert stressed the Consistoire's belief that Blum had no relation to the Jewish community and that the Jewish community in turn had no obligations toward him. Blumel claimed that Blum received "a large number of vicious, outrageous, and simply vile letters" from Jews, but did not accuse the Consistoire of instigating them (Blumel, p. 8).

47. *L'Univers israélite*, June 26, 1936.

48. The Union patriotique sponsored a meeting in January 1937 against "Bolshevik

materialism." Among the speakers was Jean Goy, a noted anti-Semite. Although Kaplan was originally scheduled to speak, public pressure forced the Consistoire to turn down the invitation. Lambert, in a rare display of independence, bitterly attacked the religious body for even considering participating in the meeting. (*L'Univers israélite*, January 22, 1937.)

49. A notable exception was William Oualid. See, for example, his statement concerning the World Jewish Congress synopsized on page 83.

50. Native concern with remaining inconspicuous often went to absurd lengths. A report issued by the administrative commission of the rue de la Victoire synagogue in 1933 noted that a religious concert had to be postponed because many natives backing it thought that, in view of events in Germany and the fact that "Jewry is the *ordre du jour*" in Frenchmen's conversations, it would have been inopportune to have their names on publicity posters. (Report found in the archives of the ACIP, B127, Lettres reçues, 1933, Synagogues, temples, oratoires.)

51. See, for example, *L'Univers israélite*, September 15–22 and November 10, 1933.

52. *L'Univers israélite*, October 4, 1935.

53. *L'Univers israélite*, December 18, 1936. Amarti, a native humorist, summed up the differences in attitude of immigrants and natives toward Frankfurter when he remarked that the immigrant community "quite simply risks creating heroes—I prefer saints" (*Samedi*, October 31, 1936).

54. In April 1933, during the Passover holiday, the Consistoire rejected the idea of reciting prayers for German Jews, arguing that Passover was an inappropriate time for prayers of contrition (*L'Univers israélite*, April 28, 1933). The religious body was not averse to using religious prayers when it suited its purpose. During the strikes of the summer of 1936, for example, rabbis continually called for a return to prayer and meditation. See, for example, the article in *L'Univers israélite*, August 21–28, 1936.

55. For a statement by the Comité français, see *Cahiers juifs*, March 1933, pp. 150–52.

56. For Oualid's discussion, see the archives of the ACIP, AA21, Conseil d'administration, 1929–35, meeting of May 22, 1934. For other sympathetic views, see the articles by Pierre Paraf in *Le Journal juif* (March 1, 1935) and by Oualid in *L'Univers israélite* (July 6, 1934).

57. For an example of this position, see the archives of the ACIP, B130, Lettres reçues, 1934, Procès verbaux du section administrative et financière, meeting of May 15, 1934.

58. As Lambert argued in *L'Univers israélite* on March 1, 1935: "Should a Hungarian student, just because he is a member of a Zionist group, have the same right as the Chief Rabbi of France or Edmond Fleg [a prominent French Jewish intellectual] to elect French delegates to the World Congress?"

59. See, for example, the anonymous letter printed in *L'Univers israélite* on March 29, 1935.

60. A copy of the statement is found in the archives of the ACIP, B129, Lettres reçues, 1934, Sociétés diverses.

61. Sephardic natives had their own refugee problem. Many Jews from the Near East and from North Africa fled to Paris after anti-Semitic riots in their homelands. The anti-Jewish riots in Constantine in the summer of 1934 were by far the most serious of these. For an examination of the Sephardic refugee problem in the 1930s, see the article by Joseph Meleh in *Archives israélites*, August 22, 1935.

62. For favorable discussions of German Jews, see the article by Henri Hertz in

L'Univers israélite (May 3, 1933) and the statement by Oualid at the Assemblée générale of the Consistoire held on April 28, 1933, and reproduced in *Archives israélites*, June 8, 1933.

63. For information on the activities of the High Commission in France, see *Paix et Droit*, May 1934, pp. 8–10. The Comité national also worked closely with HICEM, the international federation of Jewish relief organizations.

64. The statement is reproduced in *L'Univers israélite*, June 30, 1933.

65. In 1933 there were some thirty organizations in Paris concerned with Jewish immigrants and refugees, including one called the *Caisse juive pour l'aide aux refugiés allemands par le développement en France d'industries et de fabrications artisanales d'articles jusqu'ici importés d'Allemagne* (The Jewish Fund to Aid German Refugees through the Development in France of Industrial and Handcrafted Articles Previously Imported from Germany).

66. The most prominent native was the ever-present Robert de Rothschild. Among the non-Jewish members were the archbishop of Paris, a number of Radical deputies, and Justin Godart, a leading lawyer.

67. See, for example, the article by Lambert in *L'Univers israélite*, October 12, 1934.

68. *L'Univers israélite*, July 28, 1933. The French government reciprocated by granting state-owned buildings to the Comité national for use as temporary places of refuge.

69. See, for example, the article by Bielinky in *L'Univers israélite* (October 27, 1933), in which he argued that before fleeing to Germany, many Polish Jews fought against the Kaiser in World War I and thus defended France's vital interests.

70. For a discussion of German Jewish organizations in Paris in the 1930s, see *La Terre retrouvée*, March 25, 1936. For native disenchantment with German Jews, see the discussion in the article in *L'Univers israélite*, February 16, 1934.

71. In an article published in *L'Univers israélite* on July 28, 1933, Janine Auscher claimed that many native Jews regarded German Jews as enemies of France. In reply she argued that the best way to make a friend out of an enemy was to help him in time of trouble.

72. According to A. Tcherikover, in his article "Di Tragedie fun a shvakhn dor," *Oyfn Shaydveg*, April 1939, p. 11, if the amount of money given to German refugees in Paris in the 1930s were divided evenly among the French Jewish population, it would have come to about three or four francs per person.

73. According to Roblin (p. 72), there were 8,730 German Jews in Paris in 1931. By 1938 the figure had risen to 15,711. In addition there were as many as 50,000 refugees who passed through Paris in the 1930s on their way to other countries or back to Germany. Still others arrived illegally and were never officially listed in government records.

74. See, for example, the letter sent by the Consistoire to the Bullowa family of New York, found in the archives of the ACIP, B130, Lettres reçues, 1934, Correspondance Bullowa.

75. The declaration is reproduced in *L'Univers israélite*, August 2–9, 1935.

76. For a discussion of the various colonization schemes studied by the Popular Front government, see *Samedi*, January 23, 1937. Marius Moutet, the Minister of Colonies under the Blum government, had been a close confidant of both the Consistoire and the Fédération in the early 1930s when he was a Socialist deputy. He continued to maintain contact with the two organizations throughout his tenure in the Popular Front government.

77. Cited in *Le Matin*, November 19, 1938.

78. J. H. Dreyfuss, *Israël et la France: Sermon prononcé le 1ᵉʳ jour de Pâques 5693 (11 Avril 1933) au Temple israélite de la rue de la Victoire* (Paris: Consistoire Israélite de Paris, n.d.), p. 5.

79. In an article published in *L'Univers israélite* on December 17, 1937, for example, Lambert argued that it was "acceptable" to ask French diplomats to intervene with the Polish government on the question of the plight of Jews in Poland. He was quick to point out, however, that such an intervention would be justified in the "name of humanity" and did not imply granting special favors to Jews.

Government officials often called upon native leaders to advise them on the refugee problem. In 1933, for example, Julien Weill, Chief Rabbi of Paris, was appointed to a subcommittee on refugees of the Ministry of Foreign Affairs.

80. *L'Univers israélite*, March 31, 1933. In the editorial, the journal explained that native leaders had remained silent for two months out of deference to the wishes of the French government and because they feared any protest action would adversely affect the situation of German Jews.

81. Natives were particularly gratified by French attempts to create the so-called Stresa Front, which centered around an accommodation with Fascist Italy. Almost every few months one could find an article in *L'Univers israélite* describing how Fascism differed from Nazism. It is for this reason that natives also generally opposed Jewish involvement with left-wing groups seeking to mount a struggle against the "Fascist menace." For a typical discussion of Fascism, see *L'Univers israélite*, November 3, 1933.

Native attitudes toward Italy remained unchanged even after Mussolini imposed anti-Jewish legislation in late 1938. In the October 1938 issue of *Paix et Droit*, Alfred Berl talked of Mussolini's anti-Semitism in the following terms: "If he engages in anti-Semitism, it is not by conviction but by proxy, Italy having chosen to bask in the light of the German star."

82. See, for example, *L'Univers israélite*, February 24, 1933.

83. *L'Univers israélite*, March 1, 1935. See also Lambert's article in *L'Univers israélite*, May 15, 1936.

84. *L'Univers israélite*, November 5, 1937.

85. Cited in *Le Matin*, November 19, 1938.

In a speech delivered at a LICA banquet on November 26, Léon Blum alluded to Weill's statement: "I will say everything I think, here, even if I offend other Jews, even if it means protesting against the statements made or published recently by men who, at least from the religious point of view, are considered to be representatives of Jewry. I can think of nothing in the world so painful and so dishonorable as seeing French Jews attempting at this moment to close the doors of France to Jewish refugees from other countries. Let them not delude themselves into believing that they are assuring their security. There has never been a time in history when security has been achieved through cowardice, whether it be nations, human groups, or individuals" (cited in Blumel, p. 6).

86. *Chalom*, January 1933, pp. 12-15; September 1933, p. 17; December 1933, pp. 10-11.

Rabinovitch has since become well known in French Jewish circles, writing under the pseudonym Rabi, and is the author of a general work on French Jewry, *Anatomie du Judaïsme français*.

87. As he noted: "The fate of Israel is not the fate of France. The ideal of the Jewish people is not the Declaration of 1789" (*Chalom*, September 1933, p. 17).

88. Even within the Consistoire, one could hear faint hints of support for the idea of a "Jewish policy," if not for specific Jewish protest action. See, for example, the article by Serge Weill-Goudchaux on Frankfurter in *Le Journal juif*, February 14, 1936.

89. See, for example, the article by A. Fleury-Wahl in *Samedi*, May 29, 1937.

90. For information on the protest held in February 1933, see *Cahiers juifs*, March 1933, p. 240.

91. Most of the battles between LICA supporters and anti-Semites occurred in the "Pletzl," which the latter periodically entered to break windows, molest residents, and deface buildings. LICA was particularly concerned with preventing the showing of films in Paris that were imported from Germany. On at least one occasion, LICA supporters entered a movie theater and refused to leave until a German film was taken off the screen.

92. For details on the debate, see *L'Univers israélite*, December 8, 1933. Native dissidents eventually formed their own organization, the *Comité de défense des juifs persécutés*, which, although preaching a militant stand against Nazism, refused to ally with political parties. For information on the Comité, see *L'Univers israélite*, December 22, 1933, and May 18, 1934.

93. Cited in *L'Univers israélite*, November 29, 1935.

94. The statement was reproduced in *L'Univers israélite*, December 17, 1937. In January 1937 LICA changed its name to the *Ligue internationale contre le racisme et l'antisémitisme* (LICRA) to signify its widened concern with all forms of oppression against minority groups. The organization continued to be popularly known as LICA, however, and assumed its original name after World War II.

95. Léon Blum, *Souvenirs sur l'Affaire* (Paris: Gallimard, 1935), p. 27.

6   The Jewish Question
      and the Jewish Response,
      1933-37:
      Eastern European Immigrants

By and large, eastern European Jews in Paris showed a greater understanding of the Nazi phenomenon than their French coreligionists. Even before the rise of Hitler, one could find immigrants who foresaw the exit of Jews en masse from central Europe.[1] When the Nazis finally did come to power, most European Jews recognized the fundamentally new nature of the anti-Semitism that they espoused. Far more serious than the Jew-hatred immigrants themselves had experienced in eastern Europe, Nazi anti-Semitism seemed more grandiose in its proposals for the solution of the "Jewish question." Few immigrants before the war could envision just what "solution" lay in store for many of them, but even those who dimly understood the Nazi phenomenon clearly sensed its threat to Jews in Europe.[2]

Immigrant concern with Nazism was reflected in the many analyses of anti-Semitism published in the Paris Yiddish press. Some immigrants, including Dr. Alfred de Gunzbourg, head of the Russian Jewish community in Paris, sought to trace the development of Jew-hatred from ancient times, when Jews were singled out because of their unwillingness to assimilate, through the Middle Ages, when a religious component was added, and finally to modern times, when traditional modes of anti-Semitism were combined with pseudoscientific notions of racial purity. Others, like Joseph Hollander, a German refugee, argued that the Jew was the eternal scapegoat and that in the words of Hollander, "if there were no Jews in the world, they would have had to have been created." Still others with left-wing tendencies stressed the role of anti-Semitism as a device used by the Nazis to divert public attention from the real dangers of capitalism and Fascism.[3]

No matter what their particular explanation, however, most immigrants centered their analyses around the tragedy of the German Jew. Hitler's racial definition of a Jew, they reasoned, meant that no Jew could erase his identity no matter how hard he tried. The consequences of this were direst for German Jews who had placed great faith in the liberal doctrines of emancipation and individual freedom. In the frantic drive to integrate themselves into the nation, German Jewry had destroyed all of the traditional modes of defense that Jews had created against the hostile society. Now burdened with an identity that they had rejected totally, German assimilants proved powerless to react to the danger that threatened them. Instead, they continued to deny their Jewishness while protesting their loyalty to the Reich. [4]

The immigrants' argument against German Jews could well have applied to their French coreligionists. Indeed, a writer in *Pariser Haint* in 1933 openly stated that French Jews had learned from the German tragedy that "assimilation is a pipe dream, that it can never work." [5] Similarly, immigrants condemned the natives' attempts to disassociate themselves from eastern European Jews who were allegedly responsible for anti-Semitism. If any Jews were responsible for anti-Semitism, immigrants argued, it was the native banker and financier and not the impoverished immigrant masses. [6] Immigrants were equally critical of the natives' frantic attempts to counter xenophobia in France through public displays of unwavering loyalty to the nation. As one immigrant writing as a "loyal reader of *L'Univers israélite*" noted in a letter to the journal: "It is this fearful concern to be more royalist than the king, more Catholic than the Pope, that has us believe that in order to be good Frenchmen, we must always be in agreement with the Minister of Foreign Affairs in office." [7]

Despite their similar analyses of the French and German Jewish dilemma, eastern European Jews in Paris proved unwilling to equate French anti-Semitism with Nazism. Although greatly concerned with the rise of xenophobic feeling in France, they could not accept the notion that Frenchmen were consciously anti-Semitic. The only comprehensive analysis of anti-Semitism in France I could find in the Paris immigrant press in the 1930s spoke of hatred of Jews as merely one manifestation of a general fear of the strange and of the exotic. [8] The small group of rabid anti-Semites found in movements like *Action française* and *Solidarité française* were dismissed by Jews long used to vicious pogroms as "untalented *shlemazls*" (bumblers). Even at the height of antiforeigner legislation and the injection of racial ideas into French political life, immigrants still clung desperately to the belief that Frenchmen would never succumb to the Nazi form of anti-Semitism. Thus, for example, while

Nisan Frank, a leading Yiddish journalist in Paris, voiced fears in an article published in *Pariser Haint* on January 4, 1935, that "we live in a world where no one can guarantee [what] tomorrow [will bring]," he also reaffirmed his confidence in France and in its principles of brotherhood and fraternity.[9]

Immigrant Jews in Paris concluded from their analysis that they would not make the same mistake as German Jews. The only hope, they argued, lay in an immediate Jewish response to the threat of anti-Semitism both in central Europe and in France. But what exactly could a group of some 150,000 Jews in Paris do to counter an enemy that grew stronger with each passing day? Would it not be best to rely on French leaders for the salvation of their brethren?

The policy of relying on France for effective action against Nazi persecution found ready supporters among older immigrants. All had arrived in France at a time when favorable economic conditions facilitated their integration into French life. A large number had volunteered in the French army in 1914 and had returned from the trenches imbued with patriotic ideals of *la patrie* and *la gloire de France*. Mingling with native Jews, they soon learned of the debt that Jews allegedly owed to the French Revolution for their emancipation. France, the birthplace of modern democracy, would always support humanitarian efforts to aid Jews.[10]

Equally important in the older immigrant's decision to rely on French government leaders was his deep-seated distrust of newer immigrants. There were many settled eastern European Jews who believed along with natives that more recently arrived immigrants were responsible for anti-Semitic outrages in Paris. The "uncultured" mannerisms of the newer immigrant, his insistence upon speaking Yiddish, his penchant for left-wing activity and noisy protest demonstrations, his distrust of non-Jews—all were said to increase xenophobic sentiments among Frenchmen.[11] Nor did older immigrants take kindly to the demands that newly arrived Jews made upon the established Jewish community. Most of the relief organizations created by older immigrants, like their native counterparts, seemed more interested in impressing upon new immigrants the need for respect of French Jewry than in catering to their needs.[12]

Although most were not French citizens, recently arrived immigrants were not averse to calling upon French leaders to aid Jews. In the months after Hitler's accession to power, *Pariser Haint* was filled with articles lauding France's hospitality to refugees.[13]

Arriving from countries ruled by aging monarchs and autocrats who were more than willing to use anti-Semitism as a means of rallying public support, eastern European Jews in Paris were convinced that only democracies could save Jews from persecution. It was not surprising, therefore, that groups like the Fédération des sociétés juives de France continually deluged government officials with requests for more lenient treatment of refugees already in the country and for those still waiting to find a place of refuge.[14] Immigrants also demanded publicly that France as the leading democratic nation in the world intervene for the Jews in the League of Nations. Nor did eastern European Jews hesitate to suggest alternative foreign policies that they felt would be more beneficial to Jewish interests.[15]

Immigrants were especially hopeful of governmental assistance after the victory of Léon Blum and the Popular Front in June 1936. As we shall see, the conviction that a more progressive government would be more sympathetic to the plight of Jews in central Europe and in France led many eastern European Jews in Paris, despite their fear of Communism, to vote for Popular Front candidates in the elections of April–May 1936. Immigrants did not hide their enthusiasm over the prospect of having a Jew as premier of France. Blum was warmly applauded at Jewish protest rallies, and more than one *shul* prayed for his welfare after the Popular Front victory.[16] Immigrant leaders like Shmuel Jatzkan, the editor of *Pariser Haint* until his death in late 1936, made much of the fact that Blum, unlike most of his native coreligionists, did not try to hide his Jewish identity.[17] A man who could write articles on Zionism in the Yiddish press and whose mother was rumored to have kept a kosher home and not to have allowed anyone to work in her house on the Sabbath could only, it was felt, be sympathetic to the Jewish cause.[18]

The immigrants' enthusiasm for the Popular Front belied an underlying mood of cynicism and despair whose origins can be traced back to early 1935. The results of the plebiscite in the Saar in January and the passage of legislation in France in late 1934 which effectively prevented the employment of aliens in certain trades aroused great consternation in the eastern European Jewish community. Already in February 1935, A. Alperin, the leading editorialist in *Pariser Haint* and later to become its editor-in-chief after the death of Jatzkan, was denouncing the refusal of world leaders to speak out in protest against Nazi persecution of Jews.[19] Similarly, the negotiations carried on between Laval and German leaders in mid-1935 led at least one Yiddish writer to suggest that Jews could only save themselves by "demonstrating, yelling in every corner of the world and basically responding by all means that we have at our disposal."[20] Even moderate spokesmen like Jatzkan expressed fears that the French government might betray its own principles of humanitarianism by signing an agreement with Hitler.[21]

Immigrants were also disappointed by the failure of international attempts begun in early 1935 to seek a solution to the Jewish refugee problem. The decision by the League of Nations to establish a High Commission on Refugees was itself received with mixed emotions. Though welcoming the effort to seek an international solution to the plight of refugees, immigrants in Paris realized that the creation of the commission resulted from the unwillingness of individual countries to accept any more refugees; and without the readiness of countries like France and Great Britain to take an active interest in the fate of stateless Jews, an international solution was impossible. As Alperin cynically concluded in January 1935, since the League was beholden to the so-called "democratic powers," it must necessarily fail in its attempt to help refugees.[22]

Although the idea of a specific Jewish policy against Nazism was not to be fully developed by immigrants until 1935, Jewish protests in Paris against Hitler began soon after the Nazis' accession to power. After a two-month period of relative silence in which immigrant leaders were urged by the Consistoire to refrain from all demonstrations,[23] the Fédération organized a protest meeting on March 28, 1933. This was quickly followed by other meetings, including two held on April 3 and 5, sponsored by Jewish war veterans' groups; another held on April 5, sponsored jointly by the Fédération, the Union universelle de la jeunesse juive, and the Alliance israélite universelle; and a mammoth demonstration in Trocadero on May 10, attracting over 5,000 people.[24] The moderation of the statements by the various Jewish and non-Jewish speakers and the failure of immigrant leaders to act sooner, however, angered many eastern European Jews who felt that organizations like the Fédération were kowtowing to the demands of natives that immigrants play down Jewish protest.[25]

The period also saw the development of a program to boycott German goods sold in Paris. The action was initiated in March 1933 amidst great opposition. More militant immigrants like Haim Chomsky, a student activist from Poland, and Alperin supported it as one of the few means by which Jews could directly affect the functioning of the Nazi state. Indeed, as early as April, *Pariser Haint* was talking of the concessions Jews might accept from Germany in return for ending the boycott.[26] Many immigrants, however, opposed the action. Leaders of the Fédération, like Jefroykin, under the influence of the Consistoire, questioned the motives behind the boycott and pointed to Adolf Hitler's statement in late March that he would increase repression of German Jews if world Jewry did not end the boycott. Others feared disastrous repercussions in the Paris Jewish community, which maintained strong economic ties with German business firms. The movement also failed to attract large native-run stores in Paris without whom the action could not be successful.[27] By 1936, despite the extravagant claims of its supporters, the boycott action had all but collapsed.[28]

From 1933 to 1935 the attitudes of most immigrants in Paris had wavered between faith in the sincerity of French government leaders and a growing conviction that only Jews cared for the fate of European Jewry. The failure of the democracies to protest against the Nuremberg Decrees of September 1935 sent profound shock waves through the entire eastern European Jewish community. The decrees had been viewed as an acid test of government sympathy. The blatant racialism underlying their enactment seemed to be in direct opposition to the fundamental beliefs of Western democracy. The silence of diplomats and statesmen could only be interpreted by immigrants as a rejection of these beliefs in the name of some transitory hope for peace. The passage of the Nuremberg Decrees also meant the escalation of Nazi persecution of Jews. The legalization of Hitler's racial policy called for a similar escalation of Jewish protest in western Europe.

Signs of increased militancy could already be seen in May 1935 after Rothschild's unfortunate statements at the Consistoire's general assembly. In answering the charges levelled against immigrants by the president of the religious organization, Alperin noted that such statements only showed that French Jewish leaders did not wish to mingle with eastern European Jews. It followed that immigrants should have nothing to do with natives.[29] Even Fédération leaders who had previously willingly accepted the criticisms of natives now demanded that Rothschild make a public apology.

The call for action was sounded in the Yiddish press after the summer lull. In late September 1935 N. Lirik, writing in *Pariser*

Haint, argued that Jews must rid themselves of the notion that the world would help them and instead search to find how "we alone will overcome the totally new situation which has been imposed upon us in Germany and which can spread throughout Europe." The question was no longer whether the outside world had abandoned the Jews, but rather: "Are we prepared for it [that is, the lack of outside support]? Can we find enough moral strength to overcome it and thus remain unbroken and strong within?"[30] Chomsky mirrored these notions when he argued in December that the Nuremberg Decrees meant an attack not merely on religious and economic life but on Jewish existence itself.[31]

Such statements presaged the emphasis upon psychological preparedness that would mark immigrant attitudes in the waning months of peace. Unlike immigrant concerns in 1939, however, the demand voiced by militants in 1935 and early 1936 that the community prepare itself for the Nazi assault did not assume Jewish impotence. If world Jewry could no longer count upon outside support in its struggle for existence, writers like Chomsky and Lirik argued, it was still capable of mounting a concerted defense effort on its own.

In an article published one month before the passage of the Nuremberg Decrees, Chomsky outlined the dimensions of a specific Jewish policy. Among the many proposals he put forth were the extension of the boycott, the intensification of protest meetings, the mounting of a counterpropaganda campaign, opposition to the 1936 Olympics, which were to be held in Berlin, and the demand that Jewish political leaders speak out in protest.[32] The grudging realization that many of these programs could not be accomplished without the active participation of the more wealthy and influential elements of the eastern European Jewish community led *Pariser Haint* militants to intensify their pressure upon the Fédération. Articles in the immigrant press continually sought to instill pride in the Jewish struggle and thus to counter arguments of resignation and passivity put forth by native leaders. All Jews, a concerned Amarti wrote in *Le Journal juif* in February 1936, should be happy and honored "to belong to the most unjustly calumnied people on earth."[33] Immigrants also pointed to the Nuremberg Decrees as final proof that Jews, no matter what their personal beliefs, could not escape their Jewish identity.[34] Similarly, attempts were made to show that specific Jewish action would be efficacious and that if it were not initiated soon, disastrous results would ensue.[35] Militants seemed heartened by the bitter reaction of Fédération leaders to the failure of France and Britain to prevent Germany's occupation of the Rhineland in March 1936.[36]

Yet despite the demands by militants for an intensification of Jewish protest, the Fédération proved unable and unwilling to mount a concerted campaign. In part this stemmed from the organization's desire to seek an accommodation with the native community. It thus remained quite willing to accede to Consistoire demands that immigrants tone down their public protests. In part the fault lay with society leaders themselves who refused to provide money to the Fédération to finance its various activities. A final factor was the rise of a left-wing Jewish protest movement, the *Mouvement populaire juif*, which quickly assumed the leadership of the Jewish protest campaign. Although, as we shall see in the discussion of the left-wing Jewish response to anti-Semitism, the Mouvement made several overtures to the Fédération to join in its activities, the latter refused to become involved in what it regarded as a political movement. Caught between native organizations that demanded it remain silent and a left-wing movement that offended its political sensibilities, and unable to mount its own campaign because of lack of funds, the Fédération drifted aimlessly in the 1930s.

The dilemma of the Fédération can best be seen through an examination of its involvement in three aspects of Jewish activity mounted in the interwar period: public protest, aid to German refugees, and the movement for a World Jewish Congress. Despite the dim view it took of public protests, the Fédération did sponsor a number of rallies and demonstrations in the 1930s. In general, these meetings were held in response to specific events in Germany, eastern Europe, and France. With the exception of the spate of meetings held soon after Hitler's accession to power, few if any were considered as the springboard for further Jewish protests. The speeches by immigrant leaders at the various meetings reflected the influence of the Consistoire. Thus men like Jefroykin and Judcovici talked at length of Nazi barbarism but rarely criticized the French government directly for failing to respond to it. Instead, they masked their concern in vague statements about "moral obligations" and the "spirit of democracy" that eventually would lead government leaders to take strong action. Immigrant audiences were warned that involvement in domestic politics would alienate Frenchmen and might lead government officials to tighten restrictions on the influx of refugees to France. The role of immigrants was to make Jewish demands known to all Frenchmen, Fédération leaders argued, and not just to those of one particular political persuasion. Limited in its effectiveness and cautious in its demands, the Fédération-sponsored demonstration soon became a mechanical response to any tragedy befalling Jews. It was a far cry from the Jewish response envisioned by militants like Alperin and Chomsky.[37]

A similar development could be seen in the Fédération's activity to aid German Jewish refugees in Paris. The Fédération was the first Jewish organization in Paris to establish a relief agency for Jews fleeing from Nazi Germany. At first, the organization's leaders had hopes of expanding their relief work and establishing it on a permanent basis. Despite their increasingly close contacts with the Consistoire, immigrant leaders like Jefroykin were convinced that the native relief effort was discriminating against the *Ostjuden*. It was the responsibility of eastern European immigrants in Paris, he argued, to aid their *landsmen*. Jefroykin also hoped that immigrant involvement in the refugee relief program would stimulate interest in other community programs.[38]

The failure of member societies to contribute adequate funds to the relief effort, however, left Jefroykin's hopes unfulfilled. Although continuing to maintain a small refugee bureau in its central headquarters on the Place de la République, the Fédération was forced to cede its position as the major relief organization to the wealthier Comité national français, which refused positions of authority to eastern Europeans.[39] For the most part, the organization had to remain satisfied with merely criticizing the native-run Comité for discriminating against eastern European refugees.[40]

The Fédération was again to take an active interest in the refugee problem during the period of the Popular Front. Thanks to its frequent interventions with left-wing political leaders in the early thirties to aid individual refugees, it was able to cultivate a number of relationships that bore fruit in 1936. In particular, the organization maintained close contacts with Marius Moutet, the Minister of Colonies in the Popular Front government, and was largely responsible for his decision in 1937 to investigate the possibility of settling refugees in the French territories of Madagascar, New Caledonia, and New Hebrides.[41] These plans were quickly shelved after the defeat of Blum's government in June 1937, however, and the Fédération was never again to play an important role in the solution of the refugee problem.[42]

The Fédération was one of the staunchest supporters of the World Jewish Congress in the Paris Jewish community. The attempt by European governments to deal with the refugee problem through the creation of an international commission under the auspices of the League of Nations reflected a growing concern among both Jews and non-Jews that the "Jewish question" could not be solved on the local level. The Fédération, in particular, was motivated to seek allies outside of France because of its continuing inability to mount an effective protest action in Paris. The organization's decision to support the congress also stemmed from pressures exerted by Zionists within the Fédération. Influential members like Marc Jarblum, an important leader of the *Poalé-Sion Hitachdouth* and later president of the Fédération, and Léonce Bernheim, the head of the French committee for the congress, were convinced that the immigrant organization could only be effective if it rallied to the demands for a Jewish homeland put forth by the congress movement.[43]

In spite of the enthusiasm that the movement for a World Jewish Congress generated among immigrants in Paris,[44] Fédération leaders seemed uneasy over the refusal of native organizations to participate in the international Jewish conclave. Men like Jefroykin and Bernheim publicly voiced their fears that no movement could attain respectability and influence among non-Jews without the involvement of native Jewish organizations.[45] From its inception, the largely immigrant Comité français pour le Congrès mondial juif made continual appeals for native participation. In particular, the Comité sought to recruit support among prominent French leaders, hoping thereby to convince natives that the congress could not in any way be considered by non-Jews as an "international Jewish conspiracy." The few natives like Oualid who expressed sympathy for the congress were trumpeted in the immigrant press as true proponents of the ideal of *klal yisroel.*[46] Other Western Jews like Stephen Wise, the American Reform rabbi, were invited to Fédération banquets to preach the message of Jewish unity to skeptical natives.[47]

The movement for a World Jewish Congress in Paris, like much of Jewish protest in the capital in the 1930s, proved far less successful than had been originally hoped. Although a delegation of Jews living in France was sent to all three congresses held in the period before the war, the refusal of native organizations to participate deprived the movement of any influence in French government circles. The absence of native Jewish representation also prevented the movement from becoming a launching pad for a unified Jewish protest action in Paris as many immigrants had hoped. The executive committee of the congress did establish a central bureau in Paris in 1936 to act, in the words of one of its leaders, as a "sort of Jewish government" to represent Jewish interests in all international negotiations. Without the active support of "Jewish notables," however, it could do little.[48]

Although, as we have seen, there were a number of caustic critics of the Fédération's failure to coordinate an active Jewish protest campaign in Paris, both militants and moderates agreed on the necessity to avoid all political involvement. The Fédération's position of political neutrality cannot be explained away simply by the reliance of its leaders upon the Consistoire. There was strong opposition among eastern European Jews in general to involvement in politics and particularly in left-wing political activity. In part, this stemmed from the influence wielded in the organization by Russian immigrants, many of whom had fled Russia after the Revolution of 1917.[49] Opposition also came from religious members who remembered only too well their continual battles with Communists and Bundists in eastern Europe. Although more politically minded leaders like Jarblum, himself a member of a socialist Zionist group, viewed the rise of the Popular Front movement with great sympathy, most members of the Fédération feared the association of Jews with Communists and other "disrupters of society."[50] If Jews wanted to engage in politics, Jefroykin stated in a declaration issued by the organization in February 1935, let them engage in "Jewish politics."[51]

Writers in *Pariser Haint* echoed the Fédération's sentiments. Although some immigrant militants expressed admiration for the ideals of socialism and Marxism, they regarded Soviet Communism as anathema to Jewish interests. Zionists for the most part, they were particularly incensed by what they regarded as Jewish Communist collusion with Arabs in Palestine against Jewish inhabitants. Unimpressed by Communist appeals to the Jewish masses in Paris, they saw the creation of popular movements like the Mouvement populaire juif as the exploitation of Jewish issues for narrow ideological ends.[52]

In examining the attitudes of the Fédération and of the militant writers in *Pariser Haint* toward political issues, one finds that, like the natives, they opposed Jewish involvement in politics only as it manifested itself in Communist activity. The Fédération's close association with Radicals and Socialists sympathetic to the Jewish plight has already been mentioned. Similarly, the immigrant organization saw no conflict with its position of political neutrality in urging Jews in Paris to vote against anti-Semitic candidates in the May 1935 municipal elections.[53] Although not openly supporting any candidate, *Pariser Haint* made sure to point out before the second ballot which candidates were Jewish and which were not, the implication being that a Jewish candidate would best represent his coreligionists' interests.[54] Immigrant leaders were less covert in their support of candidates in the elections of April–May 1936. Jatzkan, in an article published in *Pariser Haint* shortly before the elections, discussed the problem of Jewish voters. The Jewish voter had a difficult choice; never had France been split into such polarized camps. Although Jews generally voted Left where they found more sympathy for their plight than on the Right, Jatzkan concluded, they must recognize that

we have well-known friends of the Jews who do not belong to the Popular Front, and it would be a great mistake on our part if we were to oppose them. The Jewish voter therefore cannot vote blindly to the Left but must vote on an individual basis, that is, taking into account the character of the candidate with reference to his activities and attitude toward Jews which, in general, are reflective of his attitude toward democratic principles.[55]

Jatzkan's statement points up the dilemma of many nonpolitical immigrants faced with the increased politicization of French life in the 1930s. Jews could not plead political neutrality when confronted with a generally sympathetic left-wing movement such as the Popular Front and a large number of right-wing candidates openly hostile to the "foreign invasion." Yet the participation of Jews with revolutionary movements led immigrant leaders to caution Jewish voters not "to vote blindly to the Left." In at least one case, that of the "Pletzl," these fears led Fédération leaders to support a right-wing candidate with contacts among anti-Semites.

The elections held in the "Pletzl" provide an interesting insight into the nonpolitical immigrants' dilemma. The deputy seat for the fourth *arrondissement* was contested among five candidates: Maurice Hirschowitz, a Socialist and the obvious choice of Fédération leaders; Albert Rigal, the Communist candidate; Robert Lange, a radical; Michel Pares, a right-wing candidate and, in the words of *Pariser Haint*, "enough of an anti-Semite"; and Edmond Bloch, the founder of the Union patriotique des Français israélites and a member of the anti-Popular Front *Union nationale.* In the first round of elections, Rigal received 4,127 votes, Bloch 3,261, Hirschowitz 2,951, Lange 2,389, and Pares 2,371.[56] As a result, Hirschowitz and Lange dropped out of the race in favor of the Communist, while Pares threw his support to Bloch. The lines were now drawn between a non-Jewish Communist and a Jewish right-wing candidate with support from anti-Semitic elements.

The reactions of immigrant leaders were contained in an article published in *Pariser Haint* soon after the first round of elections. The elderly Jew "interviewed" by the paper seemed more concerned over the victory of Rigal than over Bloch's acceptance of the support of anti-Semites.[57] By early May the position of immigrant leaders on the second ballot had been formulated. In an article published on May 1, the editors of *Pariser Haint* explained why Jews should vote for Bloch. Noting that there were 4,000 Jewish voters in the "Pletzl," the anonymous writer questioned whether they would "vote for the Communist Rigal, who is an extremist candidate in the eyes of many Jews, or . . . better, vote for the Jewish candidate who is not in the Popular Front?" In arguing for the election of Bloch, the article described his active participation in Jewish life as head of the Union patriotique and his long association with "Pletzl" Jewry. The writer judiciously avoided any mention of Pares' support or of Bloch's own opposition to immigrant membership in the Union patriotique. The weak arguments furnished by *Pariser Haint* masked the real fears of immigrant leaders, fears which were more honestly expressed in the statement by Jatzkan directly before the second ballot: "One should not forget the Communists' motives which are not in the interests of the Jews. People will think that all Jews are Communists, which will only work to the advantage of the enemies of Israel."[58]

Despite the warnings by Fédération leaders and writers in *Pariser Haint*, Jews in Paris voted overwhelmingly for Popular Front candidates. Immigrants in the "Pletzl" simply refused to believe that a right-wing deputy would better serve the interests of the Jewish community than a Communist supporter of the Popular Front, and Rigal was voted in by a narrow margin.[59] Jatzkan, in an article written after the elections, refused to comment on his support of Bloch but talked instead of the peaceful nature of the elections, which he argued showed "the civilized nature of Frenchmen."[60] Although *Pariser Haint* and the Fédération eventually welcomed Blum and the Popular Front as a government sympathetic to the plight of Jews, they were never to lose their fears of Communist participation. More than one immigrant leader wished out loud during Blum's cabinet that the PCF would quit the coalition.[61]

By the time Blum's government fell in June 1937, the Fédération's position as the central representative of the Paris immigrant community was being seriously threatened by the rising left-wing Jewish movement. But even before the advent of the Mouvement populaire juif, there were signs of a growing malaise within the organization. Its accession to the demands of native leaders undoubtedly pleased those Parisian Jews who looked to an accommodation between natives and immigrants. At the same time, however, it alienated many who looked for a strong Jewish protest action in a period when the reliance upon the benevolence of the French government was beginning to be seriously questioned. The pleas by Fédération leaders that the organization could not engage in political activity without alienating its membership only intensified the anger of those immigrants who saw the necessity of choosing between Left and Right.

In a sense the Fédération, like the Consistoire, was a victim of the increasing politicization of French life in the years between 1934 and 1937. The attempt by leaders like Jefroykin and Jatzkan to restrict the "Jewish question" to a humanitarian or moral issue seemed strangely out of place in a political atmosphere where even the most trivial questions became major bones of contention between Left and Right. At times the Fédération could not avoid becoming involved in French politics. Its rigid anti-Communism and its continued reliance upon the Consistoire led it in at least one instance to support a right-wing candidate. When the immigrant organization succeeded in remaining aloof from politics, it refused to chart its own independent Jewish policy. The Fédération thus remained in limbo—neither part of French politics, and thus unable to influence those in power or those vying for power, nor apart from it in the sense of creating its own independent policy. No wonder then that the price which the Fédération paid for maintaining an apolitical position was immobility and impotence.

The genius of the left-wing movement in the Paris Jewish community and the major reason for its success, at least for a time, in creating a huge following among immigrant Jews was its recognition of the need to ally the "Jewish question" with French politics. The development of a Jewish Communist-led mass movement was not to come until the mid-thirties, however. In the period between 1933 and 1935 the immigrant Left and particularly Jewish Communists remained tied to a rigid dogma that isolated them from the rest of the Paris Jewish community.

The Jewish Left's analysis of anti-Semitism in the early thirties stemmed directly from its analysis of capitalist society. Nazi persecution of the Jews, left-wing immigrants argued, was only a small part of a general attack upon the European masses. Anti-Semitism could not exist without class division. It was an important tool used by the bourgeoisie to turn worker against worker and thus to dull class consciousness. As a Jewish Communist explained anti-Semitism in a novel written by Bertrand Fontenelle: "It's a bone that people are given to gnaw on in order to divert their anger, to let the guilty ones off the hook.... Daniel, you must understand why anti-Semitism is linked to the existence of the capitalist regime. If you don't want one, you must fight against the other."[62]

Left-wing immigrants pointed to the class divisions within the Jewish community to explain the effect of anti-Semitism upon Jews. Although admitting that all sectors of Jewish society were attacked by anti-Semites, the Jewish Left argued that rich Jews suffered much less.[63] The frantic drive by native Jews to differentiate themselves from immigrants was interpreted by left-wing elements as a willing acceptance of the racist myths of the anti-Semites. Further, to the extent that anti-Semitism retarded the development of revolutionary consciousness, the Jewish bourgeoisie as all bourgeois were said to benefit from its propagation among the masses.[64] The Jewish Left also made much of what they called "Jewish Fascism," manifesting itself in organizations such as the Union patriotique and the Zionist Revisionists. "The legitimate child of the aspirations of the Jewish bourgeoisie," as one left-wing brochure stated, Jewish Fascism was only one reflection of the general capitalist attack upon the working masses.[65] Indeed, a study conducted by *Naie Presse* in February 1937 revealed that both Vladimir Jabotinsky, the leader of the Revisionists, and Edmond Bloch were considered by its readers to be among the ten greatest enemies of the Jewish people.[66]

At first, left-wing immigrants refused to believe that France was less prone to anti-Semitism than eastern Europe. Rigidly tied to the doctrine of class against class and imbued with a revolutionary fervor stemming from years of illegal activity in eastern Europe, Jewish Communists and Bundists scoffed at arguments that Fascism and anti-Semitism could never become major forces in democratic countries. If France was praised by natives and older immigrants as a "land of hospitality," left-wing immigrants arriving in the early thirties, when restrictions upon aliens were beginning to be imposed, thought of it only as a "land of expulsion."[67] At most, France was said to give rich Jews an opportunity to become leaders in big industry, politics, and the academe. As far as the Jewish masses were concerned, however, class-conscious Jews knew instinctively that, in the words of one young Communist militant, "when crises arose, when competition increased, when it became unnecessary to calm the uneasiness of the popular masses—the bourgeoisie implemented its old proven ploy—anti-Semitism.[68]

The anti-*klal-yisroeldike* sentiments of the Jewish Left made it unsympathetic to any notion of a specific Jewish protest action. In the period before the creation of the Mouvement populaire juif, Communists deliberately attempted to point out class differences in the Paris Jewish community that prevented any unified Jewish action.[69] Even groups like LICA that engaged in militant activity were viewed with disdain because of their willingness to ally with "reactionary" forces in the Jewish community.[70] The roots of the antagonism between left-wing immigrants and militant Jewish activists in the early thirties lay with their differing attitudes toward the question of a specific Jewish protest. The rigid class analysis of the Jewish Left showed that the unity of the Jewish community could not be achieved in capitalist society and that the only hope for the Jewish masses lay in an alignment of the "Jewish question" with the general problems facing the French working class. Thus a Communist could write in *Naie Presse* in January 1934 that immigrants were concentrating on the "meaningless struggle between Germans and Jews" instead of turning their attention to the problem of Fascist oppression of the European working classes. Jewish workers in France did not wish to be placed in the same category as Polish or German nationals who desired separate consideration for their distinctive problems. Their only desire was to integrate themselves into the French working class.[71]

It was not surprising, therefore, that Communists and Bundists opposed almost every Jewish protest action organized by the Fédération and by LICA in the period before the rise of the Popular Front. The boycott action, for example, was denounced by a writer in *Naie Presse* as illusory in a world of capitalist competition. While well-meaning immigrants refused to buy German goods, he concluded, Zionists and rich Jews were carrying on a lucrative trade with Germany. Similarly, A. Galitzine, the editor of the Yiddish Communist paper, attacked the World Jewish Congress in 1935 as a

"Zionist trick" to divert attention from the real problems facing
Jews in their particular countries.[72] The Jewish Left had equally
unkind words for the attempts by both natives and immigrants to
aid German refugees. French Jews were denounced as being more
interested in ridding France of "bothersome" eastern Europeans
than in actively aiding them, while the Fédération's committee was
accused of pandering to Zionists by showing special favoritism to
those refugees who desired to emigrate to Palestine.[73]

The decision of Jewish Communists and Bundists to work closely
with French left-wing groups to combat both Fascism and anti-
Semitism followed logically from their analysis. Yet left-wing
immigrant leaders faced many problems in trying to convince newly
arrived eastern European revolutionaries of the need to band
together with French groups. Arriving from Poland and Rumania
and losing none of their revolutionary zeal, many were shocked by
the "petit bourgeois" nature of both the PCF and the SFIO. Long
accustomed to underground activity, they were dismayed by the
halfheartedness with which French Communists and Socialists
approached the question of class conflict.[74] Others could not
accustom themselves to working in a legal party with a huge
bureaucracy and an ample supply of funds. Still others, hoping soon
to return to eastern Europe, took little interest in French politics and
looked down upon the French working-class movement as weak and
ineffectual.[75] Left-wing Jewish leaders were also hindered by the
concentration of immigrants in the "Jewish" trades, which effectively isolated them from any contact with French workers.

The first active Jewish participation in left-wing demonstrations
occurred in the days immediately following the riots of February 6,
1934.[76] The *Comité intersyndical*, the coordinating body of all
Jewish sections in the CGTU, sent representatives to march in a
funeral procession held on March 4 for a worker killed in the
February 6 melee. Yiddish signs reading "Down with Fascism"
could be clearly seen scattered among the crowd. Jewish workers
also participated in small numbers in the general strike of February
12, the most militant among them succeeding in closing down a
number of *ateliers* in the "Jewish" trades.[77] The May 1 demonstration of that year attracted a stronger following of Jewish workers,
but the small number of unionized immigrants and the fear of losing
their jobs kept most Jews away.[78]

The threat of Fascism posed by the riots of February 6 had
brought French Socialists and Communists together to discuss

possible unified activity. Similarly, Jewish Bundists and Communists were led to create a United Front against "Fascism" within the Jewish community. At first the steps toward Jewish left-wing unity were halting. In early 1934, in response to pressures from the CGTU, the Comité intersyndical grudgingly entered into discussions with Bundist and anarchist elements within the Jewish trade union movement. Labor leaders like J. Monikowski, the leading Jewish representative on the Comité intersyndical and the head of the Jewish section in the leather trades union (*maroquinerie*), however, openly opposed the discussions as "a farce" which would only enable "Trotskyists" and other extremist groups to spread their doctrines among Jewish workers. The only unity beneficial to the Jewish worker, Monikowski concluded, was unity with the French working class.[79]

By July 1934, however, the rigid class against class tactic of the Jewish Communists was beginning to break down. Like their French counterparts, Jewish Communists saw the United Front as a means of extending their influence over the large mass of nonunionized workers and artisans. The decision to enter seriously into negotiations with other left-wing movements was also motivated by the demands of leaders of the Bundists and of the *Linke Poalé-Sion*, a left-wing faction of the Zionist Jewish Socialist Party, who were frightened by rising xenophobic feeling among Frenchmen.[80]

The goals of the United Front, comprising the Jewish subsection of the PCF, Medem-Farband (Bundists), and Linke Poalé-Sion, were outlined at its first organizational meeting, on July 28, 1934.[81] Of primary importance was the need to combat antiforeigner legislation and particularly those laws affecting the employment of immigrant workers and artisans. Second, the three organizations called for strong action against xenophobia among French workers and reaffirmed the commitment of the Jewish masses to the ideals of proletarian internationalism. Thirdly, they announced an attack upon Fascism and in particular upon "Fascist" elements in the Jewish community.

From its beginnings, however, the United Front was split by grave dissension among its three founding members. Jewish Communists, with an eye toward spreading their influence among the Jewish community at large, seemed reticent to accept the more militant demands of the other two groups. Thus, for example, they refused to include in the Front's program the Bundists' proposal that the movement concern itself with the struggle against the French capitalist regime. Nor would they countenance any discussion of the need to combat "clerical-reactionary elements" in the Jewish community, which Medem-Farband demanded. To do so, the Jewish subsection argued, would alienate the many sincere religious Jews in the community. Finally, Jewish Communists rejected the Linke Poalé-Sion's proposal to include a program for unrestricted emigration to France, for they feared that it would alienate French workers faced with unemployment and low wages.[82]

Bundists, for their part, opposed the participation of the Linke Poalé-Sion in the Front, arguing that the group was more Zionist than revolutionary. Similarly, they looked askance at what they regarded as Communist opportunism, and particularly the refusal of the Jewish subsection to take a clear-cut stand on the question of revolution.[83] The Linke Poalé-Sion, in turn, was skeptical of the sincerity of the Jewish Communists, remembering only too well their bitter feuds in eastern Europe. Bundists, of course, were dismissed outright by the Zionist group as sectarians whose rabid anti-Zionism disqualified them from participating in any unity movement with the Linke Poalé-Sion.[84]

Despite internal dissension, the United Front did manage to engage in a number of protest actions in the 1930s. The Front was the most prolific distributor of pamphlets and flyers in the Jewish community, with subjects that ranged from "Jewish Fascism" to antiforeigner legislation.[85] In addition, the three organizations marched together until 1937 in the annual May Day parade and in the procession to the Mur des Fédérés to honor the defenders of the Commune. The Front was also active in petitioning CGTU leaders for a more sympathetic attitude toward immigrant workers and artisans. The basic disagreements among the three groups were never to be resolved, however, and in fact were to become more sharply defined as the Jewish Communists drifted more and more to a position supporting a unified Jewish community above class differences.

The transformation of the Jewish Communists from the defenders of the small and insignificant Jewish working class to a major force in the Paris Jewish community as a whole was accomplished through the creation of a Mouvement populaire juif or Jewish Popular Front. The rise of the Jewish Popular Front was concomitant with the development of the Popular Front movement in France and, indeed, one of its main purposes was to link the so-called "progressive forces" in the Jewish community with the national struggle against Fascism. There were other factors, however, germane only to the Jewish community that led to the creation of the movement.

From the Communists' point of view, the creation of a popular movement provided them with an opportunity to escape their rigid class analysis of Jewish society. Trained in an illegal movement which by necessity stressed the coming revolution rather than the present reality, Jewish Communists generally were slow to recognize the incompatibility of their rigid ideal of class conflict with the reality of the Jewish immigrants' economic situation in Paris.[86] The gradual realization by militants that they would not be returning to eastern Europe, however, forced them to confront the fact that there was no sizable Jewish working class in the capital. The peculiar nature of the "Jewish" trades—the preponderance of artisans and *façonniers*, the large number of women, the blurred line between *patron* and worker, and between *patron* and *façonnier*, the importance of Jewish ties which often overrode class hostilities—all now began to be understood by left-wing immigrants. For a while Jewish Communists sought to avoid the issue through semantic differentiations between authentic Jewish workers and Jewish "laborers."[87] Within time, however, the example of the PCF as well as the sense of increasing isolation with the immigrant community led to a loosening of even these definitions and their replacement by a notion of "progressive forces" in the Jewish community that transcended the idea of class.

The broadening of the Communists' view was reflected in a number of articles published in *Naie Presse* in the months following the creation of the Mouvement populaire juif in August 1935. Thus F. Korn, writing on August 10, openly stated that the goal of the movement was to win the Jewish petit bourgeoisie over to its side. Korn went on to praise *landsmanshaftn*, previously a major target of Communist criticism, for giving immigrant Jews in Paris a sense of community. Responding to attacks by more "dogmatic elements" on the Jewish Left, Korn, in an article on January 26, 1936, denied that the appeal to Jewish artisans was *klal-yisroeldike*. "We must accept the petit bourgeois masses as they are," he noted, "and not as we would like them to be."[88]

Nor were Jewish Communists above wooing natives to the new movement. In an article published on October 23, 1935, for example, Zosa Szajkowski wrote that "it was wrong to think that all

6,000 members of the Consistoire are bankers or stockholders in Rothschild's northern railroad line." Among the members, he noted, one could find a large number of French Jewish merchants, shopkeepers, artisans, and intellectuals who, like the immigrants, suffered from the economic crisis. Since the Consistoire refused to recognize that all Jews were endangered by Fascism, Szajkowski explained, it was the obligation of the Mouvement populaire juif to "win over the democratic faction of French Jewry."

From its beginnings, the Mouvement populaire juif also sought to incorporate the Fédération into its organization. Indeed, the history of the Paris immigrant Jewish community in the period between 1935 and the outbreak of World War II centered largely around the struggle by the left-wing movement to wrest control over the immigrant masses from the Fédération. Organizers of the Mouvement knew only too well that there was no hope of reaching the mass of immigrants affiliated with *landsmanshaftn*, mutual-aid societies, cultural groups, and veterans' organizations without the active support of the immigrant organization.

At first, left-wing leaders attempted only to dissuade the immigrant organization from uniting with the Consistoire. After a Fédération banquet on July 6, 1935, which was advertised as the first step in the reconciliation between the native and immigrant communities, F. Schrager, one of the leaders of the Jewish subsection, wrote an article in *Naie Presse* denouncing the Consistoire as comprised of the "blackest powers in French Jewish life." In wanting to unite with the native organization, he maintained, the Fédération had chosen to ally with the Right in the struggle between the two opposing political forces in France.[89] Non-Communist supporters of the Mouvement populaire juif expressed similar sentiments. Israel London, writing in the socialist-leaning *Hebdo-Pariz* on July 12, called the banquet "no marriage, much less an agreement on the conditions for marriage [*tnoyim*]."

The appeal to the Fédération was intensified in August 1935, after a meeting was held to coordinate a united boycott action.[90] At the meeting itself, which was attended by a number of Fédération leaders, Schrager spoke of the need for the immigrant organization to follow the will of its members by joining the Jewish Popular Front. Similarly, sponsors of the meeting were carefully chosen by supporters of the Mouvement to include not only left-wing militants but also nonpolitical Jewish activists who were well respected in Fédération circles.[91] The policy was continued at a mass protest meeting held on August 5 in support of the unity campaign, at which speakers ranged from Florimond Bonté of the PCF to Father Lambert, a priest from Oran. While most speakers at the meeting talked of the struggle against Fascism, however, Jefroykin, representing the Fédération, concentrated on the boycott against German goods and steered clear of any discussion of politics. According to *Pariser Haint*'s account of the proceedings, his speech, as well as that of Georg Bernhard, editor of the *Pariser Tageblatt*, the newspaper of German Jewish refugees in Paris, were interrupted repeatedly by catcalls and cries of "Les Soviets partout."[92] Not surprisingly, the final declaration issued at the meeting made no mention of the boycott but talked instead of the danger of Fascism.[93]

Despite these incidents and the embittered protests by anti-Communist militants like Jatzkan and Alperin, the Fédération refused to rule out cooperation with Mouvement supporters.[94] Jefroykin, speaking after the August 5 meeting, supported the idea of a Jewish Popular Front but insisted that its activity be limited to the struggle against anti-Semitism, rejecting its involvement in internal politics. For the Left, he noted at the August 5 meeting, "the struggle against anti-Semitism serves only as a pretext for dragging the Jewish masses into the political struggle."[95] Other Fédération leaders, like Jarblum, actively supported the idea of a Jewish Popular Front with political ties to the French Popular Front, arguing that the struggle against anti-Semitism could not be divorced from the struggle against Fascism.[96]

The split within the Fédération came to a head in late September 1935, when a meeting was called to decide how to respond to the Mouvement's latest appeal to join. The majority, led by Jefroykin and Judcovici, maintained that an organization that represented the bulk of the immigrant and nonnaturalized Jewish population of France could not join a movement with political tendencies. Allying with the Popular Front movement, they argued further, would alienate many Frenchmen who stood neither on the Right nor the Left and yet were sympathetic to the Jewish plight. To integrate the "Jewish problem" into some larger political problem would be to ignore the humanitarian appeal of the Jewish plight and to make Jews mere playthings in the struggle among political parties.[97]

The minority, led by Jarblum and Dr. R. Reichman, the president of the Warsaw Society, spoke in terms similar to those voiced by William Oualid in May 1934 during the course of the Consistoire's deliberations over participating in the World Jewish Congress. In essence, they argued that the Fédération had to join the Mouvement populaire juif so that it could influence the latter's actions and prevent it from engaging in activities contrary to the interests of the Jews. Sensing the increasing polarization of French political life, they maintained that the Fédération could not sit idly by while the Right and Left did battle. If the Right won in France, they argued, anti-Semitic outrages would inevitably follow.

The final resolution repeated essentially the majority position. Although refusing to join the Jewish Popular Front, the Fédération agreed to participate in select activities which it deemed relevant to the "Jewish question." While rejecting affiliation, it would allow its member societies to decide for themselves whether they wished to join.

The resolution of the Fédération left the door open for member societies to join the Mouvement populaire juif. At the first meeting of the Mouvement on October 8, 1935, there were 154 delegates in attendance, including representatives from such important societies as the *Brzezhiner* and *Veracité*, as well as prominent immigrant leaders like Jarblum, Dr. Reichman, and L. Bilis, then secretary-general of the Fédération. Ironically, while there was no official representative from the latter organization, the Alliance did send a delegate, Georges Schneeberger, who talked of the need for immigrants to accept French culture and to rely on democratic and church support for aid.[98] The platform agreed upon at the meeting reflected the Jewish Left's attempt to woo as yet uncommitted immigrants.[99] The Popular Front movement, the platform began, "uniting all working-class and democratic forces in Jewish life, defending the interests of the Jewish masses everywhere, fighting against all attacks on their existence," opposed anti-Semitism and any other force that sought to destroy democratic freedom and that resorted to xenophobia and chauvinism to gain popular support. Special emphasis was to be placed upon the struggle against Hitlerism by all means including a boycott. All members of the Front were obligated to respect each other's independence and to refrain from derogatory statements. Finally, all decisions of the Mouvement were to be unanimous, and any organization or party in agreement with the platform could join.

While it is extremely difficult to find reliable figures on membership, it appears that a significant number of immigrants joined the Mouvement. Opponents of the Jewish Popular Front traced its appeal to its ability to play upon the fears of the Jewish masses in a period of despair and disillusionment. There is no denying that the Mouvement arrived at a propitious moment in the Paris community's deliberations over the appropriate response to anti-Semitism. Its commitment to effective action on internal and international Jewish problems clearly provided a positive counter-balance to the pessimistic musings over the Nuremberg Laws, the failure of international refugee relief efforts, and the implementation of antiforeigner legislation in France.

But the Jewish Popular Front also filled a political vacuum within the Paris Jewish community. In the period between its founding in October 1935 and the victory of the French Popular Front in June 1936, the prestige of the movement grew in proportion to the decline in Fédération membership and activity. Jefroykin himself admitted at the general congress of the organization, held in February 1936, that the Fédération was in dire straits.[100] The only significant campaign that the Fédération launched in the period before the victory of the Popular Front was an abortive attempt to renew its contacts with the Consistoire and the Alliance israélite universelle.[101] Deserted by many of their member societies and uncertain over the organization's future, Fédération leaders stubbornly clung to their independence. Refusing to participate in Jewish Popular Front protests, the organization lacked the means to initiate its own campaigns. The result, as we have seen, was inactivity.[102]

While the Fédération faced an uncertain future, the Mouvement populaire juif benefited from the wave of enthusiasm generated by the Popular Front in France. Immigrants generally agreed that the Popular Front was more sympathetic to the plight of Jews, both in central Europe and in France, than any other political group in the country. Not only did it oppose Fascism, but many of its leaders supported the granting of legal status to immigrants, a position which Jewish Communists exploited to the fullest in their propaganda for the Jewish Popular Front.[103] Supporters of the Mouvement were especially pleased with the results of the voting in the "Pletzl" in the April–May 1936 municipal elections. *Naie Presse* devoted most of its lead articles during the campaign to denouncing the candidacy of Bloch and arguing, in the words of one article published on May 3, that "a Jewish anti-Semite is worse than a non-Jewish one." After the elections, the newspaper could note happily that Jatzkan's warning had gone for nought and that immigrants had not succumbed to pressures from leaders who feared victories of Communist candidates.[104] Nor were Jewish Communists above parroting patriotic slogans about the immigrants' unwillingness to vote for a regime in France that "would erase the names of Jewish war dead from memory" and about their desire to live as "free and happy men in a free France."[105] The fact that most immigrants were not in France when World War I broke out and undoubtedly supported the advancing German armies in their *shtetlakh* as a welcome alternative to Tsarist rule was joyfully forgotten in the wake of the impressive victory.

Even before the elections, however, there were signs of the growing influence of the Jewish Left in the Paris Jewish community. While the Fédération stood by helpless to react, Communists and other left-wing elements spearheaded a protest campaign against the indictment of David Frankfurter in February 1936 for the murder of the head of the Swiss Nazi Party. The protest was repeated during Frankfurter's trial in December of the same year. Jewish Communists seemed to sense the importance that Frankfurter's act had for immigrants despairing of any hope for a lessening of Jewish suffering. In article after article Communist writers explained why Jews had to take rash actions against their "bloodthirsty enemies" and why Frankfurter should be regarded as a national hero who took vengeance upon those who sought to destroy his people.[106]

The appeal to emotions by the Communists had profound repercussions on their own evaluation of the nature of anti-Semitism. No longer merely the extension of capitalism, Nazism was now portrayed as an irrational movement which transcended class divisions. Previously described as an attack upon the European masses as a whole, the spread of Nazism was now viewed as particularly threatening to the existence of world Jewry. B. Tcharny, a Communist writer, drew wild applause from the largely immigrant audience at a mass meeting sponsored by the Jewish Popular Front in December 1936 when he noted that Frankfurter's victim was "a symbol of the vile, wild hordes which spread over the world with flaming torches under the banner of racial hatred, inciting, poisoning, burning down, destroying, pushing the world into an abyss of barbarism."[107]

A similar development could be seen in the Jewish Communists' reaction to the calling of a World Jewish Congress. Once denouncing the congress as a "Zionist conspiracy," Lerman, voicing the opinions of the Jewish subsection, spoke in March 1936 of the need for revolutionary organizations to support all international efforts to publicize the Jewish plight around the world. In April the Jewish subsection issued a statement that outlined a program for the upcoming congress, including the demand for full rights for Jews in all countries, the elimination of the Nuremberg Decrees, and legal status for foreigners in France. In the end, Communists were not allowed to participate in the French delegation to the congress, in large part due to the influence of anti-Communist leaders of the delegation like Jefroykin and Israel Naiditch, a prominent head of a Paris *landsmanshaft*. In its discussion of the congress, however, *Naie Presse* largely ignored the rebuff and concentrated instead on the failure of the meeting to deal with many important issues that directly pertained to Jews in eastern Europe.[108]

The Jewish Popular Front also gained support in the community as a result of its aid to the Loyalist cause during the Spanish Civil War. Immigrant Jews in Paris were particularly active in supporting the so-called Bottwin Battalion, a ragtag company of Jewish volunteers recruited from various countries in Europe. While some immigrants from Paris went off to fight, others remained in the capital to aid volunteers' wives and children or to collect supplies of food and cigarettes for the front. Some workers in the "Jewish" trades spent the little leisure time they had making clothing for volunteers. The aid program was not restricted to left-wing immigrants, however. With the exception of Consistoire leaders, who took a neutral stand on the war and emphasized atrocities committed by both sides, most natives and immigrants tended to support the Loyalists against what they regarded as the forces of Fascism.[109]

One of the aims of the Mouvement populaire juif had been the defense of the interests of the thousands of workers and *façonniers* in the "Jewish" trades, who, because of their alien status, were not covered by state social services. Yet, with the exception of a small number of union members and a few left-wing artisan organizations, Jewish laborers took little interest in the movement. Throughout the 1920s and early 1930s the fear of being exposed as "illegal" laborers had led immigrant workers and artisans to reject affiliation with any organization and, in particular, those associated with left-wing activity. By 1935, however, there were signs of increased militancy among immigrants in the "Jewish" trades. As more and more would-be Jewish proletarians were forced to become *façonniers* because of government restrictions upon the employment of aliens, their influence upon other Jewish artisans increased proportionately. The prospect of the victory of a government more sympathetic to the plight of eastern European immigrants in Paris was also an important factor in the increased militancy of Jewish workers and artisans.

Already in September 1935 the three major trades which saw the largest influx of militants—men's clothing, rubber raincoats, and leather coats—successfully carried out strike actions against *entrepreneurs.*[110] In October 1935 Jewish *entrepreneurs*, seeking to gain more pay for their piecework in order to pay the increased wages of the victorious workers, began a three-month strike action against Galeries Lafayette, a leading department store and *maison de couture.*[111]

By June 1936 the "Jewish" trades had seen almost seven months of tension between *entrepreneurs* and *maisons de couture*, workers and *patrons*, and *façonniers* and *patrons*. It was not surprising, therefore, that the "Jewish" trades were caught up in the wave of strikes which broke out in France concomitant with Blum's accession to power. In general the strikes were spontaneous, Jewish union leaders having been caught completely unaware.[112] On June 5, workers occupied the first of many Jewish factories, and two flags, one red and one tricolor, were hoisted outside its windows.[113] Strikes continued to spread even after the initiation of national bargaining on June 10 because most *patrons* ran businesses that were too small to be considered in any national contract discussion. The result was that while French workers gained their demands within a month, immigrants in the "Jewish" trades were forced to fight on, in some cases well into 1937. And although strikes in the "Jewish" trades had pretty much petered out by September, it was actually not until March 1937, after long and involved bargaining, that immigrant workers finally achieved a forty-hour work week.[114]

Many left-wing leaders had hoped that the participation of eastern European Jews in the strike wave would bring them closer to French workers. Yet the strikes as they developed in the "Jewish" trades only tended to sharpen the differences that separated the two groups. The necessity for Jewish workers and artisans to continue the strike action well after the agreement on the national contract was only one reflection of the fact that the "Jewish" trades were, in the words of A. Rayski, a Jewish trade union leader, "a small island . . . an exception to the general rule."[115] The complex working relationships in the clothing trades created confusion among immigrants as to exactly whom to strike against. In the men's clothing trade, for example, workers first struck against *entrepre-*

neurs before deciding to band together with the latter against the *maisons de couture.*[116] Similarly, although *façonniers* participated in surprisingly large numbers in the strike action, many chose to act as scabs. Even when contracts were signed between *patrons* and workers, they were often broken by scheming *atelier* owners seeking to take advantage of cheap labor supplied by "illegal" *façonniers.*[117] In some cases, immigrant *façonniers* returned to work after only a few days on strike, having been opposed in their demands for piecework payment by unions seeking to bring them under a general work contract. In other cases, *façonniers* and *entrepreneurs*, uncovered by wage and hour agreements between workers and *patrons*, continued to strike despite the protests of Jewish union leaders.[118]

Indeed, the strikes in the "Jewish" trades, by pointing up the peculiarities of the immigrant economic structure, tended to reinforce the long-standing xenophobic sentiments of French workers. The problem of French-Jewish labor tension was clearly understood by Jewish trade-union leaders as early as 1934. In an article published in *Naie Presse* on January 22, 1934, Rayski explained the factors that led to conflicts between French and Jewish workers. The Jewish worker was concentrated in small *ateliers*. Because there were fewer Jews in large industry as a result of the economic crisis, there was little opportunity for French and Jewish workers to meet. Even when they came together in trade unions, the immigrant's ignorance of French prevented any meaningful communication. Those French workers who lived in Jewish areas or who worked in the "Jewish" trades were unaware of the fact that, while they left their *ateliers* at seven o'clock, *façonniers* often worked well into the night in adjoining hotels. In 1934 xenophobia among French workers culminated in an article in the December issue of the CGT's organ, *Le Peuple*, which denounced home-laborers as a danger to unionism and called for a restriction of the number of foreign workers in the textile trade. By 1936 such sentiments had taken on racial overtones foreboding a unified anti-Semitic front of Left and Right.[119]

Jewish Communists responded to the more militant attacks of 1936 with calls for "proper behavior" on the part of immigrants. Not only did this imply the end to the *façonnier's* working late into the night but also changes in the immigrant's attitudes, speech, and mannerisms. In many cases, Communist criticism paralleled the native's attacks upon the "visibility" of eastern European Jews.[120] Jewish trade-union leaders now spoke for the first time of the illusions created in eastern Europe about employment in France and of their sympathy for trade-unionist demands that there be no more workers introduced into the "Jewish" trades. "No matter what their situation is in Fascist countries," the Jewish propaganda commission of the *Union des syndicats* of the Paris region declared in November 1937, "they [Jews] should refrain from coming to France."[121]

The increase in tensions between French and Jewish workers was only one reflection of the decline of the Jewish Popular Front movement. Ironically, the victory of the French Popular Front spelled doom for its counterpart in the Paris Jewish community. The belief that the Blum government would take action to help immigrants seemed to be fulfilled by the decision of the Popular Front government in June to grant work permits to political refugees.[122] Jewish Communists contributed to the immigrants' myopia by continually emphasizing the success of Blum's government in solving problems of particular concern to eastern European Jews in Paris. Thus they pointed to the strong stand that Blum took against Fascism and by implication anti-Semitism, the signing of the Matignon Agreements which benefited all Frenchmen, and the rescinding of Laval's antiforeigner legislation.[123] In strengthening the immigrant's faith in the Popular Front, however, Jewish Communists also created the belief that Jewish protest action was no longer necesssary. The result was a noticeable slackening off of Jewish Popular Front activity in the months after Blum's accession to power.

The decline of the Jewish Popular Front also stemmed from pressures exerted by the PCF upon Jewish Communists, the prime movers of the Front. From my discussions with former militants, it appears that the PCF at first looked favorably upon the idea of a Jewish Popular Front. In the absence of any primary material on the decisions of the party, one can only surmise that the Popular Front movement in the Jewish community was accepted by party officials within the general framework of the drive for increased Communist influence among the French masses as a whole. With the advent of the Blum government, however, the Front fell into disfavor. Its conscious attempt to separate "Jewish" issues from general questions in France was in conflict with the PCF's emphasis upon national unity. Slogans like "La France aux français" freely borrowed by French Communists from right-wing movements implied criticism of all groups that sought to maintain an identity apart from the majority of Frenchmen. Such slogans also dovetailed with the

Communists' recognition of a growing xenophobia among French workers, a development that itself spelled trouble for the Jewish Popular Front.

A reading of *Naie Presse* during the period of the Popular Front reveals great concern by Jewish Communists over the implied criticism of the PCF. The creation of the Mouvement populaire juif was accompanied by much discussion of the alleged ties between immigrants and the progressive ideals of France. Already in July 1935, for example, Schrager was urging immigrants to participate in the annual festivities held on Bastille Day.[124] *Naie Presse*, in an ingenious blend of national mythology, Marxist theory, and Jewish pride, also ran lengthy articles on Jewish participation in the French Revolution and in the Commune.[125] Echoing the PCF's concern with France's future, Jewish Communists like Korn and Galitzine argued for legal status for immigrants on the basis of the contribution they could make to "a growing France with a stagnant birthrate."[126] When there was an obvious conflict between the demands of immigrants and the interests of the Popular Front, it was the latter that invariably won out in Jewish Communist discussions. Thus Lerman could argue in January 1937 that Jewish workers would not go out on strike despite the miserable conditions in the textile trades because they knew that worker unrest would only play into the hands of "Fascists" who were continually trying to prove that the Popular Front bred social anarchy.[127] As time went on, the accomplishments of the Jewish Popular Front were discussed solely in terms of its reliance upon the "democratic and proletarian forces" in France as a whole.[128] L. Waldman, a prominent member of the Comité intersyndical and a leading spokesman for the Mouvement, went further when he noted in August 1936 that "there has never been a special 'Jewish' problem for our French comrades and they have always worked on the supposition that anyone who is exploited and stripped of his nationality has the right to join the great family of the unionized worker that carries on the struggle for a better tomorrow."[129]

From its inception, the Mouvement populaire juif had come under strong attack from more dogmatic Jewish Communists and from Bundists. In particular, more left-wing elements denounced Jewish Communists for seeking to gain influence among the Jewish petit bourgeoisie at the expense of the interests of the Jewish working class. Loyal to a class definition of society and generally uninvolved in the day-to-day workings of the Jewish trade-union movement, most radicals failed to recognize the preindustrial nature of the "Jewish" trades and in particular the large number of artisans whom they employed. Others, like Schrager, who eventually joined the Bundist movement after defecting from the Communists, did not oppose the formation of the Jewish Popular Front but felt that Jewish Communists, in their eagerness to form a mass movement in the Paris Jewish community, had ignored their revolutionary goals.[130]

The Bundist position was explained by Raphael Riba, one of the leaders of the Medem-Farband, at a meeting of the United Front held in April 1936.[131] Although recognizing the need to win over the Jewish petit bourgeoisie, Riba questioned the methods used by the Jewish Communists. The artisan class, he argued, could not be won over as long as it maintained its own organizations. Referring to the Jewish Communists' attempt to woo *landsmanshaftn*, Riba denounced the concept of a "partnership" of working-class and petit-bourgeois organizations in a progressive coalition. More specifically, he demanded that the Jewish Popular Front oppose the Fédération, which was "a clerical-reactionary" organization, and Zionist groups that created illusions among the Jewish masses and diverted attention beyond the borders of France. By widening the Front, he concluded, Jewish Communists had created a situation in which no one knew any longer whom the enemies of the Jewish masses were.

Bundists and Communist dissidents were also critical of the Jewish Communists' espousal of French patriotism. As proponents of international revolution, they were repelled by the Communists' narrow appeals to French nationalism. Sensitive to xenophobic feeling in France and never well integrated into the French working-class movement, they questioned the sincerity of the PCF and the newly created CGT and their statements in support of the Jewish masses in France and in central Europe.

The skepticism of Bundists and Communist dissidents proved well founded. By 1937 the gains made by workers and artisans in the "Jewish" trades, as in much of the French economy, had all but been wiped out.[132] Rightly or wrongly, Jewish workers and artisans blamed their plight on the Jewish sections of the CGT and on the Jewish subsection of the PCF, both of which were felt to be too closely allied to the Popular Front government and to its disastrous economic policies. Immigrants were also disappointed by the failure of the CGT to control xenophobic feeling among French workers. As the economic crisis worsened, so too did the attacks upon foreign workers.[133] The failure of Blum to actively aid the Loyalists in Spain was interpreted by many immigrants as an unwillingness by the Popular Front government to oppose the Fascist menace. If Blum would not intervene to aid Spain, many reasoned, why would he help stateless Jews?[134]

The most crushing blow to Jewish faith in the Popular Front, however, was the abolition of the Jewish subsection of the PCF in March 1937. As we have seen, the Jewish subsection had been the prime mover in the creation of the Mouvement populaire juif. The group had managed within the space of only a few months to mount a large Jewish protest movement, involving numbers far beyond its membership, in the Paris immigrant community. Its willingness to cooperate with organizations like the Fédération, although often not completely sincere, seemed to bode well for the eventual unification of the immigrant community. The abolition of the section and the meekness with which Jewish Communists accepted the PCF's decision, however, dashed all hopes that the Communists had finally liberated themselves from their dogmatic past.

The events surrounding the dissolution of the Jewish subsection are shrouded in mystery. Lacking primary sources, one must piece together the story from incomplete and often biased secondary sources.[135] The decision of the PCF to eliminate its foreign language sections coincided with its disenchantment with the Popular Front and its decision to return to an emphasis upon purely working-class concerns. Obviously, a Jewish Popular Front structured along the lines of its French counterpart would be one of the first victims of the Communists' policy of retrenchment. At the same time, the PCF seems to have feared that the Jewish subsection was becoming too autonomous in its actions. The purpose of the Jewish subsection was merely to bring the party's message to those immigrants who spoke only Yiddish. The development of the Jewish Popular Front, however, and particularly its tendency to isolate "Jewish" issues from the general problems confronting the French masses as a whole, was now viewed by party leaders as a deviation of the Jewish subsection from its proper role.[136]

In early June, Y. Lerman, speaking in the name of the party's politburo, explained the reasons for the dissolution of the Jewish group at a stormy meeting of the Jewish United Front.[137] The foreign language sections of the party, Lerman explained, had been established at a time when there was a large influx of immigrants. Today, however, there was no longer a need for such groups since "our party has grown into a powerful force, . . . [I]t has a full cadre of militants who are aware of the particular demands of every stratum of the populace, . . . [F]oreign workers understand the [French] language and know how to struggle together with their French comrades."

Lerman also discussed the party's opposition to a separate Jewish party, thereby confirming the rumor in immigrant circles that the PCF had feared the growing autonomy of the Jewish subsection. In his conclusion, the Jewish Communist leader conceded that the abolition of the Jewish subsection meant that it could no longer sit on the coordinating committee of the United Front. He was quick to point out, however, that the party's decision did not affect the Jewish Communists' continued involvement in the Jewish Popular Front. Communists would continue to participate in programs but only with the expressed consent of the PCF.

Indeed, from the time that the first rumors of the impending abolition of the Jewish subsection began circulating in the immigrant community, Jewish Communists were already at work attempting to convince non-Communist members of the Mouvement that the decision would have no effect upon their involvement in the Jewish Popular Front. At meetings of the Mouvement, members were told that the representatives of the Jewish subsection would now have a mandate from the Paris region of the party and that the Mouvement could thus count on the support of the entire party for its activities.[138] Communists were also sent into Jewish areas of Paris to explain the party's decision to immigrant militants. At most meetings, despite protests, resolutions were pushed through declaring that the assumption of leadership of the Jewish masses by the PCF effectively guaranteed that the interests of Jews would be defended.[139]

On the whole, however, immigrants were unconvinced by the Jewish Communists' arguments. Major organizations like the Poalé-Sion Hitachdouth which had previously supported the Jewish Popular Front now openly broke with Jewish Communists and refused to participate in any activity that they sponsored. Other non-Communist groups that had previously flocked to the Mouvement because they believed it to be the most vibrant force in the immigrant community similarly disaffiliated. Most immigrants simply would not accept the participation of the PCF in a movement ostensibly committed to Jewish defense. Jewish Communists, for their part, reacted to the withdrawal of immigrant support by gradually downplaying the importance of the Jewish Popular Front.

By May 1937 articles in *Naie Presse* were stating that the movement
had achieved its goals and that immigrants should once again leave
the struggle against Nazism to French working-class organizations.[140] The Jewish Popular Front died quietly with the fall of the
Blum government in June 1937.

Jewish Communists had learned a bitter lesson from the dissolution of the Jewish Popular Front. In their eagerness to become a
major force in the Paris Jewish community, they had forgotten their
"official" function as the transmitters of party policy to the Jewish
rank-and-file. In the early period of the French Popular Front,
Jewish Communists sincerely believed that there was no conflict of
roles between their leadership of a Jewish mass movement and their
responsibilities as members of the Jewish subsection of the PCF. The
party's disaffection with the Popular Front in early 1937, however,
brought the conflict into clear focus. In choosing to accede to the
wishes of the PCF, Jewish Communists sacrificed the opportunity to
increase their influence within the Paris immigrant community.
Although, as we shall see, Communists continued to play an active
role in Paris Jewish communal affairs until just before the outbreak
of World War II, they were never again to forge a "Jewish" policy
independent of the programs and policies proposed by the French
working-class movement.

In retrospect, it is difficult to see how the Jewish subsection could
have succeeded in bringing the "Jewish question" to the attention of
Popular Front leaders even if it had not been abolished. The Popular
Front, by its very nature as a provisional coalition of widely
disparate forces, was incapable of solving even the most rudimentary
problems besetting France. Its main strength derived from its
ideological commitment to unite the nation against Fascism, a
commitment that was not easily translatable into the day-to-day
functioning of government. Wracked by internecine quarrels among
its three member parties, it could hardly lay claim to effectively
tackling the "Jewish question" which required the maintenance
of a strong stand against Nazi Germany. The fact that the PCF
never fully supported the Front (it refused to accept any min-
isterial posts, for example) also made it highly doubtful that the
appeals of the Jewish subsection would be seriously considered. Even
the appointment of a concerned Jew as premier did not assure a
sympathetic ear in the government to the pleas of Paris Jewry.[141]

The dissolution of the Jewish Popular Front also marked the end
of active Jewish protest in the Paris community. The events of 1938

and 1939 certainly occasioned sharp reactions among Parisian Jewry. Few Jews in Paris, however, believed that the rallies and demonstrations held in response to these events were anything more than desperate appeals to the French government to come to the aid of European Jewry. The emphasis upon active resistance which had marked the early years of the Paris Jewish response to Nazism was to gradually give way to a concern with psychological preparedness. Despairing of any real hope of changing the course of Jewish persecution in central and eastern Europe, both natives and immigrants turned their attention inward toward the needs and problems of the Paris Jewish community itself. The search for community, and specifically the attempt to unify the native and immigrant population, was to be the major concern of all elements of Paris Jewry in the waning years of peace.

Notes

1. Ironically, the most prescient immigrant I found in my research was Bielinky, a Consistoire stalwart. In May 1932 he spoke of anti-Semitism in the following manner: "The wave continues to rise; it has already crashed against the Austrian shore in an explosive manner. What will happen tomorrow in this Europe in disarray? Will we soon see pogroms *à la russe*? Will we be witnesses to the desperate flight of thousands of families hurrying in an incessant stream to the borders of East and West, begging asylum, protection, and assistance, and all at a time when each country bans the immigration of foreigners who only aggravate domestic unrest? I ask these troubling questions because they have already been posed and because their eventuality is not impossible. Let us hope that such events will not occur" (speech by Bielinky at a conference held in Lille on May 18, 1932, and contained in the Bielinky Archives, Personnel).

2. In an article published in *Pariser Haint* on December 26, 1938, an immigrant identified only as "Greenbaum" discussed the difference between the German and the eastern European forms of anti-Semitism. Eastern European anti-Semitism, he noted, sought to lessen the number of Jews in the particular country and to break their economic and cultural hold on the population. Still regarding Jews as human beings, it did not advocate violence but rather sought redress through laws and decrees. Characterized by a looseness of ideology, it did not believe that one could rid a country of Jews completely. German anti-Semitism, on the other hand, Greenbaum argued, sought to wipe out all remainders of a Jewish presence in Germany and to rid the country of Jews "root and branch."

3. For Gunzbourg's articles, see *Pariser Haint*, September 20, 1935, and June 24, 1938; for Hollander's article, see *Pariser Haint*, August 30, 1938; for left-wing attitudes, see, for example, the article in *Naye Zeit*, April 30, 1936.

4. Immigrants refused to believe that German Jews would willingly accept their fate. In an article in *Pariser Haint* on March 16, 1933, A. Alperin concluded that German Jews were being forced to pledge their loyalty to the Nazi regime. As late as 1935 a writer in *Le Journal juif* could express his amazement that German Jews had

not yet realized that they were considered as Jews whether they liked it or not and that they were therefore not wanted in Germany (*Le Journal juif*, December 6, 1935).

5. N. Frank in *Pariser Haint*, October 20, 1933.

6. See, for example, the article by Chomsky in *Pariser Haint*, September 13, 1936.

7. *L'Univers israélite*, March 15, 1935.

8. Chomsky in *Pariser Haint*, September 13, 1936.

9. *Pariser Haint*, October 20, 1933.

10. A fascinating example of the attitudes of older immigrants toward their adopted country is supplied by Robert Sommer in his article "La Doctrine politique et l'action religieuse du Grand-Rabbin Maurice Liber," *Revue des Etudes juives* 125 (January–September 1966): 9–20. Born in Poland and brought to Paris in 1888 at the age of four, Liber soon learned the duties of a *Français israélite* at the Consistoire's *Talmud Tora* on rue Vauquelin. His love of France deepened during his period of apprenticeship under Chief Rabbi Israel Lévi, and he was seriously considered for the position of Chief Rabbi after Lévi stepped down in 1935. But, as Sommer explains, "in this period of mounting peril," Liber himself argued against the nomination of a foreign-born rabbi. Instead, Liber was appointed Chief Rabbi for the provinces, sharing the chief rabbinate with his former teacher, Julien Weill. Never rejecting his eastern European past (Sommer relates that he was one of the few French rabbis who always wore a skullcap), Liber nevertheless placed his loyalty to France above all notions of Jewish nationhood. As René Cassin told Sommer: "Perhaps Chief Rabbi Liber would have been less of a patriot if he had not been foreign-born and a naturalized citizen."

11. See, for example, the letter from S. Lerner, identified as a "well-known community leader," in *Pariser Haint*, August 22, 1933.

12. In June 1938 the *Comité d'assistance aux refugiés*, a relief organization sponsored jointly by natives and older immigrants, issued a brochure of *dos* and *don'ts* for refugees. Among other things, the brochure called on newly arrived immigrants to "be polite and discreet." (Cited in *L'Univers israélite*, June 10, 1938.)

13. See, for example, the article by Alperin in *Pariser Haint* on April 16, 1933, praising French leaders for welcoming Albert Einstein into the country.

14. Immigrant interventions reached their peak in early 1935, after a series of government decrees were issued placing restrictions on the employment of aliens. In January 1935 alone the Fédération wrote memoranda to all the deputies and senators in Parliament explaining the need for a tolerant attitude toward foreigners in conformity with French interests and calling for an international agreement on stateless Jews (Fédération, *Rapport moral et financier*, p. 14). In the same month, the immigrant organization sent delegations to over fourteen prominent lawyers, statesmen, and politicians to plead the immigrants' cause (letter from the Fédération to the Consistoire dated February 7, 1935, and found in the archives of the ACIP, B131, Lettres reçues, 1935, Associations, oeuvres: Fédération des sociétés juives de France).

15. Almost daily in *Pariser Haint* during the 1930s, one could find an article by Jarblum detailing the Jewish stake in the involved negotiations carried on between French and other European diplomats. For a typical article, see *Pariser Haint*, February 9, 1934.

16. On applause for Blum at a Jewish protest meeting, see *Naie Presse*, June 14. 1936; on prayers for Blum in *shuls*, see *Samedi*, September 12, 1936.

17. As Jatzkan stated in an enthusiastic article published in *Pariser Haint* on May 12, 1936: "Blum is not simply a Jew but a real Jew, a Jew with a Jewish heart and a

Jewish understanding, a Jew who even cares about the establishment of the Land of Israel as a Jewish homeland, and that such a Jew is ... the premier of one of the greatest countries in Europe ... is unique in modern history."

18. For Blum's articles on Zionism, see *Pariser Haint*, June 28 and 30, 1935; for the rumor about Blum's mother, see *Pariser Haint*, December 1, 1936.

19. As Alperin noted: "And the world knows nothing; people are said to be fed up with it [the 'Jewish question']. They made noise at the beginning; they were protesting then. Today, two years have passed—they have 'quieted down.' " (*Pariser Haint*, February 1, 1935.)

20. Chomsky in *Pariser Haint*, July 28, 1935.

21. *Pariser Haint*, November 15, 1935.

22. *Pariser Haint*, January 30, 1935. Similar sentiments were expressed by Nisan Frank in July 1936, after the suicide of a Jewish journalist at a League of Nations meeting in Geneva. "Poor naïve journalist," Frank concluded, "it [the League] is not a tribunal to which the Jewish people can appeal" (*Pariser Haint*, July 10, 1936).

23. In an article in *Pariser Haint* on March 10, 1933, Alperin noted that French Jews had cautioned immigrant leaders to remain silent in the first months after Hitler's accession to power so that they could take "correct steps" in "a discreet manner," a policy which Alperin himself admitted "had a good effect."

24. For information on the March 28 meeting, see *Pariser Haint*, March 30, 1933; for the war veterans' meetings and the jointly sponsored demonstration, April 5, 1933; for the meeting at Trocadero, May 11, 1933.

25. Indeed, despite his previous statement supporting the policy of French Jewry in the months after January 1933, Alperin openly accused the Fédération, in an article in *Pariser Haint* on April 1, 1933, of acceding to the demands of the native community. The participation of the Alliance in one of the protest meetings and the decision by the Fédération at its executive meeting on March 31 both to oppose the boycotting of German goods and to caution immigrants against further action would seem to corroborate Alperin's accusation.

26. *Pariser Haint*, April 16, 1933.

27. Galeries Lafayette, for example, a large Jewish-owned department store in Paris, announced in February 1936 that it would have to continue selling German goods because of competition from rival stores (cited in *Le Journal juif*, February 14, 1936).

For a discussion of Paris Jewish merchants' ties with German firms, see *Hebdo-Pariz*, November 15, 1935. Many immigrants also feared the repercussions of the boycott on German Jewish merchants. See, for example, the letters sent by a group of Paris Jewish merchants to *Pariser Haint* in protest against a statement by the president of a Jewish merchants' organization that a boycott had the support of his membership (*Pariser Haint*, May 17, 1933).

28. According to an article in *Pariser Haint* on November 7, 1933, in the first eight months of the boycott, Germany had lost over 2,000,000 francs in trade. Similarly, LICA claimed that in the same period, German trade with France had decreased by 34 percent. (Cited in *Pariser Haint*, November 27, 1933.) Figures were conspicuously lacking in the pages of the *Haint* in the years 1934–36.

29. *Pariser Haint*, May 29, 1935.

30. *Pariser Haint*, September 27, 1935.

31. *Pariser Haint*, December 29, 1935.

32. *Pariser Haint*, August 5, 1935.

33. *Le Journal juif*, February 14, 1936. Amarti ("I said," in Hebrew) was typical of a number of native and older immigrant intellectuals in Paris who went through a *crise de conscience* in the mid-thirties. In the early thirties he could often be found attacking newer immigrants in the pages of *Le Journal juif*, a newspaper run largely by older immigrants. By 1936, however, as can be seen by the above citation, he was clearly in the militant Jewish camp, fighting against the timidity of French Jews and their immigrant "hangers-on." He and A. Mitzri, cited below in note 35, appear to have been instrumental in the increased militancy of *Samedi*, a newspaper arising out of the merger of *Le Journal juif* and *Archives israélites* in 1936 and which was to become the most vehemently anti-Nazi journal in the Paris Jewish community in the late thirties.

34. The immigrants' attitude was reflected in Amarti's statement, in the article cited above, that he preferred eastern European Jews to "Westjuden," who, although identified as Jews, could not tell you why they were Jewish.

35. See, for example, the article by A. Mitzri in *Le Journal juif*, February 21, 1936.

36. Jatzkan, in a barrage of articles written in March and April 1936, denounced Foreign Minister Pierre Flandin and Premier Albert Sarraut as "loafers" who did not even know when France's security was being threatened, and attacked British diplomats for their apathetic reception of Hitler's occupation of the Rhineland (*Pariser Haint*, March 15, April 9, and April 17, 1936).

37. For a typical demonstration, see the discussion of a meeting organized in February 1937 to protest attacks upon Jews in Pshitik, Poland, in *Pariser Haint*, February 15, 1937.

38. As Jefroykin stated at a meeting of the Fédération in May 1933: "One cannot build Jewish life [in Paris] with only the Rothschilds, however influential they may be" (cited in *Pariser Haint*, May 13, 1933).

39. The Fédération's refugee bureau gave legal advice and provided credit to German refugees. Acting in conjunction with various international Zionist organizations, it was also instrumental in making arrangements for refugees to emigrate to Palestine. For more information on its activity, see *Pariser Haint*, January 6, 1934.

40. Among the many accusations levelled against the native organization were the establishment of a *numerus clausus* against eastern Europeans (*Pariser Haint*, September 6, 1933), special favors to German Jews (*Pariser Haint*, May 3, 1933), lack of long-range plans (*Pariser Haint*, May 7, 1933), insufficient aid (*Pariser Haint*, August 6, 1933), and native demands that *Ostjuden* go back to their homelands (*Pariser Haint*, August 15, 1933).

41. For immigrant attitudes toward the colonization plans, see *Pariser Haint*, January 19, 20, and 23, 1937.

42. Fédération interventions with government officials continued until the outbreak of war, however. For some examples, see *L'Univers israélite*, October 29, 1937, and November 5, 1937.

43. Of the many Paris-based organizations supporting the World Jewish Congress, the majority were Zionist. For a list of supporting organizations, see *L'Univers israélite*, July 10, 1936.

44. Eighty societies in Paris affiliated with the congress movement. There were also 5,000 individual members of the Comité français. (Figures taken from ibid.)

45. Bernheim, speaking for the Comité français in early 1935, openly admitted that "we need the Jewish bourgeoisie, whose institutions governments consider as the official representatives of world Jewry" (cited in *Le Journal juif*, February 15, 1935).

46. Immigrant militants, for their part, criticized the Comité français for what they regarded as pandering to native Jews in order to gain their support. See, for example, the article by Amarti in *Samedi*, February 12, 1938.

For a sympathetic discussion of Oualid's stand, see, for example, *Le Journal juif*, March 5, 1935.

47. The Fédération sponsored a "unity" banquet on July 6, 1935, and invited prominent members of the native community to attend. Aside from Wise, natives in the audience heard Nahum Goldmann, head of the World Zionist Organization, argue for international Jewish unity, and Shalom Asch, the noted Yiddish writer, call upon native Jewry to play a more active role in Paris Jewish life. For more on the banquet, see the Fédération's *Rapport moral et financier*, p. 27.

48. By January 1937 the central bureau had all but ceased functioning. See the criticism by Alperin in *Pariser Haint*, January 5, 1937.

49. At a meeting of a Russian *landsmanshaft* held in May 1934, for example, the president denied membership to all Jews "who mix with *goyim* [non-Jews]" and advised them to join the PCF (cited in *Naie Presse*, May 22, 1934). See also the account of a meeting of Jewish merchants in *Pariser Haint*, June 16, 1933.

50. For Jarblum's position, see his articles in *Naye Zeit*, May 15, 1936, and June 12, 1936.

51. Cited in *Illustrierte Yidishe Presse*, February 15, 1935. Jefroykin also stated that "the solutions of the Communists and of Taittinger [a prominent leader of Far Right] are all the same to us."

52. For a sympathetic view of Marxism, see the article by A. S. Lirik in *Pariser Haint*, February 24, 1933. The Yiddish paper also published translations of Leon Trotsky's attacks on the Soviet leadership, less as a service to its readers than as a valuable piece of anti-Communist propaganda.

In my interview with Alperin on January 21, 1971, the one-time editor of *Pariser Haint* reasserted his belief that Jewish Communists were the most destructive element in the Paris Jewish community in the 1930s.

53. As Alperin noted in *Pariser Haint*, speaking of the Jewish voter: "Beyond his civic duty . . . he also has a Jewish responsibility. Today he must protest with his vote and help to defeat all those who are running with overt or covert anti-Semiti[c] support" (*Pariser Haint*, May 5, 1935).

54. *Pariser Haint*, May 6, 1935. Jewish war veterans' groups and LICA put up candidates in a number of Jewish areas in order to distribute flyers and to put up posters denouncing anti-Semitic candidates.

55. *Pariser Haint*, April 19, 1936.

56. Figures taken from *Pariser Haint*, April 27, 1936.

57. *Pariser Haint*, April 28, 1936.

58. *Pariser Haint*, May 2, 1936.

59. The "Pletzl" Jew's position was summed up by one immigrant who, on the death of Henri Barbusse, the noted writer, in September 1935 stated: "He was a Communist but I would rather have dealt with him than with the Fascists" (cited in *Pariser Haint*, September 10, 1935).

According to a retrospective article published in *Naie Presse* on February 12, 1939, at least ten Popular Front deputies in Paris were elected on the strength of Jewish votes. Of these, seven were Communists. For detailed figures, see *Pariser Haint*, May 4, 1936.

In the "Pletzl" election, Rigal received 7,638 votes while Bloch received 6,545. The figures reveal that about 1,000 Jews who had voted for Hirschowitz and Lange were influenced by *Pariser Haint* to vote for Bloch, while about 2,000 switched to Rigal.

60. *Pariser Haint*, May 5, 1936.

61. See, for example, the article by Jatzkan in *Pariser Haint*, November 3, 1936.

62. Bertrand Fontenelle, *M. Goldberg aimait Minet* (Paris: Les Nouvelles Editions, 1953), p. 121.

63. See, for example, the article by Lerman in *Naie Presse*, April 14, 1936.

64. *Naie Presse*, March 17, 1934.

65. The brochure was issued by the *Sécrétariat pour l'Europe occidentale du Parti communiste juif—Poalé-Sion (Linke Poalé-Sion)* and can be found in the Yivo Archives: Yidn in Frankraykh—Poaley-Tsiyon, tsionistn, arbetloze komitetn, Arbeter Ring. See also the series "Yidn mit gelt" (Jews with Money) published in *Naie Presse*, March 1935.

66. For the complete list, see *Naie Presse*, March 2, 1937.

67. See, for example, the article by B. Tcharny in *Naie Presse*, April 28, 1934, and the unsigned article on January 20, 1934.

68. Zosa Szajkowski in *Naie Presse*, June 20, 1934. In the 1930s Szajkowski wrote many articles on the history of French Jews for the Yiddish Communist paper. Leaving the party and France in the late thirties, he immigrated to the United States, where he has become one of the most prolific researchers of Franco-Judaica.

69. See, for example, the article in *Naie Presse*, January 9, 1935. S. Feld, the writer of the article, noted that the case of a Jewish landlord who did not provide gas, electricity, or water to his Jewish tenents only showed that "you can never trust a bourgeois, even a Jewish bourgeois."

70. See, for example, the article in *Naie Presse*, May 13, 1934.

71. *Naie Presse*, January 28, 1934. See also the article by Lerman on May 13, 1934.

72. *Naie Presse*, November 22, 1934; May 26, 1935.

73. For examples of left-wing attacks on the Comité national, see *Naie Presse*, January 21, 1935, and February 5, 1935; for a typical attack on the Fédération's bureau, see *Naie Presse*, January 5, 1935.

74. In our discussions, Kénig related that a number of his fellow Communists were shocked to find that PCF members sang and danced to the *Internationale* at cell meetings. In eastern Europe, the mere mention of the song would have led to a ten-year jail sentence.

75. *Naie Presse*, in this period, published relatively few articles on France. Most of its attention centered on Polish revolutionary movements. A poll conducted by the newspaper in March 1934 revealed that 75 percent of its readers were most interested in articles on the Soviet Union and on international politics. The study also found that there was a great demand for more articles on Poland. Details of the poll can be found in *Naie Presse*, March 14, 1934. Another reflection of the "foreigner mentality" of left-wing immigrants was the fact that only fifteen people attended the course on the history of French labor unions given by the popular university of the *Kultur-Liga* in 1933 (figure cited in *Naie Presse*, January 4, 1934).

76. Jews in the Belleville area erected barricades on the night of February 6 to guard against a "Fascist invasion." On the whole, however, Jewish areas remained relatively quiet throughout the evening.

77. As expected, the most successful strike action occurred in Belleville, where in at least one case police had to be called in to prevent the shutting down of a factory. According to an article in *Le Populaire* published on the day after the general strike, 95 percent of the *maisons de cuirs et peaux* and 100 percent of the *maisons*

d'habillement were closed down. For detailed information of Jewish participation in the general strike, see *Pariser Haint* (February 13, 1934) and *Naie Presse* (February 14 and 15, 1934).

78. *Naie Presse*, in its issue of May 2, claimed that "hundreds" of Jews marched under the banner of the Comité intersyndical in the traditional parade but admitted that the group included a large number of Jewish youths from various student and youth groups. A retrospective article on May 1 demonstrations published in the Communist paper on April 30, 1938, listed the number of Jewish participants as only 200.

79. *Naie Presse*, February 20, 1934.

80. The Linke Poalé-Sion actually claimed credit for initiating the idea of a Jewish United Front. See especially the article in *Arbeter Wort*, July 1934.

81. For a discussion of the meeting, see *Naie Presse*, August 4, 1934.

82. For a discussion of the Jewish subsection's position, see *Naie Presse*, July 22, 1935.

83. For the Bundist critique, see *Naie Presse*, January 4, 1935.

84. *Arbeter Wort*, May 1934.

85. For examples of pamphlets, see the Bundist Archives, Der "Bund" in Frankraykh: pamphlet issued in October 1934 on antiforeigner legislation and flyer on February 6, 1934, issued sometime in early 1935.

86. In our discussions, Kénig claimed that the question of the Jewish Popular Front occasioned bitter debate at Jewish Communist cell meetings. Many newly arrived immigrants viewed appeals to the petit bourgeoisie as a betrayal of the Marxian doctrine of class conflict. Some Jewish Communists, like F. Schrager, a major spokesman for the Jewish subsection in the early thirties, actually broke with the Communists over this question and joined the more doctrinally pure Medem-Farband.

87. Throughout the period before the rise of the Popular Front, *Naie Presse* generally referred to Jewish artisans and *façonniers* as *heropashnikes*, a Polish word that can be roughly translated as manual laborers or toilers. In this way, Communists hoped to avoid the perplexing problem of the actual nature of class divisions among the Jewish masses.

88. Korn did not seem terribly sure himself as to just what the appeal to the Jewish petit bourgeoisie implied. The main justification he furnished in his article of August 10 for winning over Jewish artisans was the fact that it was the petit bourgeoisie which made up the backbone of Fascist support. How this related to the Jewish community, however, was unclear.

89. *Naie Presse*, July 7, 1935.

90. Supporters of the Jewish Popular Front were later to regard this meeting held on July 26 as laying the groundwork for the creation of the Front.

91. Among the sponsors were Solomon Schwartzband, the assassin of Hetman Petlura in 1926 and a hero among immigrants, and Dr. Reichman, a prominent member of the Fédération.

92. *Pariser Haint*, August 7, 1935.

93. For a synopsis of the final resolution, see *Naie Presse*, August 6, 1935.

94. Typical of the comments by writers in *Pariser Haint* was that of Nisan Frank in an article published on August 16, 1935. Talking of Jewish Communists, he said: "I do not believe in the metamorphosis of a wolf who suddenly appears with stars on his shoulders. One must avoid such ... [creatures] like fire."

95. Cited in *Le Journal juif*, August 9, 1935.

96. For Jarblum's statement, see the account of the July 26 meeting in *Hebdo-Pariz*, August 2, 1935.

97. For accounts of the meeting, see *Pariser Haint* (September 26, 1935) and the Fédération's *Rapport moral et financier*, pp. 19–20.

According to an article published in *Pariser Haint* on October 2, 1935, Jefroykin stated at the meeting: "I must say openly that the Jewish bourgeoisie does more than the democratic or left-wing non-Jew when Jews are being persecuted."

98. I could find no list of the founding members of the Mouvement. *Naie Presse* covered the Fédération's general meeting of October 1, 1935, with great interest, making sure to point out those organizations that expressed support of the Jewish Popular Front (*Naie Presse*, October 2, 1935). *Pariser Haint*, on October 10, claimed that representatives of merchants' unions, artisan organizations and "a few societies" were in attendance. The paper was also careful to point out that Jarblum attended as a representative of the Poalé-Sion Hitachdouth and not of the Fédération.

For a report by Schneeberger on the meeting, see *L'Univers israélite*, October 18, 1935.

99. The platform is reproduced in *Naie Presse*, October 10, 1935.

100. For an account of the congress which understandably placed great emphasis upon the inactivity of the organization, see *Naie Presse*, February 20, 1936. *Pariser Haint* was noticeably silent on the Fédération during this period, a further sign of the decline in its activity.

101. For a discussion of the contacts between the Fédération and native organizations in late 1935, see *Hebdo-Pariz*, November 8, 1935.

102. Thus, for example, the Fédération refused to participate in the Front-sponsored rally in support of Frankfurter in February 1936. Under pressure from its largely Polish membership, however, the organization did delegate Jefroykin and Judcovici to speak against anti-Semitism in Poland at a Jewish Popular Front meeting held on March 30, 1936.

103. See, for example, the statements by Paul Vaillant-Couturier, a prominent PCF leader, and Albert Bayet, a member of the Radical party, at the Jewish Popular Front meeting held on March 30 and reproduced in *Naie Presse*, March 31, 1936.

104. *Naie Presse*, April 30, 1936. The paper used Jatzkan's support of Bloch as a propaganda tool to destroy the reputation of *Pariser Haint* and thereby hopefully boost its own readership. Headlines like "*Pariser Haint* Put on Trial by the Jewish Masses of the 'Pletzl' " were printed daily, while prominent Jewish left-wing leaders outdid each other in making absurd allegations. Typical of the latter was the statement by Lecache published in *Naie Presse* on May 13, which began: "If Jews had actually followed Jatzkan's suggestions, we would all be in concentration camps...."

105. A. Galitzine in *Naie Presse*, May 1, 1936; unsigned article, ibid.

106. See, for example, *Naie Presse*, December 6, 1936.

107. Cited in *Naie Presse*, December 23, 1936.

108. *Naie Presse*, March 7, 1936; April 7, 1936; August 18, 1936.

109. The most comprehensive work on Jewish involvement in the Spanish Civil War is David Diamant, *Yidn in spanishen krig, 1936–1939* (Warsaw: OJFSNAJ, 1967). Diamant is a long-time Communist militant in Paris, and although the work is well documented, he tends to overemphasize the role of Jewish Communists in the aid effort to the Loyalists. For a discussion of support among non-Communist elements in the Paris community, see *Pariser Haint* (August 15, 1938), *Samedi* (September 27, 1936), and the statement by Rabbi Zalman Chneerson, an influential religious leader among "Pletzl" Jews, in *Samedi* (May 15, 1937).

The exact number of Jewish volunteers from Paris is unknown, although a writer in *Naie Presse* on November 15, 1936, claimed that at that time there were more than 100. For biographical sketches of some immigrant volunteers from Paris, see *Pariser Haint* (November 26, 1936) and *Naie Presse* (October 11 and 12, 1936).

The Consistoire's position was best expressed by Chief Rabbi Weill in his Rosh Hashanah sermon delivered in September 1936. In the sermon the Chief Rabbi of Paris deplored the tragic fate of priests who were not involved in the conflict yet were brutally and senselessly murdered. For a synopsis of his sermon, see *L'Univers israélite*, September 25, 1936.

110. For information on the strikes, see *Naie Presse*, September 1935. For background information on conditions in the "Jewish" trades which led to the strikes, see the article by A. Rayski in *Naie Presse*, August 29, 1935.

111. The strike was not ended until late January 1936 and then without a clear-cut victory by the *entrepreneurs*.

112. On June 4 Monikowski published an article in *Naie Presse* explaining that Jewish workers could learn an important lesson from the metalworkers' wildcat strike that had recently broken out. In the article, he suggested that workers attend a meeting scheduled for June 22, at which CGTU leaders would discuss French workers' attitudes toward foreigners. On the same day, strikes broke out in almost all sectors of the "Jewish" trades.

113. *Naie Presse*, June 6, 1936.

114. For details of the agreement, see *Naie Presse*, March 29, 1937. The agreement did not affect *façonniers* who struck sporadically in the period from June 1936 to April 1937.

115. *Naie Presse*, June 10, 1936.

116. For a full discussion of relations between workers and *entrepreneurs* in the men's clothing trade, see *Naie Presse* (June 15, 1936).

117. See, for example, the article in *Naie Presse* (October 9, 1936).

118. The decision by *entrepreneurs* in the men's clothing trade in July 1936 to continue their strike action after bargaining had already begun led one union leader to remark that Jewish artisans had to learn "when to end a strike, when the important gains have been achieved" (cited in *Naie Presse*, July 2, 1936). On July 5 the Jewish section of the men's clothing trade warned that if *entrepreneurs* did not end their strike action, they would no longer receive support (*Naie Presse*, July 5, 1936).

119. See, for example, the statement by a French trade union official at the meeting of the leather trades union in August 1936 that in the near future the union would only accept "pure Frenchmen" (cited in *Unzer Stime*, August 15, 1936). For other examples of xenophobia among French workers, see *Naie Presse*, November 4, 1935.

120. See, for example, the article by Korn in *Naie Presse*, July 26, 1936. After describing some of the bad traits which eastern European immigrants brought with them to France, he concluded that "such things must stop in the street, in the Metro, in the home, in the theater, and in the movie house."

121. Cited in *Naie Presse*, November 2, 1937. See also the account of the meeting of the Comité intersyndical on December 5, 1936, in *Naie Presse*, December 8, 1936.

122. The decision was only temporary, however. A proposal to make the granting of permits a permanent policy was defeated in Parliament. For Blum's decision, see *Naie Presse*, June 24, 1936.

123. See, for example, the article by Y. Spero in *Naie Presse*, May 2, 1937. See also the article by Lerman on August 28, 1936, in which he argued that now that workers

had achieved their aims and the Popular Front was victorious, immigrants needed only to support the government in its attack upon the "external menace."

124. *Naie Presse*, July 8, 1935.

125. See, for example, the article by Szajkowski on Jewish participation in the defense of the Commune in *Naie Presse*, March 17, 1935.

126. *Naie Presse*, January 27, 1935, July 20, 1936.

127. *Naie Presse*, January 30, 1937.

128. See, for example, B. Tcharny in *Naie Presse*, February 12, 1937.

129. Cited in *Naie Presse*, August 10, 1936. In the article, Waldman spoke glowingly of the end of "Jewish" unions in the clothing and textile trades as a result of the influx of thousands of French workers into light industry.

130. For the views of a Jewish Communist who left the party to join the Bundists, see *Unzer Stime*, January 26, 1936.

131. Riba's speech was reproduced in *Unzer Stime*, April 18 and 25, 1936. For a Communist rejoinder, see *Naie Presse*, April 18, 1936.

132. On the Jewish workers' economic condition in 1937, see the article by L. Goldmann, a member of the Comité intersyndical, in *Naie Presse*, December 3, 1937.

133. *Naie Presse* cited an example of antiforeigner propaganda directed toward unemployed French workers in the clothing and textile trades in its October 28, 1936, issue. Referring to *façonniers'* tendency to work late into the night, which allowed *patrons* to lay off workers, a flyer distributed in working-class quarters stated: "You want to know who is stealing your bread? Take a look inside Jewish houses at night and you will see who is making you starve!"

134. See, for example, the editorial published in *Samedi* on September 5, 1936.

135. Surprisingly, none of the former Jewish Communists I interviewed had any recollection of the subsection being abolished before the war. Both Carol and Kénig denied it vociferously, while Lerman, who was delegated by the subsection to explain the party's decision to Jewish militants, could only weakly state that it was possible but that he just could not remember!

A reading of *L'Humanité* for the years 1936-37 failed to reveal any information on the activities or the dissolution of the Jewish subsection. The period surrounding its dissolution, however, did see numerous articles by union leaders, including Marcel Brenot, the head of the *comités intersyndicaux* for the Paris region, demanding a limitation on the hiring of *façonniers*. Under these circumstances, the active support of *façonnier* interests by the Mouvement populaire juif could only have angered PCF and CGTU leaders and undoubtedly was a major factor in the Jewish subsection's sudden demise. For Brenot's remarks, see *L'Humanité*, March 26, 1937.

136. According to A. Kremer in *Pariser Haint* (March 14, 1937), the PCF viewed the deviation as resulting from the infiltration of "Trotskyists" into the Jewish subsection. Bundists described the PCF's attitudes toward immigrant Communists in the following manner: "Children, it is time for you to become civilized men; you must be equal, you must assimilate" (*Unzer Stime*, May 1937).

137. Lerman's statement is reproduced in *Naie Presse*, June 6, 1937.

138. See especially the articles by Lerman in *Naie Presse*, March 2 and 21, 1937.

139. See, for example, the account of the general meeting of Jewish Communists of the eighteenth *arrondissement* held on March 12, in *Naie Presse*, March 16, 1937.

140. See, for example, *Naie Presse*, May 2, 1937.

141. Blum, himself, was sensitive to the possible conflicts between his sympathies

for the Jewish plight and his position as premier of France. In his memoirs he noted that he told a German representative in Paris in 1936 that, as a Jew and a Marxist, he should logically have refused to enter into discussions with a state that destroyed socialist organizations and persecuted Jews. In doing so, however, he would have betrayed his responsibility as a French leader to defend his nation's interests while seeking peace. (Léon Blum, *L'Histoire jugera* [Montreal: Editions de l'Arbre, 1945], pp. 330-31.)

7   The Unity Campaign, 1934-38

The drive toward a unified Jewish community in Paris in 1937 and 1938 was the clearest reflection of the turning inward of all segments of Paris Jewry after the fall of the Popular Front and the failure of the Jewish protest movement. Uncertain of support from the French government in the struggle against anti-Semitism and increasingly aware of the futility of isolated Jewish action, Jews directed their efforts toward creating a strong and cohesive communal structure in the capital as a last line of defense against enemies both within and without France. Beset by factionalism that had doomed the Jewish protest movement, Paris Jewry now sought to find points of agreement that could provide a basis for future action within the community and for a common understanding of the fate of European Jewry in the face of the Nazi onslaught.

An examination of the various unity campaigns beginning in 1934 and continuing through 1938 reveals that each group in the community generally sought unification on its own terms and for its own ends. For natives, unification meant the bolstering of their sagging organizational structure through the introduction of large numbers of eastern European Jews into the Consistoire. For immigrants, on the other hand (and this was true for both those in the Fédération and those in left-wing organizations), unification necessitated the revamping of traditional communal structures in order to meet the needs of the new Jewish settlers in Paris. While French Jews sought merely to realign their traditional institutions in response to the growing influence of immigrants, eastern European Jews looked to the creation of a new Jewish community in Paris formed from the interaction between the culture of the *shtetl* and the ideals of the West.

Native interest in a unified Jewish community stemmed mainly from concern over the decline in Consistoire prestige and activity. Although the religious organizations continued to attract a small number of new members each year, the influx could not compensate for the overall decline in membership as a result of resignations and of deaths of older members.[1] More significant was the lack of membership interest in the organization. Thus, for example, only eighty-nine members (barely 1 percent of the total membership) attended an important meeting held in October 1935 to discuss candidates for an upcoming consistorial election.[2] The elections themselves attracted only 11 percent of the membership, despite the fact that each affiliate was personally canvassed by representatives of a special membership committee.[3] More damaging still was the falling off in donations and the payment of membership dues. In 1935, for example, only about one-third of all members had paid their dues.[4] At almost every meeting of the Consistoire's administrative council, Secretary General Manuel decried the disastrous financial situation of the organization. Dozens of schemes were attempted to raise additional funds. Rabbis instituted a general appeal for funds from the pulpit on the High Holydays, a practice hitherto considered demeaning by Consistoire leaders. The organization also imposed drastic reductions in its expenditures: synagogue budgets were pared, subsidies to *L'Univers israélite* were reduced, religious schools were consolidated, salaries and pensions were cut. In the end, the Consistoire was also forced to raise the price for the performance of funerals, marriages, and bar mitzvahs.[5]

By far the most enterprising action undertaken by the Consistoire to alleviate its financial woes was the appeal to eastern European immigrants to become members. Natives had few illusions about the financial status of individual immigrants. They were undoubtedly aware, however, of the large caches of money hoarded by mutual-aid societies, for this was a major complaint of Fédération leaders in discussions with their counterparts in the Consistoire. Native leaders also felt that an influx of "new blood" into their organizations might restore French Jewish faith in the Consistoire.[6] In addition, they feared that the numerous religious and charitable organizations created by immigrants would draw support away from the Consistoire's activities. The unity of the Jewish community under the tutelage of the religious organization, natives reasoned, would restore the Consistoire to its rightful place as the central institution of Paris Jewry.[7]

Another factor that led French Jews to consider unity was their fear of immigrant agitation and an attendant upsurge in anti-Semitism. Throughout the 1930s, native attitudes toward the appropriate response to immigrants wavered between the carrot and the stick. While some French Jews talked of the need to take strong measures against immigrant involvement in French political life, others voiced approval of attempts by leaders like Oualid to win immigrants over to an acceptance of native leadership. Proponents of the hard-line approach were dealt a severe blow by the negative response of moderate leaders in the eastern European community to Baron de Rothschild's harsh words of rebuke at the general assembly of the Consistoire in May 1934 and again in May 1935. In the meantime, the worsening economic crisis in France and the growing international crisis beyond its borders had led to an increase in both immigrant militancy and French xenophobia. The time seemed ripe for a new overture to the immigrant community. Rather than chastising immigrants for irresponsible behavior, native leaders would seek to convince them of the dangers involved in political agitation and of the necessity of French leadership of a united Jewish community.

Such an approach could be seen as early as 1934 when both the Consistoire and the Alliance initiated contact with the Fédération, ostensibly to seek a rapprochement between natives and immigrants. It was clear, however, that natives had the recent events of February 6 on their minds rather than any dreams of a unified Jewish community. Thus, for example, Jacques Bigart, secretary-general of the Alliance, spoke at a meeting of the Fédération in June 1934 of the need for immigrants to recognize "la mentalité française," which rejected public displays of emotion in the name of rational compromise, and of the efforts of his organization to inculcate such values among younger immigrants.[8] At the same meeting, Adolph Caen, a member of the administrative council of the Consistoire, reminded the immigrant audience of the debt eastern European Jews owed to the established Jewish community for aiding them in their settlement in Paris.[9]

The first major exposition of the policy of rapprochement was contained in a speech by Lambert at a meeting of the Fédération in December 1934. In his remarks, the editor of *L'Univers israélite* chided French Jews for their hostility toward immigrants and called for the recognition of the eastern European element as an "important partner" in the effort to build a united Jewish community.[10] The speech was followed by articles by both Lambert and Léon Berman, a member of the Consistoire and the author of a popular history of French Jewry, that openly admitted that the native community was losing its vitality. Lambert, expressing the views of the Consistoire leadership, stressed the need for an official Jewish body encompassing all groups and, although criticizing immigrants for their harsh judgment of native organizations, called for a renewed attempt by the latter to make contact with the eastern European community. He was quick to point out, however, that native Jews should initiate all community activity in order to avoid "the ill-fated démarches by committees of foreigners who knew nothing of the realities of French life."[11]

The native leadership's call for unity found sympathetic ears among the Consistoire membership. Although some French Jews felt that talk of banding together to fight anti-Semitism would only help to increase its influence in France, most took the pragmatic view that if natives did not take an active interest in the "Jewish question" in the capital, immigrants would take independent action that would have disastrous results for all of Paris Jewry.[12] Almost all French Jews who responded favorably to the articles by Lambert and Berman agreed that any resultant action should only be concerned with Jewish problems and should not become embroiled in political affairs.

Ironically, the most enthusiastic supporters of the natives' overture to immigrants were the immigrant leaders themselves. As we have seen, the Fédération often deferred to the Consistoire on issues of domestic policy. Yet the willingness of Fédération leaders to accede to native demands that immigrants tone down their public protest or avoid political agitation did not imply a recognition of French Jews as the dominant element in the Paris Jewish community. Hard pressed by the rising left-wing movement and unable to mount its own campaign, the immigrant organization saw accommodation with the Consistoire as a much needed boost in its efforts to retain control over the eastern European community. Like the Consistoire, the Fédération saw unification only on its own terms and would not consider any plan which meant the relinquishing of its autonomy.

The conflicting interests of the native and immigrant organizations were evident at the so-called "unity" banquet sponsored by the Fédération on July 7, 1935.[13] Although the immigrant organization had invited both the Consistoire and the Alliance to send delegates to the banquet, they declined, choosing instead to send only a group of "unofficial observers." Native leaders obviously feared that official representation would be construed as a major accession to the Fédération, which had originally proposed the banquet. At the banquet itself, Baron Alfred de Gunzbourg, a Russian immigrant with close ties to the Consistoire, expressed native concern when he protested against the use of the word *marriage*, coined by a Fédération leader to describe the unification of the two communities. Each community must have its own independence, the Baron noted; they could only be "friends" and nothing more. Similarly, although Lambert reiterated his plan for a *Union juive de France* to defend all Jews, he again emphasized the need for French Jewry to take the initiative in leading the proposed organization.

The failure of the "unity" banquet brought an end to the short history of active native involvement in the unity campaign. Although Consistoire leaders were to achieve some success in organizing a loose federation of religious groups in the Paris community under their control, they were never able to convince the mass of immigrants to band together around the native religious organization as the central body of the Jewish community.[14] The reasons for the natives' failure are not hard to discern. The refusal of the Consistoire and the Alliance to send official representatives to the Fédération's banquet angered most immigrants, who interpreted the action as a direct rebuke to eastern European Jews. The native organizations were also hampered in their unification efforts by their association with the Union patriotique and the Croix de feu. Although militants on the *Pariser Haint* staff and leaders of the Fédération were generally anti-Communist, they could never bring themselves to ally with antiforeigner elements in the French populace.[15] Nor were immigrants impressed by the natives' demands that only French Jews could assume the leadership of the future Jewish community. Statements like those made by Baron de Rothschild in 1935 only led immigrants to assume correctly that French Jews were more interested in avoiding noisy demonstrations than in establishing a strong community to defend Jewish interests. Finally and most importantly, native leaders were never able to convince immigrants that the Consistoire and its affiliated organizations were anything more than decaying remnants of an outworn communal structure. The apathetic attitude of the Consistoire membership, which lay at the heart of the native unity drive, seemed to immigrants to be proof of the unsuitability of French Jewish institutions as foundations for the future Jewish community in Paris.

The unity campaign was thus to be left largely in the hands of the eastern European Jews, who despite their varying beliefs, all agreed that the future community would be led by and directed toward immigrants. The first signs of what was to become the campaign for a *kehila* or eastern European community could be seen early in 1934.[16] In an article published in *Pariser Haint* on January 27 of that year, A. Kaufman, an official of a mutual-aid society, described the isolation of Jewish immigrants in Paris. Eastern European Jews, he argued, were used to a tight communal structure with a central body, or *gemaynde*, overseeing all aspects of life. In Paris, however, newly arrived immigrants found "a handful of small and still smaller organizations, a bunch of societies, a few large active organizations, but no one central organization." What was needed, Kaufman concluded, was the creation of a cohesive community that would maintain the tight organizational structure of the *kehila* of eastern Europe yet would remain open to the influence of the new environment in which immigrants found themselves.

Kaufman had explained his concern with a *kehila* by noting that most immigrants living in Paris had decided to settle permanently and thus were interested in establishing a strong communal structure. By 1935 there were also external pressures leading immigrants to seek a unified community. Of primary importance was the anti-foreigner legislation passed in the early thirties. As we have seen, these decrees threatened the livelihoods of thousands of immigrants engaged in artisan trades. Still other immigrants, having entered France illegally, faced immediate expulsion. Only a strong central organization, many immigrants argued, could defend Jewish interests and present a coherent argument to government officials. A second factor working toward unity was the growth of left-wing movements in the community. Among the many programs discussed by the Jewish Popular Front was the destruction of the *landsman-shaft* system and its replacement by organizations more sensitive to the problem of eastern European Jews in a strange and hostile environment. The prospect of a left-wing dominated community and the threat it posed to established institutions undoubtedly moved anti-Communist immigrants and members of mutual-aid societies to act.

The years 1935 and 1936 saw an intensive discussion in the immigrant community of the problems and possibilities of a *kehila* in Paris. As was to be expected, the campaign for a strengthened community was spearheaded by militants writing in *Pariser Haint*. At first, Alperin and his associates seemed more than willing to accept the leadership of the Fédération in the drive toward community. Elaborate rationalizations were furnished to explain the organization's inactivity. Thus Nisan Frank explained in *Pariser Haint* in February 1935, for example, that the fault lay not with the leadership but rather in the refusal of its affiliates to part with their sizable caches of money.[17] Supporters of the *kehila* thought they saw a solution to the organization's financial problem in the Fédération's decision in April 1935 to go beyond societies by appealing to individual immigrants for aid.[18] In these early discussions, no one bothered to examine whether the Fédération could meet the demands of new immigrants. To do so would be to bring the whole *landsmanshaft* system into question.

Nevertheless, by September immigrant militants were beginning to have their doubts about the viability of the Fédération as the proposed central body of the *kehila*. Many of them were dismayed by what they regarded as the organization's kowtowing to the Consistoire at the "unity" banquet held in July.[19] Others were disappointed by the failure of the Fédération's appeal to individual immigrants and by the chaotic way in which the organization went about formulating its unity programs.[20] Still others were dismayed by its inability to rouse member societies to action. By late September one writer in *Pariser Haint* could note cynically that the Fédération was the "the largest beggar of the Paris organizations," living as it did on day to day handouts.[21]

Yet supporters of the *kehila* soon realized that they had no other choice but to rely on the Fédération. They obviously lacked any influence among the individual societies, which generally regarded their criticism as irresponsible if not libelous. To ally with the Consistoire was equally impossible, since the native organization was opposed to the creation of a Jewish community dominated by immigrants. Similarly, they could not approve of the activities of left-wing elements who, although increasingly influential, were seen ultimately as betrayers of Jewish interests. Their only hope lay in a restructured Fédération which would adequately meet the needs of the growing immigrant community.

But how to restructure a loose conglomeration of fiercely independent organizations? Frank summed up the problem facing *kehila* supporters when he noted in February 1936 that Paris immigrants, in their nostalgic longing for the "old country," had convinced themselves that "the society is the highest authority and that there is no higher [authority] nor any need for one."[22] Similarly, N. Dijour, a member of the Fédération's executive committee, writing in *Pariser Haint* in May of the same year, wondered aloud

whether immigrants "want to continue 'playing in societies,' planning annual balls, searching for burial plots, calling for general
meetings, and stashing away their money?" Dijour went on to
describe how, although the Fédération had some eighty societies
under its aegis, only about sixty had bothered to pay their yearly
duties. Most societies, the Fédération leader concluded, did not take
part in the organization's activities and appealed to the central body
only in times of need.[23]

Throughout their discussions, supporters of the *kehila* kept a
watchful eye on the rising left-wing movement in the Jewish
community. Although few thought that the Jewish Popular Front
would be the basis upon which a true immigrant community could
be created, they quickly recognized that Jewish Communists and
their supporters would be forces to reckon with in any struggle for
control of the immigrant populace. As we have seen, there were in
fact a few unsuccessful attempts by Fédération leaders in early 1936
to reach a modus vivendi with the Front. Much of the blame rested
with the leaders of the Mouvement, who, in their premature hopes of
infiltrating the immigrant organization, were insensitive to the
support and loyalties which the Fédération had engendered as
quasi-official spokesman of the eastern European community. A
major stumbling block, however, was the Fédération's refusal to
view a future community in any terms other than its own. Thus
Jefroykin regarded it as a major concession when he announced in
April 1936 that the Fédération would be willing to accept individual
members of political groups into the organization. He categorically
refused, however, to admit Jewish Communists en masse as a
"political bloc," arguing that to do so would be to destroy the
politically neutral nature of the immigrant organization.[24] For
immigrant leaders, it was obvious that the interests of the immigrant
community and of the Fédération as it presently existed were
indistinguishable. It mattered little that statements like Jefroykin's
seemed to run counter to the basic supposition of the *kehila*
movement, namely, that the Paris immigrant community had "out-
grown ... [its] primitive level of organizations and self-help ...
[and] is large enough and developed enough to achieve higher forms
of organization."[25]

Supporters of a unified community were heartened by a softening
of the Fédération's position toward admission of Jewish left-wing
organizations in early 1937. The change in policy seems to have
resulted from an evaluation of the role of the Jewish Left in the

immigrant community. Although the Jewish Popular Front had failed, Fédération leaders realized that its emphasis upon militant political action continued to find wide support among normally quiescent immigrants. The continual barrage of denunciations of the Jewish Left by *Pariser Haint* militants did little to diminish its strength and influence. Fédération leaders were also encouraged by an upturn in their own membership. In September 1936 the immigrant organization had eighty affiliates. By April 1937 the number had grown to ninety-five, partly as a result of the disaffection of *landsmanshaftn* with the Jewish Popular Front after the abolition of the Jewish subsection. Immigrant leaders like L. Shapiro, then secretary of the Fédération, reasoned that it was in the interests of his organization to take under its wing those groups left leaderless by the PCF's action.[26]

The new position was announced by Jarblum, always more sympathetic to the Jewish Left than other Fédération leaders, in an article published in *Pariser Haint* on April 20, 1937. The Fédération never questioned the political credentials of any organization seeking to join, he argued, thus contradicting Jefroykin's previous position that no "political party" would ever be accepted into the immigrant organization. Even Jefroykin, himself, argued for a reasonable approach to unity by noting that all groups must give up some of their independence for the sake of the community at large.[27] Similarly, Dijour pleaded with the Left not to build a community on the ruins of the old, a veiled allusion to the desire by left-wing immigrants to destroy the *landsmanshaft* structure. Reflecting the new realism, he concluded that the new wave of politically militant immigrants would be welcomed into the Fédération as soon as they ceased their attempts to impose new organizations on older immigrant members.[28]

The Fédération's unity campaign culminated in a general membership conference held on April 24, 1937. The main focus of the conference was on Jewish communal life in the provinces. In part the emphasis on Jews in the provinces stemmed from the realization by Fédération leaders that the Jewish Left had little or no influence among Jews outside of Paris. In part it reflected the bitter reality that Jewish groups in the provinces, far flung and relatively isolated, had a vested interest in a strong central organization of immigrant Jews in France, while societies in Paris seemed satisfied with the loose organizational structure of the Fédération. The conference itself only confirmed the fears of the leadership. Many of the larger societies in Paris refused to send representatives, arguing that discussions of problems in provincial Jewish communities had little relevance to Jewish life in Paris.[29] Those societies that did attend could not agree on the structure and goals of the future *kehila*.[30]

One of the few resolutions agreed upon at the conference denounced attempts to create new organizations in competition with the Fédération. The resolution was clearly directed against the Jewish Left, which, despite the abolition of the Jewish subsection, had continued to run programs and to attract immigrants to them. Contrary to the hopes of Fédération leaders, the dissolution of the Jewish subsection had only led Jewish Communists to limit their actions to the internal problems of the Paris Jewish community and not to cease activity completely.[31] If the PCF would not tolerate any specific Jewish action against Fascism, Communist militants reasoned, it would certainly not oppose programs restricted to the day-to-day activity of the Jewish community. Besides, they concluded, it would be a shame to lose the impressive support the Jewish Left had garnered during the heyday of the Jewish Popular Front.

The Jewish community envisioned by Jewish Communists was to be, in the words of Y. Spero, a member of the *Naie Presse* editorial staff, "a tightly structured and well-organized Jewish collectivity [*kibetz*], that all Jewish groups, political and social, professional and cultural, in which all Jewish authorities and officials who can and wish to work together in a France of the Popular Front" can participate.[32] This was a far cry from the "progressive forces" of the Jewish Popular Front, much less the "proletarian masses" so cherished by Jewish Communists in their sectarian period. Instead, the Jewish community proposed by the Left was to be a mirror image of France under the Popular Front banding together all members of the nation or community in a united effort against outside enemies.[33] In line with PCF demands, Jewish Communists took pains to differentiate between purely Jewish matters and those matters relevant to all Frenchmen. Thus, Spero argued in an article published in *Naie Presse* on April 24, 1937, that the Popular Front had succeeded in "exorcising the Fascist devil," so that Jews in Paris could now turn their attention to sanitariums, popular clinics, credit unions, mutual-aid groups, and other communal organizations. The emphasis on social welfare and economic betterment also meant the end of attacks upon political foes within the Jewish community. Gone were the diatribes against "reactionary" forces in the Paris Jewish community working for the triumph of Fascism. Instead,

Spero voiced the belief that "90 percent of the Jewish community can agree upon a common language, can work out a common program, and all [banding] together can make it work."

The increased interest of the Jewish Left in the unity campaign was reflected in its surprisingly mild reaction to the Fédération's conference of April 1937. In an article published soon after the conference, Spero expressed disappointment with the immigrant organization's failure to invite representatives from unaffiliated organizations. He also chided the Fédération for demanding that conference participants issue a statement declaring their intention of joining the organization and affirming their belief that the Fédération was the only representative body of immigrant Jewry in France. Despite his disappointment, however, Spero did not rule out a future accommodation with the immigrant organization.[34] Similarly Lerman noted after the summer lull in activity that there was renewed interest within the Fédération for a truly representative community. In particular he pointed to the sympathetic attitude of some members of the organization toward the Yiddish Cultural Congress held in Paris in November 1937 under the auspices of Jewish left-wing groups.[35]

Yet the Jewish Left did not seriously believe that the Fédération would be willing to forsake its independence for the sake of a community in which left-wing elements would play an important part. At the same time, PCF leaders were undoubtedly unhappy with the attempts by its Jewish militants to woo petit-bourgeois organizations at the expense of its commitment to the immigrant proletariat. In June 1937 Jewish Communist groups and Jewish sections of labor unions decided to create their own central body, the *Tsentrale fun arbeter un folks-organizatsies* (Federation of Worker and People's Organizations) or TSAFO, to act as both a replacement for the defunct United Front and a basis for a new Jewish community encompassing all "democratic" organizations.[36] After eight months of feverish activity in which militants attempted to widen their support among nonunionized and non-Communist immigrants, TSAFO finally called a general unity conference on April 24, 1938. The Nazi occupation of Austria in March evidently had acted as a catalyst for TSAFO's action, and indeed for a time it appeared that the various immigrant groups would be able finally to unite in a coordinated action. Thus *Pariser Haint* militants, sensing the danger that Jews faced as a result of Anschluss, agreed to publish the call for unity issued by TSAFO. Similarly, the Fédération agreed to discuss the matter of participation at a meeting held in late March.[37] But the immigrant organization reached no agreement at its meeting, and on March 21 it published a statement in *Pariser Haint* that made no mention of the Left's unity proposal. The final blow was issued by Jarblum in an article published in *Pariser Haint* on April 8, in which he denounced the organizations affiliated with TSAFO as tools of forces acting behind the scenes to destroy the Fédération. The president of the immigrant organization concluded the article with a firm declaration that not one society in the Fédération would join the "Communist" unity campaign.[38]

Despite its overtly political character, TSAFO still managed to attract a sizable following within the immigrant community. According to *Naie Presse* in its account of the founding meeting, there were 300 delegates from ninety organizations in attendance evenly divided between Communist and Fédération groups. An examination of the list of participants reveals that almost half of the organizations represented had been members of the Jewish Popular Front. The others were either recently created groups that had split off from older societies or provincial organizations that had not had the opportunity to participate in the largely Paris-based Mouvement populaire juif. Efforts by TSAFO leaders to play down its left-wing character—such as the refusal to allow the Comité intersyndical, the central organization of Jewish sections of labor unions, and the *Fraynd fun Naie Presse* (Friends of the *Naie Presse*) to join—fooled neither anti-Communist immigrants nor leaders of the Parti communiste français.

The dominance of left-wing organizations was evident in the keynote speech presented by B. Tcharny, a former leader of the Jewish subsection.[39] Sensitive to the fears created among immigrants by Anschluss, Tcharny began by noting that too many Jews believed that there was nothing that could be done to alleviate the Jewish plight. The experience of the French Popular Front showed, however, that much could be accomplished through the unity of the community. For those who countered that Jews lacked power, Tcharny responded that immigrants in France were assured of the aid of their non-Jewish brethren, who in crushing Fascism would rid the world of anti-Semitism. The purpose of a central representative body, then, was to show a united Jewish front to the rest of the world. Within France itself, he concluded, a central body would help to mobilize the democratic government to defend the rights of the Jewish people, to pass laws against racism, and to establish a strong counteroffensive to Fascism.

Tcharny had alluded only in passing to the internal needs of the Jewish community in France. His main emphasis was upon the alliance of Jewry with the democratic forces of France, an emphasis that bore clear markings of PCF pressure for a limited Jewish action. Jewish Communists moved quickly albeit cautiously to allay immigrant suspicions. Thus the resolution passed at the meeting spoke of ending the "shameful" split in the Jewish community and of eliminating apathy and pessimism among immigrants.[40] The "Manifesto to the Jewish People," as the resolution was titled, made no mention of the democratic forces of France but talked instead of aiding Jewish merchants and artisans, raising the cultural level of immigrants, opening new schools, increasing mutual-aid activity, and improving the legal status of newly arrived immigrants. Voicing the hope that all democratic organizations would join TSAFO, the resolution categorically denied that the participants had any desire to change the structure of existing organizations. The document concluded with a statement affirming TSAFO's commitment to engage in talks with the Fédération with the goal of gaining collective membership for the left-wing movement's affiliates.[41]

The Fédération's response was a foregone conclusion and had in fact been clearly outlined in an article written by L. Shapiro in *Pariser Haint* on April 23. Shapiro began by dismissing the TSAFO as a collection of political parties, *patronatn*, and "worthless" apolitical groups. At best the Fédération was willing to admit the latter organizations, not as a bloc, but individually according to their compatibility with the aims of the immigrant organization. Why should TSAFO seek to join the Fédération as a bloc, Shapiro argued, unless it was seeking to destroy the immigrant organization from within? Non-Communist immigrants had too many bitter memories of societies that had been infiltrated by newer immigrants who had succeeded in eventually transforming them into political organizations. An article by an unnamed society leader in the same issue continued the attack. How can Communists talk of unity, he argued, when their parent organization, the PCF, spouted nativist slogans? Reiterating Shapiro's position, the society leader concluded that TSAFO was hypocritical, creating new organizations in opposition to the Fédération and then turning around and demanding that they be accepted as members!

The sharp criticism levelled against TSAFO by the Fédération and its affiliate organizations showed that the period of *ouverture* to the Jewish Left had long since passed. Yet despite the Fédération's negative attitude, TSAFO (renamed in 1938 the *Farband fun yidishe gezelshaftn* or, in French, *Union des sociétés juives de France*) continued to appeal to the immigrant organization to affiliate.[42] Articles in *Naie Presse* tried desperately to counter criticisms directed at Jewish Communists by the Fédération. In particular, militants like Lerman sought to downplay dependence upon French working-class organizations and to stress Jewish Communist participation in community affairs.[43] At the same time, left-wing elements continued to widen the membership and activities of the Farband. A second meeting of the organization, held on July 9, 1938, during the summer lull, still managed to attract some seventy groups, including societies and *landsmanshaftn* affiliated with the Fédération. The meeting itself presented no new programs. Although condemning the adamant refusal of the Fédération to join in the unity campaign, the final resolution nevertheless called upon the Farband to make a new appeal to the immigrant organization.[44]

With hindsight, one can see that the Jewish Left's unity campaign was hampered by two main obstacles. On the one hand, it was forced because of PCF pressure to tread a thin line between so-called "Jewish" issues relating solely to the Paris community and national or international issues that supposedly affected all Frenchmen. Thus while Jewish Communists devised numerous schemes for centralizing social, educational, and recreational services in the Jewish community, they were always careful to point out that questions of anti-Semitism were best handled by others outside the community.[45] Yet immigrant concerns in 1937 and 1938 did not lend themselves to such fine differentiations. Although, as we have seen, almost all segments of the community turned their attention toward community problems after the defeat of the Popular Front government in July 1937, the question of anti-Semitism was never far from immigrant minds. If eastern European Jews in Paris recognized that they could do little to oppose the onslaught of Nazism, they still felt obligated to present a strong Jewish defense against those dangers within France that threatened Jewish interests; hence the concern with the plight of refugees, with the effect of antiforeigner legislation upon immigrant artisans, and with the growth of French anti-Semitism. Eastern European Jews remained unconvinced by the Jewish Left's emphasis upon allying with so-called democratic forces. In particular, immigrants could point to the upsurge of antiforeigner sentiment among French workers, the backbone of PCF support.[46] The Jewish Communists' optimistic assertions of the impending defeat of Fascism in France seemed ludicrous to Jews who feared that they might be expelled any day.

A second factor hindering the Jewish Left's unity effort was its insistence upon seeking an accommodation with the Fédération. The Left's position was based upon a careful analysis of the power structure within the Paris immigrant community. Despite its declining prestige, the Fédération was still the major immigrant organization in Paris. Older *landsmanshaftn* continued to attract the bulk of the immigrant population as well as a major proportion of its wealth. In order to reach immigrants, left-wing militants reasoned, it was necessary to first reach an accommodation with the one organization that still commanded their loyalty. If left-wing groups attacked the Fédération too strongly, they would send it rushing into the arms of the Consistoire, which, as we have seen, had its own designs upon the organization. If they merely ignored the Fédération and tried to set up their own central institution, they would isolate themselves from the majority of immigrants, who, after the abolition of the Jewish subsection, had reason enough to be skeptical of the sincerity of Jewish Communists. The only hope lay in infiltrating the Fédération, much in the same manner in which militants had infiltrated individual *landsmanshaftn*, and eventually taking it over; hence the insistence of TSAFO that the Fédération accept the left-wing organizations en bloc without any preconditions. The instinctive anti-Communism of Fédération leaders, and especially their suspicion of a coup d'état if left-wing organizations were to be admitted, doomed the Left's plan from the start.[47]

The problems dogging the Farband's unity effort stemmed from the Communists' ambiguous position within the Paris Jewish community. Since the advent of the Jewish Popular Front, immigrant militants had sought to play two roles: on the one hand, the Jewish arm of the PCF, and as such subservient to the policies of the French party; on the other, a major force in the Jewish community. For a while, Jewish Communists deluded themselves into thinking that the two roles merely reflected the two levels upon which they functioned; hence the separation of "Jewish" concerns from national concerns. Problems arose, however, when it became clear that the two concerns were in sharp contradiction to one another. To follow the PCF was to accept the nationalist and often xenophobic sentiments that the party espoused. To take an active role in the immigrant community meant defending Jews against the threats of expulsion and loss of livelihood associated with the antiforeigner impulse. The dilemma was to become sharply defined during the Munich Crisis.

The clash between political and nonpolitical organizations that characterized the unity campaign of 1937 and 1938 left many immigrants unsure of where to turn. Neither the Popular Front of democratic forces nor the *kehila* seemed to provide a satisfactory solution, for both sides refused to budge from their positions. A number of attempts were made by marginal groups in the community to provide a third alternative to the problem of unity in the Paris Jewish community.

One alternative was suggested by the Poalé-Sion Hitachdouth, a Zionist organization closely affiliated with the Fédération and for a time an important member of the Jewish Popular Front. In an article published in its organ, *Naye Zeit*, on May 8, 1936, the leaders of the organization sought to answer the question Popular Front or *kehila*? Although the Fédération was the most important immigrant organization in Paris, the Zionist group argued, it had no right to speak for the entire French Jewish community. The existence of the Jewish Popular Front showed that there were large numbers of politically active immigrants who did not and indeed should not belong to the Fédération. It followed, therefore, that the only organization that could represent the entire community would have to be newly created in order to accommodate political as well as nonpolitical organizations. According to the leaders of the Poalé-Sion Hitachdouth, the future central body was to be a carbon copy of the *gemaynde* of eastern Europe, that is, a Jewish council empowered by the French government to levy taxes, pass judgment on matters directly pertaining to the community, represent Jews in all governmental discussions affecting them, and generally act as the quasi-official governing body of the Jewish community.

The Poalé-Sion Hitachdouth did not have enough support within the immigrant community to mount a campaign for the realization of its plan. Even if it had done so, it is unlikely that immigrants who left eastern Europe to seek the freer atmosphere of the West would have been interested in merely recreating the autonomous communal structure of the *shtetl*. Nor could the Zionist group hope to attract support among left-wing elements. Poalé-Sion Hitachdouth had broken with the Jewish Popular Front in late 1936 after repeated arguments with Jewish Communists on the question of Communist activity in Palestine. Jarblum, its leader and most active proponent of the *gemaynde* plan, was henceforth considered persona non grata in left-wing circles. Besides, the plan was based upon conditions in the Paris community in 1936 at the height of Popular Front enthusiasm and, like the Jewish Popular Front it hoped to replace, could not have survived the important changes within the community after the fall of Blum's government.

More significant was the unity campaign mounted by LICA in 1938. Lecache's organization came to the campaign with impressive credentials. As a native-led organization, it had managed to attract a fair number of French Jewish youth and even counted among its members some prominent members of the Consistoire.[48] Even those natives who looked askance at its public protests could not but be impressed by the imposing array of French dignitaries who participated in the organization's meetings and rallies.[49] Immigrants, for their part, respected the militancy of LICA and particularly its willingness to actively defend Jewish areas in Paris against attacks by anti-Semitic bands. Fédération leaders, although often condemning what they regarded as the organization's irresponsible actions, nevertheless saw LICA as proof that there were at least some French Jews who were actively concerned about immigrants. Finally, left-wing elements could always depend upon Lecache's group to support its activities and welcomed its participation in the Jewish Popular Front.

It was Lecache's contention that only LICA with its influence in both the native and immigrant communities could band together the highly factionalized Paris Jewish settlement into a cohesive unit. His position was outlined in a series of articles published in *Pariser Haint* in April 1938.[50] In calling for a conference of all Jewish organizations on April 20, Lecache denounced the "spirit of competition" that pervaded the community. Unlike other organizations, he wrote on April 27, LICA would never create an organization that would compete with existing groups. Nor would it seek to differentiate among classes and groups within the Paris Jewish community. An attack on Rothschild, on a Jewish shopkeeper, on a Zionist, on an anti-Zionist; "all would mean an attack on me," he noted in an article on April 17. Similarly, after the April 20 meeting in which over two hundred societies participated, Lecache glowingly wrote that the "wonder" of LICA was that it was able to bring together Jews of the Consistoire, religious Jews, Zionists, and "progressive" Jews in one central body.[51]

By late June Lecache had succeeded in founding his own central institution, the *Union des sociétés juives pour l'action de LICA*, comprising some ninety-one societies, many of them affiliated with the Fédération and the Farband.[52] The purpose of the new unity campaign was made clear in an article Lecache wrote in *Pariser Haint* on July 21, 1938. Calling on all organizations in the Paris Jewish community to unite around LICA, he appealed specifically to the two major immigrant organizations. Speaking first to the Fédération, he asked if "you are ready to rid yourself of the fruitless isolation that weakens you and prevents you from speaking to the masses?" He then addressed the leaders of the Farband: "And you, the *Comité d'initiative* [of the Farband], are you ready to accept the discipline that is involved in the unity of Jews of all parties and philosophies?" Lecache concluded by noting brazenly that LICA had the influence, power, and non-Jewish friends to succeed in the unity effort where others had failed. All it needed was money from the two groups.

Lecache's appeal came too late to have any real effect upon Paris Jews, for the summer exodus from the city was followed by a period of international tension that culminated in the Munich Crisis. Yet even if Paris Jews had not been forced to redirect their attention to the plight of Jews in central Europe, it is doubtful that LICA's programs would have been accepted by either natives or immigrants.

The Consistoire had done relatively little to seek an accommodation with immigrants after the "unity" banquet fiasco of July 1935. Unable to convince eastern European Jews of the native organization's central role in the building of a united Paris Jewish community, Consistoire leaders seemed to be content with merely holding their own in the face of an ever-worsening financial situation. Under these conditions, Lecache's overtures to French Jews, coupled as they were with demands for financial assistance and merciless attacks upon "les juifs bien nés," only added salt to the Consistoire's wounds.[53]

Nor was the Fédération interested in LICA's appeal. It had enough trouble keeping pace with the Left's unity effort to be bothered with still another attempt to factionalize Paris Jewry. Like the Consistoire, the immigrant organization refused to consider any community structure that did not include the Fédération as the central institution. In this sense, its leaders had learned nothing from the failure of the Jewish protest movement. As in the period between 1933 and 1936, the Fédération in 1937 and 1938 remained a loose conglomerate of societies, powerless to act, yet fearful of relinquishing any of its independence. One might well argue that the unity effort, like much of the activity of the Paris Jewish community in the 1930s, failed because it represented a threat to the existing organizational structure of both natives and immigrants.

Of all the groups in the Paris Jewish community, the Left seemed least bound by loyalty to existing institutions. Yet the restrictions placed upon Jewish Communists by the PCF, as well as the Left's dogged insistence upon infiltrating the Fédération, limited its effectiveness. Never able to successfully define its own position within the Paris Jewish community, the Jewish Left remained torn between conflicting roles. In the end, the left-wing unity effort fell prey to the pull of organizations existing both within and without the Paris Jewish community.

In examining the charges and countercharges levelled by the major organizations in the Paris community during the unity campaign, one is struck by the narrowness of the debate. The fact that the struggle for unity was carried out solely on the level of organizations meant that the questions raised never went beyond those pertaining to community structure. As long as the Consistoire, the Fédération, and later the Farband viewed unity largely in terms of the leadership of the future community, there could never be meaningful discussions of the pressing problems besetting Paris Jewry in the 1930s. True, the debate over organizational structure of Paris Jewry was only a reflection of more important differences that divided Jews in the capital, differences that with hindsight one can cogently argue would have doomed the unity campaign anyway. Yet the insistence upon viewing unity in organizational terms prevented these differences from being aired and thereby helped to perpetuate false illusions about the future of the Paris Jewish community.

The petty concerns of organization leaders also blinded them to the role that a unified community might have played in creating a common understanding of the Jewish plight. Born amidst doubt over the viability of Jewish protest, the unity campaign reflected a desperate attempt to search for an alternative response to Nazism and anti-Semitism. Few Jews were prepared in 1936 to accept the underlying fatalism implied in the *gemaynde* proposal of the Zionist Left. Instead they chose to rely upon French "progressive forces" while establishing a community program of social and economic welfare. The collapse of the Popular Front was a crucial turning point in community awareness of the "Jewish question." Yet the response of immigrant leaders to growing despair and disillusionment in 1937 and 1938 was to carry on their separate unity efforts as if nothing had happened. Thus while Fédération leaders and their supporters continued to insist upon viewing the *kehila* structure as a mere extension of the *landsmanshaft* system and its programs of social welfare, the Jewish Left parroted slogans about the role of the French Left in saving Jewry. In either denying or ignoring the ramifications of the failure of Jewish protest and of the Popular Front, leaders of the Paris Jewish community missed an important opportunity to transform a sense of hopelessness into a renewed commitment to maintain Jewish solidarity in the face of the Nazi enemy.

Immigrant and native leaders in 1937 and 1938 took little notice of the isolated statements by Jewish "fatalists" who criticized the unity campaign as too little too late. Caught up in organizational squabbles, community leaders dismissed their Cassandra-like statements as the musings of eternal Jewish pessimists who could never acclimate themselves to living in a "New World." Yet the failure of community leaders to prepare Paris Jewry for the Nazi onslaught was to become even clearer in the last year of peace. For though the search for community was to continue until the final days before the outbreak of war, it was to be overshadowed by the growing awareness on the part of Paris Jewry of the total unwillingness of Western democracies to intervene with Hitler in order to prevent the worsening condition of Jews in central and eastern Europe.

Notes

1. Figures published in the *compte rendu* of the Assemblée générale ordinaire of the Consistoire for the year 1935 show that for every three new members who joined in the period 1930–35, there were eight members who died or resigned. The religious organization reached a high point of 7,114 members in 1932 but continually declined in the subsequent seven years until the war. For detailed figures, see the organization's *compte rendu* of its Assemblée générale ordinaire, 1935, pp. 27, 28; and *L'Univers israélite*, May 28, 1937.

2. *Pariser Haint*, October 22, 1935.

3. Figures on the elections can be found in the archives of the ACIP, AA23, Conseil d'administration, 1936–38, meeting of January 14, 1936.

4. Ibid.

5. For discussions of the Consistoire's financial situation, see the archives of the ACIP, AA23, Conseil d'administration, 1936–38, meetings of February 27 and June 25, 1936. For discussions of cuts in expenditure, see the reports of the meetings of November 3, 1936, and January 12, 1937.

6. The Consistoire even went so far as to allow Jefroykin to run as a candidate in its elections of 1935. For a discussion of Jefroykin's candidacy, see *Le Journal juif*, November 22, 1935.

7. See, for example, the article by Lambert in *L'Univers israélite*, August 10, 1935.

8. For an example of Consistoire appeals to immigrant youth, see the account of a meeting of native and immigrant youth at the house of Baron Edouard de Rothschild in *L'Univers israélite*, November 9, 1934. Adolphe Caen reflected the attitudes of the native leadership when he noted at the meeting that it was futile to try and convince immigrant parents. The only hope, he concluded, was to emancipate their sons and daughters from Jewish "particularism," which had no place in France.

9. Caen and Bigart's speeches are cited in *L'Univers israélite*, July 6, 1934.

10. Cited in *Pariser Haint*, December 30, 1934.

11. For Berman's article, see *L'Univers israélite*, January 25, 1935; for Lerman's article, see *L'Univers israélite*, February 1, 1935.

12. For some examples of native reaction to the call for unity, see the letters published in *L'Univers israélite*, February 8, 1935.

13. Information on the banquet is taken from *L'Univers israélite*, July 12, 1935, and *Pariser Haint*, July 8, 1935.

14. On the federation of religious organizations, see *L'Univers israélite*, February 8, 1935. The *Association des israélites traditionnels*, as the federation was called, was concerned mainly with arbitrating disputes among the various religious communities on questions of ritual, such as those of kashruth, marriage ceremonies, and conversions.

The Consistoire also flirted with the idea of uniting with the Union libérale, but nothing came of it. For discussions of unity with the Reform organization, see the archives of the ACIP, AA23, Conseil d'administration, 1936–38, meeting of December 15, 1936.

15. On May 1, 1935, an anonymous writer in *Pariser Haint* claimed that many immigrants did not regret the fact that an agreement between the Fédération and French Jewish organizations had failed. Eastern European Jews, he noted, had no interest in associating with organizations that openly flirted with the Union patriotique and other anti-immigrant groups.

Of course, such sentiments were quickly forgotten during the elections of April–May 1936, when Fédération leaders supported Edmond Bloch's candidacy in the "Pletzl."

16. The term *kehila*, as applied to the Paris Jewish community, was actually coined by Jefroykin in a speech given in early 1936. The idea had its origins, however, in discussions in *Pariser Haint* in early 1934.

17. *Pariser Haint*, February 15, 1935.

18. For information on the decision, see the interview with Jefroykin in *Pariser Haint*, April 10, 1935.

19. See, for example, the article by Alperin in *Pariser Haint*, June 26, 1935.

20. Frank, writing in *Pariser Haint* on September 13, argued that the Fédération had too many plans and programs and that, as a result, immigrants in Paris "have become accustomed to chaos."

21. N. Lirik in *Pariser Haint*, September 22, 1935.

22. *Pariser Haint*, February 19, 1936.

23. *Pariser Haint*, May 4, 1936.

24. Speech cited in *Naye Zeit*, April 24, 1936.

25. Dijour in *Pariser Haint*, May 4, 1936.

26. *Pariser Haint*, April 15, 1937.

27. Ibid.

28. Ibid. Dijour also noted incisively that it was hard to create a community when there was a new wave of immigration every five or ten years.

29. Jarblum underscored the leadership's disappointment when he wrote after the conference that it "was not in full harmony with the needs, requirements, and pressing demands of the present moment" (*Pariser Haint*, May 2, 1937).

Fédération leaders received further confirmation of membership apathy in June 1937, when a campaign to aid Jewish victims of pogroms in Poland attracted mostly Jews from the provinces. On the campaign, see *Pariser Haint*, June 21 and 24, 1937.

30. Vevyorke, writing in *Pariser Haint* on May 11, 1937, commented on the inability of delegates to agree on just what type of Jewish identity would be best suited to meet the demands of Paris life. In eastern Europe, Vevyorke explained, there was no real problem of Jewish identity, since the question had been "ironed out" in the course of centuries of community development. In the end, "everyone wanted to be a 100 percent Jew." In Paris too there were those who continued to hold to this ideal. Others, however, wanted their children to partake in French culture at the expense of Jewish identity. A compromise had to be worked out, Vevyorke concluded, that would be neither the "100 percent Jew" nor the "Judaic" Jew of western Europe.

31. The Jewish Popular Front had never seriously concerned itself directly with the problem of building a Jewish community in Paris. Although Jewish Communists made veiled threats of destroying the *landsmanshaft* system, the ad hoc nature of the Front and the deliberate vagueness of its programs, designed to appeal to all elements within the community, tended to rule out the Front as a possible foundation for a future community in Paris.

32. *Naie Presse*, April 17, 1937.

33. Spero in *Naie Presse*, April 24, 1937.

34. *Naie Presse*, April 17, 1937. Spero clumsily described the Fédération's actions as "putting wooden blocks on the rails over which the locomotive of our community must travel" and "taking a cannon and shooting it into a building."

35. *Naie Presse*, November 13, 1937. Jewish activity, as did much activity in Paris, came to a complete standstill in the summer as thousands of Jews fled the city for vacations in the provinces. The unity campaign thus was temporarily halted between June and October 1937.

36. For an account of the founding of TSAFO, see *Naie Presse*, June 19, 1937. At its inception, the organization had only eleven members, all either Communist-led or trade-union groups.

37. For the *Pariser Haint* publication, see its edition of March 17, 1938; on the Fédération, see *Naie Presse*, March 19, 1938.

38. Jarblum had replaced Jefroykin as president of the Fédération in December 1936, after the latter resigned for "personal reasons." On the resignation, see *Pariser Haint*, December 12, 1936.

39. The speech is reproduced in *Naie Presse*, April 26, 1938.

40. The resolution can be found in ibid.

41. Much of the meeting was taken up with a discussion of the Fédération and its demands for unity. According to one of the organizers of the meeting, the date of the meeting was postponed twice to accommodate the Fédération leadership, but all to no avail (cited in ibid.).

42. See, for example, the account of a letter received by the Fédération from the Farband in *Pariser Haint*, June 20, 1938.

43. See, for example, Lerman's article in *Naie Presse*, June 2, 1938.

44. For an account of the meeting and the final resolution, see *Naie Presse*, July 12, 1938.

45. At a meeting to protest persecutions of Jews in Rumania held on January 12, 1938, for example, Lerman spoke glowingly of "the entire French democratic world and especially the combative, enthusiastic, and freedom-loving Parisian people, who raise their voices in support of every noble cause and who have already shown that they can save innocents from the hangman" (cited in *Naie Presse*, January 14, 1938).

46. See, for example, the statement by Raphael Riba, the Bundist leader, on demands by French unionists that immigrants be expelled from the clothing trades (cited in *Pariser Haint*, October 19, 1937). *Pariser Haint* often used statements by Bundists to support its own attacks on Jewish Communists.

47. As usual, Bundists displayed a remarkably incisive understanding of the dilemma of the Jewish Left. Among other things, they were keenly aware of the effects of PCF pressure and the attraction of the Fédération for Jewish Communists. For some examples of the Bundist analysis, see the articles by A. Sener (May 2, 1938) and Y. Schloss (May 21, 1938) in *Unzer Stime*.

48. In 1938 the French section of LICA claimed some 32,000 members, an overwhelming proportion of whom were Jews (figure cited by Lecache in *Pariser Haint*, April 17, 1938).

49. Among French notables appearing at LICA functions were Léon Blum, Henri Torres, a prominent lawyer, Edouard Herriot, Jacques Duclos, and Léon Jouhaux.

50. See especially *Pariser Haint*, April 17 and 27, 1938.

51. *Pariser Haint*, May 8, 1938.

52. For a list of the societies joining the new organization, see *Droit de vivre*, July 21, 1938.

53. In an article published in *Droit de vivre* on February 5, 1938, Lecache spoke of class conflict among Jews in terms that were strongly reminiscent of the sectarian analyses offered by Jewish Communists in the early 1930s. His discussion of the native Jewish community, for example, ended with the declamation that "it is because of these bloated Jews that Hitler destroys starving Jews." At the same time, Lecache was not above asking for money from the Rothschilds. (See, for example, his article in *Droit de vivre* on October 22, 1938.) Statements such as these contrasted sharply with the conciliatory nature of Lecache's articles in *Pariser Haint* and clearly show that, in the end, LICA's unity campaign was more rhetoric than reality.

8   From Anschluss
       to the War

The period between the victory of the Popular Front
in June 1936 and the Nazi occupation of Austria in March 1938
marked a brief pause in the efforts by Paris Jewry to aid Jews in
central and eastern Europe. Although the "Jewish question" was not
forgotten by natives and immigrants even during the most euphoric
moments of the Popular Front, Jews in the capital seemed more
concerned with shoring up their own defenses against anti-Semitism
in France than with the plight of Jews elsewhere. Either willingly or
unwillingly, they left the fate of their coreligionists in the hands of
the League of Nations and the "democratic powers." What remained
of Jewish action after the victory of the Popular Front were scattered
protest meetings and ineffective relief programs organized in response to particular incidents of anti-Semitism in central and
eastern Europe.[1]

The last nineteen months of peace were to see a worsening of the
Jewish condition in Europe and a growing fatalism within the Paris
community. The demise of the Jewish Popular Front and the failure
of the unity effort had destroyed faith in the viability of Jewish
action. The bitter experiences of the Anschluss and Munich and the
continued growth of anti-Semitism in France would demonstrate
conclusively the unconcern of the world with the Jewish plight.
Powerless to affect the worsening condition of Jews in central and
eastern Europe, Paris Jewry was to find solace in a sharpened
consciousness of the Jewish tragedy, as if somehow a heightened
awareness of Jewish suffering would ease the anguish over the
inability to relieve it. Many Jews also hoped that, in the absence of
physical defense, an awareness of the fate of other communities
would at least prepare natives and immigrants psychologically for
the enemy's onslaught, which they knew would follow inevitably.

In order to trace the development of this consciousness, one must
begin with an examination of the reactions of the community to the
outbreak of anti-Semitism in Rumania in early 1938. In the wake of

pogroms in Rumania and the failure of the League to act forcefully to defend the rights of Jews in that country, both *L'Univers israélite* and *Pariser Haint* published lengthy articles expressing native and immigrant concern. The articles in the French Jewish journal were typically cautious in their appraisal and hopeful for the future, yet their underlying mood of skepticism led more than one native to demand that the editors stop publishing "bad news" that had no relevance to French Jewry.[2] As expected, the reaction of immigrant militants in *Pariser Haint* was more cynical. Chomsky, for example, writing in the paper on January 30, summed up their views in the following terms: "The interventions and petitions are left in the chancellories and the archive basements." Alperin echoed immigrant sentiment concerning the silence of the international community when he noted in February that "the League of Nations has destroyed Jewish hopes."[3] For the first time since the accession of Hitler to power, there was no public outcry in the Paris Jewish community. Native fears of xenophobic reaction combined with a growing sense among immigrants of the futility of Jewish protest to cast a pall over Paris Jewry. Chomsky described the attitude of the community as a mixture of anger, confusion, and despair: "Our hearts are being cut out and we can only turn around in circles."

Concern was intensified after Hitler's annexation of Austria on March 15. The sight of Austrian Jews arriving in Paris in droves revived memories of the German influx of only a few years before and triggered fears of a worsening of the Jewish situation in Europe. Many Jews now spoke of war as the only way of stopping Nazism; others talked openly of emigration to Palestine.[4] Native leaders moved quickly to stave off fears engendered by Anschluss. As they viewed the situation, their main task was to squelch rumors spreading among Frenchmen that Jews were trying to stir up hatred and fear of Germany. Thus, for example, Lambert wrote in *L'Univers israélite* on March 18 that French Jews had "too much tact and reserve" to ask that French foreign policy be geared to Jewish persecutions in other countries; "our love of peace quells our desires for revenge." The denial of Jewish bellicosity was combined with a reaffirmation of faith in France. In an article published in May, Lambert concluded that the best way to serve Jewry was to serve "France above all."[5] The only "Jewish" response that native leaders considered after the Anschluss was the offering of prayers for Austrian Jewry, but only on the condition that the action was not publicized in the Paris press.[6]

An interesting by-product of the Austrian crisis was a renewed interest in French Jewish circles in the question of Jewish identity. In a series of articles published in *L'Univers israélite* in March and April, various native intellectuals grappled with the perplexing problem of how to define Jewry. The debate was not merely academic. The persecutions of Austrian Jews after the Anschluss were a frightening reminder that Nazi ideology had imposed its own definition upon the Jew, a definition that seriously threatened the French Jew's tenuous balance between secular and religious life. Natives were also confronted with a nascent Zionist movement among its youth that defined Jewry in national terms.

The results of the discussions on Jewish identity were far from clear. While some natives argued that Jews were both a religious community and a nation, others maintained that Jewish separateness of any kind was an anachronism in a democratic country. Still others argued for a spiritual definition of Jewry that transcended both religion and nationality. Maurice Messica, a Sephardic member of the Consistoire, summed up native confusion when he noted in an article in *L'Univers israélite* on April 1 that Jewry "is a historic and ancient corpus, old and new at the same time ... which cannot be understood in a trifling manner." In the end, the debate served only to point up the profound divisions within the French Jewish community at a time when unity was so desperately needed to counter the growing Nazi threat.[7]

The most militant reaction in the immigrant community came not from newer immigrants centered around *Pariser Haint* but from the sons and daughters of older immigrants and natives who had taken over the management of *Samedi*. Thus while Alperin argued that it would be impossible for Paris Jews to support their coreligionists in Austria and Joseph Milner threw up his hands in despair because "the whole world has gone crazy," the editors of *Samedi* denounced the French government for its cowardice and defeatism in the face of Germany's refusal to abide by international agreements.[8] In part the moderation of *Pariser Haint* militants stemmed from pressures exerted by Fédération leaders, who had decided to work through the World Jewish Congress in petitioning the League to act.[9] In part it reflected their growing fatalism stemming from the belief that public protest would only exacerbate tensions between Frenchmen and Jews in Paris. As one writer cryptically noted in the paper in late March, eastern European Jews in Paris had always screamed and yelled about their own problems without bothering to think whether such problems had any effect upon other people.[10] Even members of the *Samedi* circle did not choose to go beyond bitter criticism in their reactions to the Anschluss. There were no public protests by nonpolitical Jews in Paris in March 1938.

And what of the Jewish Left? The only statement issued by Jewish Communists during the crisis reiterated the pat thesis that only the PCF and other French "democratic forces" could oppose the Nazi threat. The task of the Jewish masses, Lerman wrote in *Naie Presse* on March 12, was to publicize the Jewish plight. The article made no mention of the need for Jewish protest or public outcry. Instead, it called upon France to grant asylum to Jewish refugees.[11] The attitude of LICA was no more reassuring. In an article published in *Pariser Haint* on March 27, Lecache argued that Jews should not become pessimistic about the future. At the same time, however, he painted a frightening picture of the plight of European Jewry forced to flee their native lands yet finding all countries closed to them.

The behavior of Jewish organizations during the Austrian Crisis presaged the response of Paris Jewry to Munich in September 1938. On the whole, natives and immigrants seemed unprepared for the resurgence of Nazi persecution of Jews. Most of the major organizations had only recently been involved in intensive unity campaigns or, in the case of the Consistoire, in grappling with internal problems. Although the plight of central and eastern European Jewry was not completely absent from their minds, Jews in Paris had rationalized their relative unconcern by arguing that only a strong Jewish community in the French capital would be able to defend the interests of Paris Jewry and to present the case for Jewish refugees to government officials. The failure of the unity campaign left the Paris Jewish community uncertain as to where to turn.

There was a second and more significant factor, however, that explained the inactivity of Paris Jewry in March 1938. In the past, natives and immigrants had responded to events in central and eastern Europe that had gone largely unnoticed by Frenchmen. Few Frenchmen expressed grave concern in January 1933, for example, when Hitler assumed power. Fewer still followed developments within Nazi Germany after 1933 with any great interest. The Jewish protest movement in the early thirties thus attracted relatively little attention outside of the Jewish community itself. Even native Jews, who generally feared that public protest would engender anti-Semitism among certain elements of the French populace, never argued that vocal immigrants were acting against the interests of the nation as a whole.

The Austrian Crisis, however, had raised the possibility of war for the first time in the 1930s. The threat of armed intervention by France and England if Germany invaded Austria brought back memories of August 1914 when a succession of seemingly minor incidents triggered off a bloody and costly war. Frenchmen, in particular, had reason to fear war for they were well aware of the devastating effect that World War I had had upon the male population of their country. Their pacifist sentiments were considerably reinforced when both France and England backed down from their threats of intervention and stood by quietly while Germany occupied Austria.

While most Frenchmen argued for peace, many Jews secretly considered war. The annexation of Austria meant not only further German territorial aggrandizement but also a worsening of the Jewish plight. The sight of thousands of Austrian Jews fleeing westward led many Jews in Paris to question when the Nazi terror would end.[12] The failure of the democratic nations to actively oppose Hitler, the timidity of the League, the powerlessness of world Jewry—all created the feverish desire, however unrealizeable, to end the agony of Jews once and for all through a bloody confrontation with the Nazis.

No Jew in Paris dared to express such thoughts openly, of course. To do so would be to go against the popular desire for peace at any cost. Indeed, there was a noticeable upsurge in anti-Semitism in Paris directly after the Anschluss, attributable in large part to the rumor that Jews had tried to force the French government to declare war on Germany for their own interests.[13] Nor should it be forgotten that there were native Jews whose ties with eastern European Jewry were only tangential and who shrank from the idea of waging war to save their coreligionists in other countries. The result was a toning down of Jewish protest in favor of quiet diplomacy in the corridors of French ministries and of the League of Nations. Yet the problem of the conflict between Jewish interests and French national interests was not to be forgotten. It came to the fore once again in debates over the Jewish reaction to the Munich Crisis.

The period between the Anschluss and the Munich Crisis was marked by great uncertainty within the Paris Jewish community. The Nazi annexation of Austria made itself felt in France long after the Anschluss had become a fait accompli. The combination of antiforeigner feeling and the sizeable influx of Austrian Jewish refugees to Paris led the French government to issue a series of decrees in April and May directed against aliens in the country. Among the provisions of the new decrees were limitations on the number of foreign merchants and artisans in specific trades, restrictions on aliens opening up new businesses, repatriation of refugees who failed to register with government authorities, and expulsion of foreigners who could not produce valid work permits. Over 20,000 Jews in France were affected by one or more of these decrees, many of whom had lived in Paris for a number of years. Not surprisingly, there was a significant rise in the number of suicides within the immigrant community in the months following their issuance. Those Jews who could not pay for their own repatriation, and the number was in the hundreds, were summarily thrown into jail where they languished for months.[14]

The reaction of Jewish organizations in the capital was predictable. The consistorial and Fédération-run relief committees originally established to aid German refugees were hastily reactivated to deal with waves of immigrants affected by the new decrees. The number of eastern European Jews forced to seek aid, however, proved to be too great for the two organizations, and the relief effort collapsed after only a few weeks.[15] Failing to deal with the problem within the Jewish community, natives and immigrants next turned to the French government for help. French Jews sent dependable Judaeophiles in the French community like Justin Godart, a noted lawyer, to intervene with the Minister of Interior and the Prefect of Police on behalf of immigrants and refugees.[16] Despite warnings by French Jewish leaders that interventions with government officials should be left to natives and specifically to non-Jewish spokesmen, Fédération leaders sent their own delegations to the Minister of Interior. Unlike the native leadership, which sought only to appeal to the humanitarian sentiments of government officials, immigrants demanded that there be renewed discussion of colonization of displaced refugees, a question which had previously been raised during the Popular Front. In contrast to earlier arguments that Jews fleeing from persecution wanted to integrate themselves into French society if only given the chance, arguments of leaders like Jarblum now maintained that refugees could not and did not want to live in France but sought only a place where they could begin a new life undisturbed by their enemies.[17] Similarly, immigrant leaders discussed the possibility of creating refugee agricultural settlements in sparsely populated areas of the country, either as self-sustaining permanent settlements or as training centers for eventual settlement on kibbutzim in Palestine.[18]

Jarblum's statement implied that the refugee problem could not be solved on the national level. Such sentiments were not confined to the Paris Jewish community. In June 1938 an international conference on refugees was held at Evian, Switzerland, in which thirty-two countries participated. Jarblum greeted the conference as "the outpouring of the noblest human protest against barbarism" but showed his underlying skepticism by calling for a Jewish delegation to present the case for Jewish refugees. In suggesting plans for eventual settlement of stateless Jews, he was careful to avoid all mention of France. Natives were more jubilant over the conference, seeing it as further proof that the democratic powers, and particularly France, would never forsake Jews in their time of need.[19]

The results of the Evian Conference and of a follow-up conference held in London in July proved disappointing to those who had placed their faith in the democratic powers. Government representatives at the conference outdid each other in furnishing excuses for their refusal to accept refugees. Making little effort to disguise their hostility toward what one delegate called the "foreign invasion," the participants expressed concern over the lack of boats to transport refugees, the fear of German spies infiltrating countries while posing as refugees, and internal economic difficulties. Plans to send Jewish refugees to Palestine were quashed by Great Britain, which feared repercussions among Arab settlers.

Back in Paris, French Jews maintained strict silence for fear of arousing concern within the Jewish community. Immigrants meanwhile tried to make the best of what was obviously a great disappointment. Alperin, writing in *Pariser Haint* after the Evian Conference, could only weakly comment that the meeting accomplished more than was expected and pointed with faint hope to the resolution calling for the creation of a committee to meet in London in July in order to continue discussion on the refugee problem.[20] Shmuel Niger, a Yiddish journalist based in New York, was less reserved in an article written for the *Pariser Haint* after the fiasco of the London Conference. While covering the meeting, he noted, he often thought that "it was not a conference of mighty nations but rather a quiet meeting of heartless and stingy 'philanthropists,' each one feeling that the other should give—he had already 'done his duty.' " The failure of the thirty-two countries at the conference to commit themselves to a policy of admitting refugees led him to comment that the meeting could only have been "a provocation, a diabolical ploy of the Nazis: Let everyone see how powerless the democracies are; let everyone see clearly that they can only talk but cannot act on anything." Yet despite his cynicism, Niger, as were most immigrants in Paris, was forced to admit grudgingly that there was no other alternative but to depend upon the democratic powers for a solution to the refugee problem. In an argument that seemed more a rationalization for Jewish powerlessness than a sincere belief, he concluded that now that immigrant Jews had integrated themselves into western nations, they had the right to ask openly for aid, not as pitiful beggars but as full members of democratic societies.[21]

Jewish Communists were noticeably absent from discussions of plans for settling refugees and immigrants forced to leave France. As an international issue, the refugee problem was deemed to be the concern of the "democratic and progressive forces" upon which Jewish Communists relied for all questions not directly pertaining to the Jewish community. The silence of the Jewish Left may also have been a result of their fear of exacerbating xenophobic feeling among French workers, already hard pressed by rising unemployment and inflation. At most, left-wing militants envisioned their role as publicizers of the Jewish plight, as a liaison between oppressed immigrants and refugees and the organizations making up what remained of the Popular Front. This was the rationale behind the so-called legal status campaign, organized in late 1937 and continued until September 1938, that sought to impress upon French working-class organizations the need to normalize the immigrants' economic and political status.[22] What the Jewish Left refused to recognize, however, was that neither the PCF nor the CGT was willing to alienate its xenophobic membership for the sake of a handful of Jews.

The Paris Jewish community thus approached the Munich Crisis with little faith in the efficacy of Jewish action and a failing hope in the willingness of the democratic powers to come to the aid of Jews. The first signs of the impending crisis coincided with the beginning of the Jewish High Holidays. Not surprisingly, native leaders stressed religious belief in their discussions of the international situation. For the first time in French Jewish history rabbis proclaimed a special day of fasting, a practice traditionally associated with trage-dies befalling Jewry.[23] At the special service conducted at the rue de la Victoire synagogue on September 18, Rabbi Weill talked of the mission of French Jewry to show exemplary conduct in order to bring about the messianic reign of justice, bounty, and fraternity. Similarly, Rabbi Kaplan expressed the faith that God would not allow war to break out. Certainly men had sinned, he noted, but there were also multitudes who sought only to live in peace. "Will You remain deaf to their moving supplications?" he prayed to God while calling for divine blessings upon France, "so sincerely devoted to peace and to justice."[24]

The emphasis upon salvation through divine intervention implied a denial of the possibility of human action to stave off war. At the same time, the notion of the mission of Jewry, so integral to the French Jewish identity, was a clear warning that Jews in Paris should accept whatever fate awaited them. The goal of the Jew was to live an exemplary life. If he continued to be unjustly accused of fomenting war, native religionists argued, it was only because he was serving some divine purpose as a scapegoat for the sins of the world. Closely paralleling the prophetic belief in the ultimate justice of God's actions, the native position also served to justify the failure of French Jewry to react strongly to the threat of further persecutions posed by the Nazi occupation of Czechoslovakia.[25]

Natives were not the only Jews to flock to synagogues during the Munich Crisis. According to Bielinky, who personally visited the major houses of worship in September 1938, there were some 45,000 immigrant Jews at High Holiday services.[26] The *shul* served not only as a place for religious meditation during the fateful weeks of Munich but also as a vital source of information on international developments. More than one rumor of war spread among congregants at Rosh Hashanah (New Year) services, sending hundreds of immigrants fleeing into the streets in terror.[27] Even workers and artisans in Belleville came to *shul*, often for the first time since they had left eastern Europe, to voice their hopes for peace and to learn further news of events in Europe.[28]

In the period between Rosh Hashanah and Yom Kippur (Day of Atonement), the so-called *Yamin Noraim* (Days of Awe), Jews in Paris waited anxiously for an easing of international tension. As after Anschluss, they were again confronted with a wave of anti-Semitism sweeping through Paris which fed upon rumors that Jews were secretly pushing France toward war to serve their own interests. Dozens of Eastern European immigrants were arrested during the crisis, their foreign accents having led Frenchmen to mistake them for German provocateurs.[29] Lambert, writing in *L'Univers israélite* on September 30, described the period as "hours laden with anguish" and called upon Jews to band together with Frenchmen. Seeking to counter anti-Semitic rumors of Jewish warmongering, he concluded that if war should come, Jews would "serve and keep still" in the face of the attacks made upon them.

Immigrants showed a similar hesitancy to call for any public action. On September 26 the Fédération issued an appeal for "discipline, calm, and order" among immigrants and pledged that eastern European Jews in Paris would rise up to defend France as their fathers had done in 1914.[30] Similarly, *Pariser Haint* militants stressed their concern for peace and their faith in the willingness of western democracies to reach an agreement with Hitler.[31] Even Chomsky, long one of the bitterest writers in the Yiddish paper, could only suggest that immigrants go to *shul*, mingle with fellow Jews, pray for a better year, and feel at home away from the worries of the outside world.[32]

There was little new in the Jewish Left's response to Munich. More sensitive than either natives or more moderate immigrants to the anti-Semitic attacks emanating from the French masses, Jewish Communists were particularly concerned with warning immigrants to avoid all public discussions and with denouncing "political provocateurs" seeking to stir up trouble. In a statement that bore a marked resemblance to native arguments, TSAFO announced that eastern European Jews were just as concerned over the threat of war as other Frenchmen were. Thankful for the many opportunities that France had accorded Jews since their emancipation, immigrants were ready to defend their *patrie* against the Nazi "barbarians."[33] Jewish Communists also attempted to convince immigrants that the average Frenchman would have no part of anti-Semitism. Most articles in this vein, however, also made clear that the question of whether or not anti-Semitism would increase in Paris depended more upon the behavior of Jews than upon the attitudes of Frenchmen.[34]

The signing of the Munich Agreement was greeted with joy by all elements of the community. On October 2, Yom Kippur, both natives and immigrants were still unsure if peace would be maintained. Rabbis in synagogues and *shuls* spoke of the heroic traditions of the Jewish people and recalled with pride the participation of Jews in the French effort during World War I.[35] By October 3, when the detailed results of the Munich Conference were finally made known to the populace, Alperin could write that Jews were thankful to leaders of the democratic nations for avoiding war. Similarly an article in *L'Univers israélite* published on October 7 proclaimed Jewish fidelity to France. Recalling the recently passed High Holidays and the upcoming festival of Succoth (the Feast of Booths), the anonymous writer noted: "We prayed for peace. God heard our prayers. On Yom Kippur we were granted forgiveness, and now with peace of mind we can sit in the *Succah*, the *Succah* of Peace, with faith that the salvation of Israel will also be forthcoming."

The failure of the democratic powers to "save" Israel, however, tempered the enthusiasm of most Jews in Paris. While there were Jewish *munichois* found largely among the most assimilated elements in the community,[36] most Jews recognized that the peace of Europe also brought the extension of Nazism into yet another country where Jewish lives would be threatened. More prescient members of the Paris community realized that Munich had only been a stopgap measure with no assurance of a lasting peace. Even natives, normally reticent to voice disapproval with French foreign policy, seemed skeptical that Chamberlain's negotiations with Hitler had been anything more than a temporary truce to allow for further rearming.[37]

Both during and after the crisis, there was a general expectation in the community that the Great Powers would discuss the "Jewish question" at Munich. The willingness of the Western powers and Nazi Germany to "solve" the Sudeten problem was seen by many Jews in the French capital as a recognition of the plight of displaced persons which could only bode well for a solution to the Jewish refugee problem. Such expectations were naïve, to be sure, and undoubtedly stemmed from both pent-up frustrations over the apathy of the Great Powers toward the plight of Jewish refugees and a misunderstanding of the tangential nature of Jewish concerns in international diplomacy. The artificial attempts by Jewish journalists in the community to find positive value in the Munich Conference belied an underlying sense of hopelessness that led easily to flights of fantasy. Nisan Frank spoke more openly of the attitudes of most Paris Jews when he described the presentation of the Jewish case at the Four-Power meeting as negotiations with the Devil to save Jewish souls. "After all," he concluded, "what do we have to lose?"[38]

By far the most perceptive appraisal of Munich and its effect upon European Jewry was offered by Josef Fischer, a Zionist leader in Paris, in an article published in *La Terre retrouvée* on October 1.

The Munich conference, Fischer wrote, had destroyed a number of political myths while creating some dangerous precedents. First, the willingness of the democratic nations to negotiate with Hitler without consulting Czechoslovakia meant that the notion of the equality of peoples had collapsed. This had dire consequences for Jews in particular, the Zionist leader wrote, for as the weakest nation in Europe, they might well become the next victims of a "new ethic," which willingly dispensed with weaker nations for the sake of a fleeting peace among the Great Powers. Secondly, the Munich Agreement had created a policy of compromise between democratic and totalitarian powers. Henceforth anti-Semitic forces would have a voice in international conferences on refugees, thus making a mockery of what had previously been a sincere if unsuccessful effort to aid Jews. Finally, and most importantly, the occupation of the Sudetenland meant that Germany was seeing its pan-German dreams realized. The consequences of this for Jews as well as for the rest of Europe, Fischer concluded, were too horrible to contemplate.[39]

Paris Jews had little time to muse over the ramifications of Munich. The anti-Semitic rumblings heard in France during the early days of the crisis did not subside after the signing of the Munich Agreement. Once the initial enthusiasm over the maintenance of peace had worn off, Frenchmen looked for reasons why their country had come so dangerously close to war. As we have seen, the image of the Jew as warmonger found great currency in Paris. Ironically, anti-Semites were aided in spreading their doctrines by the public statements of Paris Jews. The continual emphasis that Jewish leaders placed upon the readiness of both natives and immigrants to defend France was pointed to as proof that Jews really wanted to wage war.[40] Anti-Jewish feeling was also fostered by the continuing economic rivalry between immigrant *façonniers* and French workers in the clothing and textile trades.[41] Some Frenchmen, concerned over the concessions made by France and England to Hitler, accused Jews of wanting a rapprochement between democracies and totalitarian governments. The fact that such statements clashed with the image of the bellicose Jew made little difference to Frenchmen seeking an explanation for the bewildering succession of events in September and October 1938.[42]

Two events in November made the situation of Paris Jewry still more uncertain. In early November, the government of Edouard Daladier issued another series of decrees that placed restrictions upon aliens in France. In essence, the decrees restricted foreigners in their choice of work, right of employment, right to housing, and right to organize. In addition, the government made known that deportation would be used frequently to "regulate" French economic life.[43] Hardest hit were the thousands of Jewish refugees who had entered France illegally. As a result of the new decrees, anyone entering the country without a regular visa would be refused a *permis de séjour*, while anyone caught without such a permit would be subject to immediate expulsion.

Of equal concern to Paris Jewry was the assassination of Ernst vom Rath, the Third Secretary of the German Embassy in France, by Hermann Grynzpan, a young Polish Jew who had seen his parents sent off to a concentration camp. In reprisal, Nazi leaders initiated the infamous Krystalnacht of November 9–10 in which bands of citizens roamed Jewish quarters in the major cities of Germany looting shops, destroying synagogues, and attacking residents. For the first time in Nazi Germany, persecution of Jews had gone beyond legal restrictions to officially sanctioned violence.

The reaction of Paris Jewry to the two events ranged from despair to sheer panic. Although natives were unaffected by the new decrees, they were shocked by the insensitivity displayed by the French government toward the plight of Jewish refugees. Unwilling to criticize the government's action for fear of being accused of unpatriotic activity, however, French Jews could only respond with an appeal for passive acceptance of the decrees.[44] The reaction of French Jews to the vom Rath assassination showed the abnormal fears that motivated their actions in the period after Munich. On November 18 *L'Univers israélite* published an open letter to the mother of the murdered Nazi in which the editors expressed great sorrow on the death of her son. At the same time, the letter implored her to show some pity for Jews persecuted in Germany while arguing that it was unjust to blame all Jews for her son's death. In their concluding remarks, the editors sought to downplay the seriousness of Krystalnacht. The events of November 9–10 were obviously the work of the rabble, the letter wishfully explained, and not of German notables who undoubtedly felt indignation and horror at the violence perpetrated against Jews.

The main concern of native Jews during this period was to demonstrate their total agreement with the decisions of the French government at Munich. This, in turn, implied a concerted attempt to refute the notion that Jewish interests demanded a more active opposition to Nazism. The astounding letter to vom Rath's mother was only one result of the twisted and tortured logic involved in this attempt. The statement by Chief Rabbi Weill in November that peace was more important than the plight of Jews in central Europe may also be seen in this context. Even when natives attempted to defend Jewry against anti-Semitic attacks, they were careful not to differentiate between the suffering of Jews and the plight of other oppressed groups. Thus, for example, Consistoire rabbis preached numerous sermons in late 1938 and early 1939 in which they spoke of the persecution of members of all faiths by the enemies of religion. If they mentioned any particular group, it was generally not fellow Jews but priests in Spain who were allegedly murdered by both sides in that nation's civil war.[45] In the few examples of public statements on the "Jewish question" in the months after Munich, natives generally supported their arguments with quotes from such questionable French spokesmen as Colonel de la Rocque and the Comte de Paris, the heir to the Orléanist throne.[46] In the Paris community at large, influential French Jews made use of their contacts in the "bourgeois" press to reaffirm Jewish support of international peace.[47] When more militant members of the Consistoire made the rather mild suggestion that French Jews demand that the government take anti-Semites to court for offenses against the Republic, they were met with stony silence.[48]

Most eastern European Jews in Paris had little time to think about countering anti-Semitic stereotypes. The impact of the decrees upon the immigrant community was devastating. Immigrants who had been living in France for several years were now threatened with expulsion or loss of livelihood. The most common reaction among immigrants was utter confusion. Yiddish newspapers were deluged with questions about stipulations in the new decrees. The confusion was so great that *Pariser Haint* was forced to set up an ad hoc committee of lawyers to sort out all difficulties. Those few immigrants who were not directly affected by the decrees pondered over the implications of the government's action. Some argued that the antiforeigner decrees were only the beginning of a wave of anti-Semitism that would engulf France. Others saw it only as a terrible error in judgment on the part of government officials which would be righted in the near future. Another question that occasioned much debate was the appropriate Jewish response to anti-Semitism. While some immigrants claimed that Jews should not mix into French politics lest they become too "visible" in a period of xenophobia, others countered that it was futile to try to appease anti-Semites, who would regard Jewish nonparticipation as a sign that Jews were seeking to separate themselves from the rest of French society.[49] Bewildered by government policy and doubting the viability of Jewish action, eastern European Jews in the French capital were paralyzed by the shock of Munich.

The vom Rath assassination and Krystalnacht only reinforced the paranoia of immigrants. The Fédération, for its part, was forced to issue yet another statement calling for calm and order in Jewish areas of Paris. At the same time, it emphatically denied that Grynzpan had any contact with the Paris immigrant community.[50] *Pariser Haint* militants added little understanding to the situation. Although condemning immigrant leaders for remaining silent, the only concrete suggestion they offered was an appeal to England and the United States to open their doors to Jews. There were no hints of possible action to be taken by either immigrants in Paris or by the French government. To talk of public agitation would be to risk further anti-Semitic attacks.[51]

As was to be expected, the Jewish Left offered few new solutions to the "Jewish problem." Once again Lerman was delegated by the PCF to impress upon immigrants the need to ally with the French masses. The events surrounding Krystalnacht brought a cry of despair from Jewish Communists but few suggestions for Jewish response. Although denouncing Jewish leaders who sought to parrot the western nations by begging Hitler's mercy, the Jewish Left, like much of the Paris community, had no plans for public protest.[52] Jewish Communists were living on the glories of the Popular Front. Just how long the idea of an active interest in the Jewish plight by French "democratic" forces could survive in the face of rising xenophobia, however, was open to question.

In examining the response of the community as a whole, one finds that the various factions were in general agreement at least on what Jews should not do. A demonstration against anti-Semitism was organized in late November by an interfaith group, but the Jewish representatives in attendance judiciously restricted their comments to a discussion of French ideals and avoided the question of Jewish persecution.[53] As a general rule, organization leaders avoided public speeches, protests, mass meetings, and even *démarches* to government officials. The reasons for the relative silence were the same for all groups. First, both natives and immigrants realized that in a period when French foreign policy dictated an increasing accommodation with Nazi Germany, it would have been foolish to separate Jewish interests from the interests of the nation as a whole. Not only would it have been futile, since it was clear by 1938 that no Western power would risk war for the sake of any other nation, much less a stateless people, but it also would have been extremely dangerous, since xenophobic feeling was already rampant in France. Secondly, the events of September and November had created near panic among immigrants in Paris. To arouse Jewish ire would only foster vain hopes of a solution to the problems besetting European Jewry and might lead to irresponsible actions patterned after the vom Rath assassination. Jewish community leaders certainly had ample reasons for playing down public protest in the months after Munich. What bothered some elements within the community was the failure of its leadership to understand that an acceptance of Jewish impotence did not have to lead to hopeless despair and pessimism.

Among the critics of Jewish inactivity were those who took advantage of the silence of the community leadership to vent their spleen against old enemies. Bundists again cautioned the immigrant masses against an overdependence upon the French working-class movement. As in the past, most of their attacks were levelled against the Jewish Communists, whom they felt were too willing to accede to PCF demands to remain silent during a period of international tension. In the end, Bundists remained tied to a sectarian view that seemed increasingly irrelevant to an understanding of the tensions in Europe in the late thirties. It was small comfort for Jews in Paris to learn, for example, that there was little difference between the "imperialistic interests of the democratic powers" and the "expansionist tendencies of the Fascists." The Bundists' emphasis upon relying on the international proletariat seemed equally meaningless in the face of the liquidation of the Left in Germany and rising anti-Semitism among French workers.[54]

A far more significant critique was offered by native and immigrant youth in the pages of *Samedi*. As we have seen, *Samedi* was the only journal in the community during Anschluss to discuss openly the effect of Nazi expansionism upon European Jewry. It was not surprising, therefore, that the paper took a militantly anti-Nazi stand during and after the Munich Crisis. The nature of *Samedi*'s criticism was two-fold: a debunking of faith in the French government and a denunciation of the Paris Jewish leadership. While both natives and immigrant organizations loudly proclaimed their belief in the benevolence of the French government, writers in *Samedi* accused French leaders of being lax in the struggle against internal anti-Semitism.[55] Although careful not to attack the Munich

Agreement per se, the paper's supporters did not mince words in their criticism of France's failure to live up to its ideals. In particular, writers denounced the government's antiforeigner decrees. An article by Amarti on January 14, 1939, for example, described the fate of a Jewish refugee upon arriving in France as that of "a stray, a tennis ball, a client for asylum at the mercy of philanthropic bureaus, a prison fixture, a trembler in the crosswalks, in a word—a refugee." If he were lucky, Amarti concluded, he might find a job, "on the condition, obviously, that he is allowed to work." It was not only opposition to Zionist attacks upon British policy in Palestine that led one writer in *Samedi* to note that England (and not France) was the home of democracy.[56]

The attack upon the French government was coupled with a denunciation of the passivity of the native Jewish leadership in Paris. For *Samedi* supporters, native Jewish fears were excessive and reflected a form of "Jewish masochism," the conviction that by demeaning Jews one could gain the approbation of the outside world.[57] The paper was especially critical of the willingness of French Jews to forsake immigrants and refugees in order to save their own reputation. In the article cited above, Amarti noted that it was not unusual for immigrants working illegally to be betrayed by "a native, one of those Jews who has nothing to forget for the simple reason that he has never learned anything, in a word, a Jew whose name recalls both the Hebrew Bible and German geography . . . [one] who will denounce you to the authorities, jealous of the bread you eat."

The tragic mistake of native Jewish leaders, *Samedi* writers argued, was to believe that Jewish interests were compatible with appeasement. Nazi Germany had declared war on the Jews, articles in the paper proclaimed, and the sooner French Jewry realized this grim fact, the better it would be.[58] *Samedi* supporters rejected the notion put forth by many French Jews that Nazism was imposed upon the German people by force. There was no "other Germany," an article noted in January 1939; Germans were "criminals" who had accepted Hitler and the Nazis freely and willingly.[59] The duty of French Jewry, then, was not to align Jewish interests with those of France but rather "to do as much evil to Germany as we can, and by all the means in our power."[60] The paper shrank from openly proclaiming that Jews should actively support war, however. War could only be made by mighty nations, an anonymous writer argued in January 1939, and not by a powerless people.[61]

In the end, then, there was no group in the Paris Jewish community that would openly state what every Jew secretly knew: the only way that European Jewry could find relief from its misery was through the destruction of Nazism. The statements in *Samedi* to the contrary, few Jews in Paris thought that there was an unbridgeable gap between their interests and the interests of the Western democracies. Even the most oppressed immigrants hoped that in the near future, France would see the error of her ways. It was a slim hope, to be sure, but it was the only hope they had.

The events of September 1938 had diverted attention from the internal problems besetting the Paris community. Already in December there were signs of at least a partial return to "normalcy." At the annual congress of the Fédération in early December, members again engaged in bitter debates over whether to join with the Consistoire or the Farband in future action to aid refugees and immigrants.[62] By January 1939 *Pariser Haint* had resumed their denunciation of Jewish Communists as enemies of the Paris community. Similarly, the Jewish Left returned to their concern with the increasing hostility between immigrant *façonniers* and French workers in the clothing and textile trades.[63]

Behind the day-to-day activities, however, lay deep-seated fears left by the Munich Crisis. The failure of the Western democracies to oppose Nazi expansionism and to aid Jewish refugees forced to flee Nazi-occupied areas could not be erased from the minds of Jews in Paris. If Western democracies could not be counted upon to oppose Hitler, many asked, what force could? The Jewish Left's alternative of reliance upon "progressive" forces seemed foolishly naïve to most Jews, either because of their ingrained anti-Communism or as a result of a reasoned examination of the attitudes of the French masses toward Jews. The emphasis of consistorial rabbis upon spiritual values undoubtedly provided comfort and solace to those Jews who maintained an unbowed faith in divine salvation, but the narrowness of their religious identity and their continual deference to French government officials offended both pious immigrants and native militants. Nor could the "solutions" of *Pariser Haint* and *Samedi* offer any great hope to a despairing community. It was one thing to talk of Jewish impotence and of the foolishness of utopian dreams. It was quite another to transform anguish and resentment into a commitment to face the future as a united community.

One alternative which was the subject of much discussion among both natives and immigrants in the six months before the outbreak of war was the "return to the ghetto" argument. Although never a movement in the strict sense of the word, the "return to the ghetto" philosophy was an important component of the reevaluation of the "Jewish question" in the waning months of peace. Unique among the various solutions proposed to a despondent Paris community, it not only demanded that Jews in the French capital confront the hopelessness of their situation but also offered the basis for a renewed strength based upon Jewish tradition and culture. The varying ways in which elements within the Paris community responded to the ideology provide a fascinating insight into the mood of Paris Jewry in the wake of Munich.

It is difficult to state exactly when the idea of a "return to the ghetto" first found expression in the Paris community. The nostalgic longing for the "old country" is a constant theme in the history of the eastern European Jewish community in Paris and indeed provided the basis for its organizational structure. But the movement for a "return to the ghetto" was directed mainly at natives who had never experienced *shtetl* life or immigrants who had long since forgotten it. Indeed, it was the contention of the movement's exponents that many of the troubles besetting Jews in Europe stemmed from their alienation from the values of the ghetto.

The first mention of the notion of a "return to the ghetto" that I could find in the Paris Yiddish press was contained in an article published in *Pariser Haint* on March 29, 1937. The idea of isolating Jews from the rest of society as a means of self-defense had found support among Jewish intellectuals in Poland, and as a subsidiary of the Warsaw Yiddish daily, the *Haynt*, the *Pariser Haint* thought it necessary to comment upon it. In the article, the anonymous writer argued against a "return to the ghetto," concluding that in Paris, at least, immigrants had to recognize that they had left eastern Europe forever. For over a year, nothing more was said on the movement. Then the debate surfaced again in mid-1938 in a series of articles published in *Pariser Haint*. The fact that two of the three articles were written in July 1938, before the onset of the Munich Crisis and during the summer lull, however, restricted their impact to a few intellectuals in the Paris Jewish community.

The statements by Moshe Fuchs, a New York journalist who had only recently arrived in Paris, on July 3 and A. Kremer on July 12 reflected a significant change in the attitudes of *Pariser Haint* militants. Thus, although Fuchs wrote that it was wrong to think that assimilation was a negative development, "a fatal mistake," he also noted that it was naïve to believe that Jews had a historical mission to bring humanism into the world. As he explained: "The role of providers to the world and bearers of sacrifices for the sake of some illusory world humanism just does not appeal to us." Assimilants had accomplished much, Fuchs admitted, but Jews could never benefit from the fruit of their labors. Ironically, the very success of Jewish assimilants brought about their own downfall since it created jealousy among the non-Jews they helped.

Kremer went one step further in his arguments. For the first time in the Paris community, he called for a "return to the ghetto," a turning away "from evil, wickedness, the lust for material goods and a return to humanity, justice, and a sane environment where not only Jews but all men who cannot exist in this world will find a home." This was not envisioned as the reestablishment of a ghetto. Indeed Kremer made a special point of denouncing those who spoke of reaching a modus vivendi with dictatorships so that Jews could retreat into self-imposed isolation. Anti-Semites would never allow Jews to live in a ghetto, he noted; the Jew was necessary as a visible symbol of all that was evil in society. If the idea of emancipation was bankrupt, he concluded, "autoemancipation" as first espoused by the Zionist thinker Leon Pinsker was not. Jews should therefore fight for the establishment of a Jewish State and for full rights in the Diaspora.[64]

The Jewish Left participated indirectly in these early discussions of the "return to the ghetto." On November 16, 1938, *Naie Presse* published an article by Joseph Opatashu, a Jewish Communist in New York, on the new ideology. Jewish isolationism, Opatashu argued, resulted from bewilderment in the face of the victories of the "dark forces" in the world. In the midst of despair, however, Jews had forgotten that there had also been progressive developments in Europe, the French and Russian Revolutions to cite only two. As long as there were people willing to carry on the traditions of liberal democracy, the "Thomas Manns," Opatashu called them, Jews had nothing to fear. If Jews were so concerned about going back to their roots, he concluded, why didn't they examine the socialism of the prophets, the "Jewish way" to progress and liberation?

Similar sentiments were expressed by Abraham Menes, the noted Bundist writer, in an article published in *Pariser Haint* on December 22. Although Menes emphasized the need for Jews to interest themselves in their own distinctive culture, he also supported the assimilants' argument that the Jews were missionaries in the world.

Even if one denied any spiritual or ethical imperative on the part of
world Jewry, he argued, each Jew was nevertheless viewed by others
as a reflection upon all other Jews. In an obvious allusion to
supporters of Jewish self-defense, Menes noted that it was naïve to
think that Jews could solve the "Jewish question" alone. The only
hope lay in the progress of humanity.

The four articles cited were indicative of the variety of opinions on
the "return to the ghetto" idea within the immigrant community.
While Zionist thinkers like Kremer argued for a return to the ghetto
in the sense of a harking back to the values of eastern European life,
and particularly the notion of Jewish self-defense, Jewish leftists like
Menes rejected the notion of a withdrawal from European society as
self-defeating and reactionary. In these early discussions, there was
no thought of a physical return to the ghetto. Nor was such a
solution to be suggested in later discussions before the war. At most,
Zionists would argue for the creation of a Jewish State, not as a
means of isolating Jews but of normalizing their condition. For both
supporters and opponents of Jewish withdrawal, the experience of
western Europe was too ingrained to contemplate a physical return
to the ghetto.

The first months of 1939 saw an intensification of the debate
among Paris Jews. Surprisingly, the impetus came not from immigrants but from native and immigrant youth banding around the
newly published journal *Affirmation*. In a series of articles published in February and March, supporters of the paper outlined
their attitudes on the "Jewish question." The essential vice of Jewish
existence in the Diaspora, Jacques Calmy wrote in February, was the
continual dependence upon the goodwill of others. The lessons of
recent history had shown, however, that in seeking the aid of outside
groups, Jews inevitably compromised themselves. At times their
dependence upon others was even detrimental to Jewish interests.
The logical conclusion to be drawn from Jewish history, Calmy
argued, was that "we can only count on ourselves."[65]

The emphasis upon self-defense also implied a disassociation
from political liberalism. In a remarkable article published in
Affirmation on February 3, Arnold Mandel, who previously had
been found in the native camp attacking eastern European roman-
ticism and obstinacy, attempted to destroy the shibboleth of native
Jewry that only democracies would protest against the persecution of
Jews. Even if the natives' contentions were true, Mandel argued, it
still would not justify the identification of Judaism with democracy

"in the political sense of the term." Ideological systems were ephemeral. Their continued existence did not depend upon the goodwill of those who espoused them but rather on "a complex economic reality and on the often changing attitudes of the chaotic multitudes." Mandel shocked French Jews when he argued that recent events presaged the disappearance of liberalism. The question remained, then: "Will Jewry consent to die along with it? No! We must prepare for the most severe test. One day we may find ourselves under the domination of a nearly universal network of dictatorial systems and of a universal anti-Semitism. And, in the meantime, we must continue to survive."

Mandel's statement was significant not only for its grim mood of resignation in the face of Nazism but also in its underlying attack upon the very basis of native beliefs. The skeptical attitude toward what Mandel cynically called the "goodwill of noble men," the distrust of the masses, the dismissal of democracy as too weak to survive the onslaught of dictatorship—all ran counter to the political mythology of French Jewry. So too did the brashness with which Mandel asserted his Jewishness. For Mandel, Jewish identity set the individual apart from society, indeed from history itself. Unlike most French Jews, he did not feel it necessary to justify his Jewish affiliation. To do so would be to admit that Judaism like democracy was ephemeral. Instead, the duty of Jews was to maintain their identity in the face of all political, social, or economic challenges. For writers in *Affirmation*, Jews were merely to continue to exist in order to fulfill their obligations as Jews.[66]

Despite the militancy of their stand, the writers in *Affirmation* made only a minimal contribution to the discussion of the Jewish response to Nazism. Their main interest, as the title of their journal explained, was to affirm Jewish identity in the face of Nazism. Their only frame of reference was the French Jewish experience, and it was against the ideas of their fathers that they rebelled. For many of these youths, the "Jewish question" had never been of great concern. Largely assimilated into French society, they now found an unwanted identity imposed upon them by outside forces. It was only natural under these circumstances that they would seek to transform the anti-Semitic stereotype into a source of pride; hence their emphasis upon the act of affirming Jewishness. Beyond the act of affirmation itself, there was little discussion. Few among them had a comprehensive enough understanding of Judaism to examine its values and ideals in any detail. What was missing in the many articles on the "Jewish question" published in *Affirmation* was an answer to the question of exactly what Jewishness entailed.[67]

Writers in *Samedi* also sought to tackle the perplexing problems involved in the "return to the ghetto" debate. Less troubled by personal questions of Jewish identity, most of their attention centered on the failure of the French Jewish leadership to actively defend Jewish interests. From the World Jewish Congress to "the profiteers of Jewish philanthropy," no segment of the Jewish establishment remained unscathed.[68] Like the group around *Affirmation*, supporters of *Samedi* bitterly attacked the limited Jewish identity of French Jews that led them to reject any alternative that was not religious.[69] Similarly, they did not shrink from proclaiming the impending demise of economic and political liberalism in the face of rising authoritarianism within and without France.[70] Yet unlike the *Affirmation* circle, writers in *Samedi* could never really bring themselves to accept the inevitability of the Nazi victory. Beneath the diatribes against France and against the naïvete of Jewish liberals lay a deeply ingrained belief that France would soon right itself and lead the Western democracies in victory over the foes of both the nation and the Jews.[71]

By far the most interesting exposition of the "return to the ghetto" ideology was contained in a short-lived periodical called *Oyfn Shaydveg* (On the Threshold), published in two volumes in April and August 1939. Although accepting articles from Yiddish intellectuals throughout the world, the periodical was published in Paris and it was in the Paris community that its statements were most closely read. In the introductory article of the first volume, the editors outlined the basic concerns of the contributors: "We are living in a period of the impending liquidation of the era of emancipation with its humanitarian and democratic principles. We have become a nation of refugees facing closed doors, of *haymloze* [stateless persons] without the prospect of finding a new home."[72]

A reading of the articles contained in *Oyfn Shaydveg* reveals a surprising unanimity of views among the most divergent elements in Jewish life in the prewar period. Contributors from the Paris community, such as Abraham Menes and Jacques Jefroykin, a militant Zionist youth leader and the son of the former president of the Fédération, for example, had far different views on the solution to the "Jewish problem," yet they both began from essentially the same analysis of the Jewish plight in Europe. That analysis was most succinctly stated by A. Tcherikover in an explanatory introduction.[73] In his essay, the noted Jewish historian talked of the shock of the progressive and anti-Nazi world when it learned of the "capitulation" of democratic forces at Munich and the atmosphere of fear and despair in the Jewish communities of the world after the failure of the Evian Conference. The events of 1938 had also led to much soul searching within the world Jewish community and particularly the concern with finding "a new basis for Jewish existence in a world where democratic principles are losing their hegemony." For the first time in modern Jewish history, there was talk of isolating Jewry from the rest of the world, of returning to religious tradition and to the idea of the Chosen People as a means of psychological defense against the Nazi enemy. Though rejecting religious belief as the basis for Jewish unity, Tcherikover concluded with an appeal for a return to the values of eastern European Jewish life. The ghetto was part and parcel of Jewish existence, he noted. It was there that the indestructible "Jewish soul" was born and had developed.

One of Tcherikover's main theses had been that the Jewish Left, despite its self-proclaimed liberation from eastern European life, was actually closely linked to the culture of the ghetto.[74] Statements such as these were bound to bring a sharp protest from Jewish Communists. The Jewish Left was also drawn into the "return to the ghetto" debate by the general mood of despair in the immigrant community that fostered such theories. Hard pressed by the PCF and fearful of a further escalation of xenophobia among French workers, Jewish Communists recognized the "return to the ghetto" movement as a major obstacle in its continuing attempt to integrate the Jewish masses into the general struggle of French "democratic" forces against Nazism.

The first major attack upon the "return to the ghetto" ideology by Jewish Communists in Paris came in January 1939 in the form of an article written by Lerman in *Naie Presse*.[75] The article itself was poorly conceived and badly written, an indication of the haste with which Jewish Communists moved to counter what they considered a formidable threat. Thus, for example, Lerman seemed so concerned with lumping Jews together with other victims of Fascism, in order to "put the Jewish question in its proper perspective," that he ignored the objective conditions (the statelessness of Jewish refugees and the anti-Semitic component) that made the "Jewish question" so unique in the 1930s. Similarly, in lashing out indiscriminately at

Jewish financiers, religionists, and "certain socialist circles" (that is, the Bundists, whom he claimed denied historical materialism for the sake of mysticism), he showed a crass insensitivity to the psychological fears that lay behind the "return to the ghetto" ideology. Caught up in the struggle against "cancerous lamenters and pessimists," the Jewish Communists failed to see the positive thrust of renewed strength in the face of adversity that grew out of the "return to the ghetto" ideology.

Jewish Communists distorted the nature of the ideology still further by labelling it as objectively reactionary. In a throwback to pre–Popular Front mythology, they talked of the "return to the ghetto" movement as a tool of the clerics and bourgeois philanthropists to mask the true nature of the Jewish plight. Dispensing with reasoned analysis, they fell back upon simplistic explanations of what was in reality a complex ideological rift within the Paris community. Thus A. Galitzine, one of the editors of *Naie Presse*, wrote an article in which he glibly explained the conflict between "reactionary" and "progressive" forces in terms of the struggle between "ghetto and emancipation, between regression and enlightenment, mystical beliefs and secularism, capitulation and battle."[76] Similarly Dr. Haim Sloves, secretary of the Jewish Communist cultural federation, in an article published in the jubilee issue of *Naie Presse*, glibly talked of the need to "reawaken the spiritual energy of our people," without realizing that his statement could well have been made by the "professional moaners and panic-makers" that he and his fellow Communists so bitterly attacked.[77] The creation of an isolationist antitype to the more optimistic ideals of the Jewish Left may well have made good propaganda among immigrants in Paris. It only hindered attempts, however, at understanding the Jewish plight at a time when a clear perception was so desperately needed.

Native Jews did not participate directly in the "return to the ghetto" debate. Nevertheless the appeal voiced by consistorial leaders to return to the spiritual values of Judaism bore a marked resemblance to the immigrant search for renewed strength in Jewish tradition. By far the most striking element in native rhetoric after Munich was the appeal to the ideals of religious martyrdom. In sermons and newspaper articles, Jews were asked to recall their heritage of suffering and self-sacrifice as if they, like Christ centuries before, were destined to die in order to atone for the world's sins. Underlying this notion was the conviction held by many

French Jews that pity and sympathy were more effective in rousing world opinion than public protest. The emphasis upon religious fatalism was clearly indicated in a statement by Lambert: "Neither meetings nor spectacular demonstrations will ever replace religious practice. The Shema [the prayer proclaiming God's oneness and His unity with the Jewish people] recited by a martyr about to die has been more effective in our history than changes in human nature or legal action which comes too late."[78]

In seeking models of resignation in the face of crisis, French Jews went beyond Jewish tradition to embrace Christian motifs. The allusion to Jews as Christ-like was a common theme in native discussions after Munich, and religious sermons stressed the close association between the sinfulness of men and the divine salvation which must inevitably follow. Native journals abounded in statements by prominent Christian theologians pointing up the close ties between Christianity and Judaism and calling upon Jews in France to return to their spiritual roots. Such appeals to the "Judaeo-Christian heritage" served not only to warn Frenchmen against the evil of anti-Semitism but also to assert native opposition to immigrant isolationism implied in the concept of the "return to the ghetto." At the same time, however, the reliance upon Christian spokesmen such as Jacques Maritain and Father J. P. Bonsirven tragically pointed up the absence of spiritual leadership and direction within the French Jewish community at a crucial moment in its history.[79]

By far the most prevalent mood among immigrants was what one writer cynically described as "optimistic fatalism."[80] In essence, this position derived from the "return to the ghetto" ideology. The examination of the failure of emancipation had led to a call for a strengthening of the Jewish community, a harking back to the values embodied in the tightly structured life of eastern Europe. In particular, Jewish isolationists stressed moral preparedness for harsh periods of persecution, much as eastern European Jews had done centuries before. Jews had survived pogroms and persecution before, they argued; as long as Jews remained together, there was no reason to believe that they would not continue to survive.

What supporters of the "return to the ghetto" refused to recognize was that a commitment to Jewish survival necessitated a fundamental restructuring of the Paris Jewish community. The statements of immigrant leaders to the contrary, the values and traditions of eastern European Jewry were inextricably linked to the institutions and community structure of the *shtetl*. If the "return to the ghetto" was to be viable in the context of the Paris Jewish community in the 1930s, its members would have to reject the factionalized and decentralized community structure that emancipation had demanded in return for acceptance of the Jew. The failure of the unity campaign showed that neither native nor immigrant leaders were willing to take that step. Lacking structural support, the "return to the ghetto" ideal was never to rise above the level of intellectual debate within the Paris Jewish community.

More militant elements in the community, despite their great concern, were unable to offer a more meaningful alternative. As we have seen, the main concern of native and immigrant youth in 1939 was to affirm Jewish identity in conscious rejection of assimilation. True, some young immigrants also talked of a "return to the ghetto" in terms of Jewish self-defense, but there were few attempts to define the form that such action would take. In a sense, they were defeated by their own arguments. Their emphasis upon facing the bitter reality of Jewish existence only reinforced the belief in the utter hopelessness of the Jewish situation. After endless discussion and debate, the only conclusion that native and immigrant youth could arrive at was that, as one native youth noted in an article in *Affirmation*, "Things are going badly."[81]

In the end, both natives and immigrants were forced to fall back on the only alternative open to a powerless and stateless people: the intervention of the Great Powers. Before the fall of the Popular Front, the dependence upon the benevolence of France was only one of many responses in the Paris community to the rise of Nazism. The confidence expressed by French Jews in the unity of French and Jewish interests and the enthusiasm surrounding the establishment of an immigrant community in the capital led to an active presentation of the Jewish position on contemporary issues, both in private discussions and in public debate. In the early 1930s such activity was aided by the openness and self-confidence of French statesmen, faced with various domestic and foreign policy options. By the late thirties, however, France had opted for policies that it would pursue doggedly until war broke out. In most cases these policies were in direct conflict with Jewish interests. The only alternative open to Jews thus became a desperate hope that France would soon return to the ideals of the French Revolution.

The year 1939 marked the one-hundred and fiftieth anniversary of the beginning of the French Revolution. The discussions in the

Paris Jewish community surrounding the celebration of the anniversary provide a final glimpse at Jewish attitudes toward France before
the outbreak of war. The fact that the celebration took place at a
time when the nation was undergoing a *crise de conscience* in the
face of the continued success to Nazism made the task of measuring
the reality of 1939 against the ideal of 1789 that more pressing.

For natives, the anniversary of the French Revolution provided yet
another opportunity to display their loyalty to the nation. Once
again the mythology of Jewish emancipation was proclaimed, less an
article of faith than as a propaganda statement directed at doubting
Frenchmen. Thus, Chief Rabbi Maurice Liber spoke at a meeting of
native Jewish youth in June 1939 of the "emancipation" of Judaism
in 1791. From the time of the Revolution, he stated, the Jewish faith
had ceased to be practiced secretly and had taken its place beside
the great monotheistic religions derived from Judaism. No longer
was it shameful to practice Judaism; Jews could henceforth play an
important role in helping to realize the ideals of the Revolution.
Liber concluded with a statement paralleling the ideals of the
French Revolution with those of Judaism. This time, however, he
placed special emphasis upon the spiritual concerns of the two
systems of thought, a reflection of the religious thrust of French
Jewish statements in the waning days of peace.[82]

The anniversary of the French Revolution also saw an assertion of
Jewish patriotism and sacrifice. In May, for example, a delegation
of prominent French Jews travelled to Douaumont where they paid
homage to the many Jewish volunteers who had died there in battle
during World War I. At the shrine, Rabbi Kaplan spoke of the
union sacrée as "a magnificent élan of self-denial" that bound Jews
to France and obligated them to submit to its laws.[83] At times the
concern with Jewish patriotism bordered on the morbid. An article
published in *L'Univers israélite* on June 23, after a French sub-
marine sank in the China Sea, for example, contained the following
statement: "May we be permitted to salute, among those sailors who
died at their post for France, a humble sailor whose name we
recognize as belonging to the Jewish spiritual family, Max May." In
a statement directed more at non-Jews than at members of the
"Jewish spiritual family," the editors concluded: "Certainly, we
regret the other deaths as well but we cannot help noting with a
certain pride that it is good, it is right, for a French Jew to occupy a
place among his comrades in the common sacrifice."

Such statements reflected the feeble nature of French Jewish efforts to win acceptance among fellow Frenchmen. The emphasis upon the glories of World War I in 1939 was not unlike the Consistoire's flirtation with right-wing groups after February 6, 1934. In both cases, the concern was with forging another *union sacrée* to counter the factionalism within France that had led to outbreaks of anti-Semitism. In both cases French Jews had failed to see the degree to which such concerns were bound up with a rejection of the politics of the Third Republic. More importantly, the concern with Jewish war dead, and indeed with the French Revolution, indicated a failure to face the realities of the present. Longing for a past that could never return, French Jews sought to erase the "Jewish question" from their minds. When they did talk of the Jewish plight, it was generally in terms of the need for a spiritual renewal of the world. Like the prophets whom they quoted so profusely, natives in the 1930s saw only an idyllic past and a messianic future.

It is difficult to gauge the attitudes of eastern European Jews in Paris during the celebrations honoring the French Revolution. Many societies that would normally have taken part in patriotic programs were severely hampered in their public activity by a government decree passed in late April that required that all activities sponsored by groups not directly concerned with religious matters receive government approval.[84] Immigrants, themselves, were still reeling from the effects of the decrees of November 1938. The number incarcerated in special concentration camps and prison stockades for inability to pay their own passage out of the country continued to increase with each passing day.[85] Nevertheless, the Fédération managed to hold what it called a "solemn demonstration" on June 15 to commemorate the Revolution. The meeting itself was poorly attended. Like the Consistoire, the Fédération seemed greatly concerned with presenting a picture of complete allegiance to the nation. Immigrant leaders who delivered speeches talked mainly of the indebtedness that eastern European Jews owed to France and carefully avoided any mention of the plight of refugees or immigrants affected by the new decrees. Nor were they averse to parroting native slogans about the uniqueness of the French Jewish experience. It is significant, for example, that one of the main speakers was Paul Grünebaum-Ballin, the vice-president of the *Comité des Amis de l'Abbé Grégoire*, a native Jew who previously had restricted his speech-making to French Jewish functions. In fact, with the exception of the large number of prominent left-wing politicians who were in attendance, the Fédération demonstration could well have been mistaken for a consistorial affair.[86]

The most impressive celebrations in the Paris community were those sponsored by the Jewish Left. Far more even than natives, Jewish Communists made the anniversary the center of their activities in April and May 1939. Among other things, Jewish Communists published a brochure in French detailing what the Revolution meant to Jews (to remind some Frenchmen, "admittedly a small number," a writer in *Naie Presse* noted, of the high principles that their ancestors had fought for) and set up a scholarship for a Jewish student who would write a thesis on the Jews and the French Revolution.[87] Not to be outdone by the Fédération, the Farband held its own meeting in which prominent French personalities, including Jacques Duclos, Romain Rolland, Cardinal Verdier (the archbishop of Paris), and Jean Zay (the Minister of Education), participated. At the meeting, B. Tcharny spoke of the horrible conditions under which Jews lived before the Revolution, while the Yiddish Popular Choir intoned *La Marseillaise*.[88] Even the Bundists were not immune from the enthusiasm surrounding the celebration of the French Revolution. In an article published on June 30 in *Unzer Stime*, a writer identified as Y. Golus (the Yiddish word for Diaspora) talked of Jewry before the Revolution as alien, ghettoized, and tyrannized by despotic rulers. "Golus" concluded that the Jewish people could well serve as an example of an ethnic culture that could integrate itself into a nation state.

Despite what in some cases were sincere and heartfelt sentiments, the motivating factor behind the Paris Jewish community's celebration of the anniversary of the French Revolution was fear. Each group in the community sought to outdo the others in attestations of loyalty to the nation. The deemphasis upon the "Jewish question," the recruitment of non-Jewish speakers, the rehashing of the story of Jewish emancipation—all were reflective of the concern with demonstrating the debt that Jews allegedly owed to France. It is admittedly difficult to sort out the propagandistic statements from the fervently held beliefs. One can say, however, that the very fact that Paris Jews in 1939 were still seeking to convince Frenchmen of their adherence to the ideals of the nation indicates the degree to which natives and immigrants still clung to the desperate hope that France would return to its role as the defender of liberty in Europe.

Although war was not to come until September, the Paris Jewish community had begun preparing for an eventual outbreak of hostilities as early as April. The impetus for the early preparation came from a government decree issued in April that allowed aliens to volunteer for the French Army. The response from Jewish immigrants and refugees was overwhelming. Many eastern European Jews saw volunteering as a means of publicly demonstrating their loyalty to France. Others hoped to avoid expulsion or imprisonment. Still others interpreted the decree as a reversal of French foreign policy toward Nazism and moved quickly to support it. Finally, there were those who hoped that by volunteering they would be assured of taking revenge against Germany if and when war broke out.

Jewish organizations in Paris were quick to take advantage of the immigrants' enthusiasm. Almost all of the major groups in the community set up offices to register Jews who pledged to join the French Army in case of war. Although figures are unavailable, contemporary estimates placed the number of registrants in the thousands.[89] In addition, organizations publicized the decree in the Jewish areas of the capital in an attempt to recruit as many refugees and immigrants as possible. By late April, the recruitment program had reached such a fever pitch that the Ministry of National Defense was forced to issue a declaration criticizing Jewish organizations for their overzealousness and demanding the suspension of further registration.[90]

The recruitment of Jewish refugees and immigrants was not the only step taken by Paris Jews in April to prepare for war. At the meeting on April 25 the Consistoire's administrative council ruled on a number of decisions concerning consistorial employees who would be mobilized in case of war. A letter from the rabbi of the *Société du culte traditionnel israélite* dated May 22, 1939, and found in the archives of the Consistoire reveals that natives had made plans for "evacuating" sacred objects from Paris in case of attack. In the archives one can also find a letter from one of the religious organization's affiliated societies, dated March 20, 1939, which talks of a request made by the *mairie* of the eighteenth *arrondissement* to use consistorial buildings to lodge Frenchmen fleeing from the frontiers in case of war.[91]

Immigrant organizations took few steps to assure their continued functioning in case of war. Less concerned with their own importance than the century-and-a-half old Consistoire, neither the Fédération nor the Farband made any attempt to preserve documents or replace drafted employees in the waning months of peace.

Eastern European Jews in Paris spent the last months before the outbreak of war not in calculated planning for wartime contingencies but in extreme despair over the future of European Jewry.

The Paris community fell into a state of almost complete inactivity in the last three months of peace. Natives justified their lethargy with statements about the need for spiritual renewal among European nations and frequent allusions to Jewish sacrifice. Immigrants, for their part, rejected the natives' religious fatalism in favor of the more "optimistic" fatalism of the "return to the ghetto" ideal, but there was little visible difference in their behavior. The Paris Jewish community thus drifted aimlessly, rent by factionalism and frustration in the face of an enemy which it was powerless to oppose.

When war finally threatened Europe in August, most Jews in the French capital simply refused to believe that hostilities would actually break out. As late as the last week in August, the three major journals of Paris Jewry were publishing articles voicing their belief that peace would be maintained. The appeals for peace were phrased in characteristic ways. Thus *L'Univers israélite* published a prayer in which the Consistoire rabbinate asked God to bless the efforts of all peace-loving men to avert war and especially those of Premier Daladier, who was quoted approvingly as declaring that he would do everything humanly possible to avoid war.[92] *Pariser Haint* talked of the betrayal of the democratic powers yet reaffirmed its faith in the ideals of the French Revolution that would see the nation through the impending ordeal.[93] Finally, *Naie Presse* announced triumphantly that Western political leaders would no longer be willing to make concessions, having realized the tragic mistake of Munich. The writer of the article also expressed his conviction that only a pact with the Soviet Union would save the peace.[94]

The differing emphases of the various groups were also clear in their reactions to the French declaration of war on Germany. While Chief Rabbi Liber delivered a sermon in which he talked of the Lord, God of Hosts, destroying the pagan hordes, the Fédération and *Pariser Haint* called upon immigrants to volunteer for the French Army both to take revenge against the Nazis and to fight for the glory of France. Jewish Communists, for their part, published a statement written by Jewish volunteers from Belleville which spoke of their desire to prove themselves good Frenchmen so as to earn the right to help in the rebuilding of postwar France.[95]

For eastern European Jews in Paris, the war came more as a relief than a burden. Ever since the accession of Hitler to power in 1933, immigrants in the capital had been living under constant strain caused by the persecution of their coreligionists in central and eastern Europe. By 1937 signs of a resurgent anti-Semitism were also beginning to appear in France. Powerless to counter the Nazi threat and increasingly despairing of help from the outside world, immigrant Jews in Paris faced an uncertain future. Although fearful of war, they could not bear the alternative of a peace at the expense of their fellow Jews. An anonymous writer spoke for the majority of the eastern European Jewish community when he noted in *La Terre retrouvée* in September 1939 that Jews had awaited war since January 1933.[96]

Such sentiments were not fully shared by French Jews. Most natives had written off the refugee problem as hopeless, arguing that French Jewish organizations had done as much as was humanly possible to care for Jews fleeing from Nazism.[97] True to their religious tradition, French Jews approached the war as *Français israélites* rather than as *juifs français*. If they seemed unperturbed by the prospect of war, it was only because they viewed the outbreak of hostilities through the optic of the ideals of the French Revolution— less a clash of Great Powers, World War II was the confrontation of two unalterably opposed ideologies, democracy and totalitarianism.[98] Most French Jews were blissfully unaware that this view was not shared by the majority of Frenchmen. Even the experience of Vichy and of the massive deportation of Jews in 1942 could not shake their belief that the French Jewish experience was unique in Jewish history.

And what of the Jewish Left? Unlike other groups in the community, the outbreak of war created more problems for Communists than it solved. Up until the last days of peace, Jewish Communists were proclaiming their willingness to wage war to defend French democracy. The Jewish Left seemed to have a definite psychological advantage over other elements in the community since the enemy was clearly defined from both a Jewish and a left-wing perspective. The signing of the Nazi-Soviet Nonaggression Pact on August 23, however, put an end to the unity of the Jewish and Communist attitudes toward Nazism. The conflict between the Jewish Communists' roles as forces in the Jewish community and as loyal members of the PCF once again asserted itself.

It is difficult to piece together a clear picture of the Jewish Communists' reaction to the Nazi-Soviet Pact. The PCF's declaration of neutrality led to the government abolition of all Communist publications, including those in the Jewish community. As a result, the historian examining the crucial events surrounding the pact is left without the most important source for information on the attitudes of Jewish Communists, *Naie Presse*. Nevertheless, the Yiddish paper did publish until the end of August, and I have managed to gain some additional information from interviews conducted with former Communist militants in Paris.

At first there seemed to be great confusion among Jewish Communists in Paris. Georges Kénig, in personal interviews, spoke of the shock and disbelief with which the news of the pact was received in the offices of *Naie Presse*. Most of the employees of the newspaper were convinced that there was some mistake in telegraph transmission and simply refused to accept the truth of the news bulletin. An article by Kénig published on August 23 reflected the confusion in Jewish Communist circles. Forced into the unenviable position of justifying an action with which he was obviously not in complete agreement, he tried valiantly to show how the pact stemmed logically from the failure of the Western democracies to present a strong defense against Nazism. The arguments were weak and unconvincing, and Kénig was forced to admit in the article that events moved so quickly that it was hard to keep track of them. Interestingly, Kénig made no reference to Jews in the article. Jewish Communists could find no way to justify the Soviet action from a Jewish point of view.

It did not take long for Jewish Communists to resolve their dilemma. Although there were those who accepted the Soviet action wholeheartedly, the majority of immigrant militants who met in emergency meetings on the nights of August 23 and 24 simply refused to justify a "party line" that spelled doom for European Jewry. A special editorial published in *Naie Presse* on August 25 publicly announced the decision made by the majority of Jewish Communists. More than ever, the editorial read, Jews were ready to defend France. The issue also contained a declaration issued by the Farband that called upon eastern European Jews to volunteer.[99]

September 1939 thus saw many Jewish Communists in open opposition to the PCF. For the first time in the 1930s, they had taken a stand on the side of Jewish interests against the interests of the party. Jewish Communists deepened the rift by joining resistance movements soon after the Nazi occupation of France, in a period when the PCF was still calling for strict neutrality. The rift was to be healed only in 1941 when the Nazi invasion of the Soviet Union brought Communist elements into the Resistance. The crisis surrounding the signing of the Nazi-Soviet Nonaggression Pact was never to be forgotten by Jewish Communists, however, and indeed proved to be a foretaste of the many disillusionments experienced by Jewish militants in the 1940s and 1950s.

Notes

1. For typical examples, see the activities in the Paris community after the pogroms in Brisk, Poland, as recorded in *Pariser Haint* and *Naie Presse*, May 1937.

2. A cartoon published in *L'Univers israélite* on February 4, 1938, for example, showed an angry native reading the French Jewish journal. The caption read: "First, there was Germany, then Poland, then Rumania. If this continues, I am going to cancel my subscription."

3. *Pariser Haint*, February 1, 1938.

4. On talk of war, see the article by A. Stern in *Pariser Haint*, March 17, 1938; on talk of emigration, see *La Terre retrouvée*, March 15, 1938.

5. *L'Univers israélite*, May 27, 1938. Lambert coupled his affirmation of loyalty to France with a denunciation of "foreigners" who warned that anti-Semitism was on the upsurge in France. Immigrants should practice moderation, he cautioned; they should not speak in public lest someone should hear their foreign accent.

6. For a discussion of the prayers, see the archives of the ACIP, AA23, Délibérations du Conseil d'administration, 1936–38, meeting of March 15, 1938. Religious leaders also stressed hope for the divine salvation of Jews. In a Passover sermon given by Rabbi Mathieu Wolff, for example, Israel was described as the *Had Gadya*, the lamb who in a traditional holiday song is saved from death by God's intervention. For Wolff's sermon, see *L'Univers israélite*, April 15–22, 1938.

7. On Jews as a nation and a religion, see the article by Colas Miclissant in *L'Univers israélite*, March 18, 1938; on the denial of Jewish separateness, see the article by S. Marcovici-Cleja on March 25, 1938; on a spiritual definition, see the article by Maurice Messica on April 1 and 8, 1938. Traces of the debate could still be found in *L'Univers israélite* as late as July 29, 1938.

8. For Alperin's statement, see *Pariser Haint*, March 15, 1938; for Milner, March 16, 1938; for a representative article in *Samedi*, see the issue of March 26, 1938.

9. For a discussion of the Fédération's efforts, see *Pariser Haint*, April 1, 1938.

10. Kremer in *Pariser Haint*, March 22, 1938.

11. Lerman concluded the article with a stern warning against Jewish agitation: "The united Jewish masses must not work separately. Our work consists of interesting all democratic institutions of the world in our plight."

12. See, for example, the article by A. Stern in *Pariser Haint*, March 17, 1938.

13. For an examination of the growth of anti-Semitism in Paris after Anschluss, see the article by Lecache in *Pariser Haint*, April 1, 1938. In the article, the leader of LICA called for an intensification of Jewish protest in Paris.

Lecache was bitterly attacked by *Pariser Haint* militants who feared that he would create panic among immigrants. He was led eventually to issue a second article on April 10 in which he explained that he had not meant to imply that Jews should arm themselves and go into the streets.

14. On immigrants affected by the decrees, see Kremer in *Pariser Haint*, May 13, 1938; on suicides, see *Naie Presse*, June 3, 1938. For information on Jews in jail, see *Naie Presse*, July 6, 1938.

15. According to an article in *Pariser Haint* on May 10, 1938, the native relief organization was being deluged by 500 immigrants a day, mostly "illegal" artisans thrown out of their jobs, while the Fédération office handled over 100 a day.

16. Godart was the head of a delegation which called itself the *Comité de défendre les droits des juifs en Europe Centrale et Orientale*. On Godart's intervention, see *L'Univers israélite*, December 29, 1938.

17. *Pariser Haint*, May 15, 1938. For Jarblum's statement, see *Pariser Haint*, June 6, 1938.

18. For a discussion of agricultural settlements, see *Pariser Haint*, June 9–11, 1938.

19. For Jarblum's statement, see *Pariser Haint*, June 21, 1938. For native sentiment, see *L'Univers israélite*, June 20, 1938.

20. *Pariser Haint*, July 17, 1938.

21. *Pariser Haint*, August 16, 1938.

22. For a discussion of the campaign, see the speech by B. Tcharny to the Legal Status Congress, cited in *Naie Presse*, January 18, 1938.

23. For the rabbis' statement, see *Pariser Haint*, September 18, 1938.

24. Cited in *L'Univers israélite*, September 23, 1938. For Yom Kippur sermons expressing similar ideas, see *L'Univers israélite*, October 14, 1938.

25. This was clearly shown in an appeal issued by Chief Rabbi Weill in September. In the appeal, Weill quoted the prophetic promise, "In calm and tranquility you will be saved," but made sure to remind Jews not to congregate in front of synagogues during and after religious services. The appeal is found in the archives of the ACIP, B134, Lettres reçues, 1939.

26. Bielinky Archives, Arts, actualités: undated article entitled "Les Fêtes de Yamin Noraim."

27. Ibid. See also, *Pariser Haint*, October 6, 1938.

28. *Naie Presse*, September 26, 1938.

29. In its issue of October 1, 1938, *Droit de vivre* described three such incidents: two Jews speaking Yiddish near the Gare de l'Est who were accused of defending Hitler; three Jews in the Faubourg du Temple district who were alleged to have incited young people not to answer their draft notice; and two Belleville immigrants who were alleged to have shouted, "Vive Hitler! Vive Allemagne!"

Pressure from LICA and other militants within the Jewish community led the Minister of Interior to initiate a government inquiry into police brutality against Jews during the crisis, but the results of the inquiry were never made public.

30. The appeal was reproduced in *Pariser Haint*, September 26, 1938.

31. See, for example, the articles by Stern in *Pariser Haint*, September 15–17, 1938. Stern called Chamberlain's trip the "last and most serious attempt to save the world from catastrophe" (*Pariser Haint*, September 15, 1938).

32. *Pariser Haint*, September 25, 1938.

33. For the complete statement, see *Naie Presse*, September 27, 1938.

34. An article written by "A Parisian" in *Naie Presse* on September 30 was typical. The writer cited an incident in which a Jew accosted a Frenchman in the street and denounced him as worse than a German. The Frenchman, the writer noted, was astounded and did not realize that it was a provocateur. The publication of such incidents reflected the Jewish Left's willingness to accept the anti-Semitic stereotype

of the warmongering Jew. Its emphasis upon "proper behavior" clearly helped to reinforce the stereotype.

35. For some examples of speeches, see *L'Univers israélite*, October 7, 1938, and *Pariser Haint*, October 6, 1938.

36. For a discussion of Jewish *munichois*, see Mandel, *Les Temp incertains*, p. 202. Emmanuel Berl was probably the most prominent member of the Jewish *munichois*. For a discussion of his views, see *Samedi*, January 7, 1939; and Pierre Lazareff, *Deadline* (New York: Random House, 1942), p. 203.

37. See, for example, the article by Alsaticus in *L'Univers israélite*, December 2, 1938.

38. *Pariser Haint*, October 23, 1938.

39. Fischer also argued that the retreat of the western powers at Munich only increased the need for Jews to emigrate to Palestine. He doubted, however, that England would allow a massive influx of Jewry until international tensions subsided.

40. Anti-Semites could also point to the great publicity given to immigrant volunteers who, as in 1914, flocked to join the French Army during the Munich Crisis. For information on volunteers in September 1938, see *L'Univers israélite*, October 7, 1938.

41. At the height of the crisis, the *Syndicat de la chapellerie* plastered the walls of Paris with posters denouncing home-laborers. The posters clearly pointed out that most *façonniers* were immigrant Jews. Bitter attacks were also levelled against Jewish workers at union meetings. Pressure from LICA led the union to issue a new poster which attacked those unwilling to negotiate with the Syndicat but made no mention of Jews. For further information, see *Droit de vivre*, October 22, 1938.

42. For a discussion of the conflicting images of the Jew, see the article by Lambert in *L'Univers israélite*, November 11, 1938.

In his work *France and Munich* (New York: Harper, 1939), p. 227, Alexander Werth commented on the rise of anti-Semitism in France during and after the Munich Crisis by noting that Blum hesitated to advocate a firm policy in September 1938, in part because of a "certain self-consciousness created by propaganda which argued that 'Jews want war, because they hope to destroy Hitler.' " See also Werth's comments in *The Twilight of France* (New York: Harper, 1942), p. 344.

43. For a list of the new government decrees, see *Naie Presse*, November 15, 1938. See also the excellent analysis in *Samedi*, November 12, 1938.

44. See, for example, the article by Lambert in *L'Univers israélite*, November 11, 1938.

45. See, for example, the sermon reproduced in *Bulletin d'information de Comité de défense et de vigilance*, January 13, 1939, p. 6. The *Bulletin* was started by French Jewish leaders in 1938 to counter accusations made by anti-Semites against Jews.

46. See, for example, ibid., p. 2. During this period, the Consistoire seriously considered participating in a right-wing movement organized to fight Nazi racism and Bolshevik materialism.

47. See, for example, the statement by General Weiller in *Le Matin*, December 3, 1938, contained in an article entitled "Les Israélites français veulent la paix au dedans et au dehors."

48. See, for example, the article by Fernand Corcos in *L'Univers israélite*, November 25, 1938.

49. For a summary of these arguments, see *Pariser Haint*, October 21, 1938. For a mildly optimistic statement, see the declaration issued by the Fédération in *Pariser*

Haint, November 4, 1938; for a more militant argument, see the article by Kremer in *Pariser Haint*, October 25, 1938.

50. For the statement, see *Pariser Haint*, November 8, 1938.

51. For representative statements, see *Pariser Haint*, November 13 and 18, 1938. The only reference to the response of immigrants in Paris per se was a description of their Jewish heart torn between hope and despair "like a ship on a stormy sea" in an article by Chomsky in *Pariser Haint* on November 13, 1938.

52. For reactions to Krystalnacht, see *Naie Presse*, November 20 and 22, 1938. In the article published on November 20, Rayski did talk of the need to establish a "Jewish policy" but gave no details.

53. The meeting, held on November 22, was organized by an interfaith group, the *Ligue nationale contre l'antisémitisme*, and included mainly French political and religious leaders. *Pariser Haint*, in its article on the meeting published on November 23, argued that the demonstration showed the world that anti-Semitism would never triumph in France.

54. I could not find issues of *Unzer Stime* for October and December 1938. This is not surprising since the Bundist paper was published irregularly until 1939, when it became a weekly. The Munich Agreement was discussed in *Unzer Stime* in July 1939. In particular, see the articles published on July 21 and 30. In personal discussions, Hillel Kempinsky, the archivist at the Bund archives in New York, also offered some valuable insights into the Bundist reaction to Munich.

55. See, for example, the article by Fernand Corcos in *Samedi*, November 5, 1938.

56. *Samedi*, December 17, 1938.

57. Ibid. For an example of *Samedi*'s attack upon the French Jewish leadership, see the criticism of the statement by Rabbi Weill in the issue of November 26, 1938.

58. See, for example, *Samedi*, January 14 and 21, 1939.

59. *Samedi*, January 21, 1939. The paper was often criticized for its militantly anti-German stand. See, for example, the letter from a reader in ibid.

60. *Samedi*, January 14, 1939.

61. Ibid.

62. For a discussion of the congress, see *Naie Presse*, December 3, 1938. The resolution that was finally passed called for joint action with the Consistoire. Only seven votes were cast in favor of a resolution supporting action with the Farband.

63. For an examination of conditions in the Jewish trades, see the article by Lerman in *Naie Presse*, January 18, 1939. Jewish artisans generally did not respond to the general strike call of November 30. For a discussion of Jewish participation in the strike, see *Naie Presse*, December 1, 1938.

64. For other articles on a similar topic, see *Pariser Haint*, July 27, 1938, and December 27, 1938. See also the statement by Jefroykin cited in the issue of December 21, 1938.

65. *Affirmation*, February 24, 1939. See also the article by David Knout, the editor of the journal, on March 3, 1939.

66. Mandel arrived at his rather militant Jewish stand in 1939 after brief flirtations with anarchism, communism, native Jewish identity, and Zionist revisionism. His novels, which trace his own development through the maze of Jewish ideologies in France in the 1920s and 1930s, are of inestimable value for an understanding of the Paris Jewish community in the prewar period.

67. The attitudes expressed in *Affirmation* invariably mirrored those of its hard-working editor, David Knout. A Russian student in Paris in the 1930s with only

tangential ties to Jewish life, Knout was attracted to Zionist revisionism, with its emphasis upon the need for a militant Jewish response to the Nazi threat. Active in the Jewish resistance in France during World War II, he settled in Israel after the war, where he died in 1955.

68. For sample articles, see *Samedi*, January 28, 1939, February 11, 1939, and April 22, 1939.

69. As Simon Marchal noted in an article published on May 27, 1939, for example, French Jews "who in their desire ... to preserve their position in a country where they live as respected citizens, have forgotten that if Judaism is only a religion for them, it is often mingled with Jewish nationalism in the minds of the masses who live in Germany, Italy, Poland, Hungary, and elsewhere."

70. See especially the extremely perceptive article by Wladimir Rabinovitch, the writer who in 1933 had proclaimed the necessity of a "Jewish policy," in *Samedi*, April 29, 1939. Among other things, Rabinovitch pointed to the decline in parliamentary opposition, rule by decrees, and the closed economy as signs of declining liberalism in France.

71. An article in *Samedi* published on March 11, 1939, for example, described the end of restrictions on immigrants as the culmination of "the true [French] Revolution."

72. *Oyfn Shaydveg* 1, no. 1 (April 1939): 4.

73. For Menes' article, see ibid., pp. 53–72; for Jefroykin's article, see ibid., pp. 224–26; for Tcherikover's introduction, see ibid., pp. 5–28.

74. As he noted, left-wing immigrants "have one foot in the ghetto and will not, or cannot, free themselves from its heritage" (ibid., p. 23).

75. *Naie Presse*, January 8, 1939.

76. *Naie Presse*, May 7, 1939.

77. *Naie Presse*, February 12, 1939. The statement about "professional moaners and panic makers" is taken from an article by Kénig on May 3, 1939.

78. *L'Univers israélite*, July 28, 1939.

79. For a typical statement, see the article by Jacques Maritain in *L'Univers israélite*, February 10, 1939.

80. Chender in *Affirmation*, June 9, 1939.

81. Ibid.

82. For Liber's statement, see *L'Univers israélite*, June 30, 1939.
The program of the meeting at which Liber spoke reads like a scenario of Jewish emancipation in the French Revolution:
   I. "La Marseillaise"
   II. Address by the president
   III. "Hymn to Liberty" (1800) sung by students
   IV. The Liberating Work of the Revolution. Discussion.
   V. A. Summary of "The Motion in Favor of the Jews," by Abbé Gregoire
      B. Speech presented at the docket of the National Assembly on October 14, 1789, by Berr Isaac Berr
      C. "The Wandering Jew Appears before the National Assembly," poetry by L. Wihl.
   VI. "Hymn to the Statue of Liberty" sung by students
   VII. The Revolution and Judaism. Discussion.
   VIII. A. Speech presented to the National Assembly on August 26, 1789, by the Jews of Paris

B. Correspondence in Hebrew announcing the convening of the Estates
General and the taking of the Bastille
IX. "Bara" and "Viala" sung by students
X. Berr Isaac Berr's reply to the archbishop of Nancy, April 1790
XI. Ronde for the Festival of Spring (1790)
XII. "The Song of Departure"
(Cited in Sommer, "La Doctrine politique," pp. 17–18, fn. 1.)

83. Kaplan's speech was reproduced in *L'Univers israélite*, May 12, 1939. The pilgrimage to Douaumont was also notable for its inclusion of the Union patriotique, shunned by the Consistoire since 1937. Whether the religious organization intended to renew contact with the patriotic organization is unclear, although the fact that Kaplan and thirty Jewish students traveled to Douaumont in a bus furnished by the Union patriotique would seem to show that relations between the two groups were improving.

84. For details on the decree, see *L'Univers israélite*, April 21, 1939. Typically, the native journal applauded the government action. With an eye to the more "troublesome" elements in the Paris Jewish community, *L'Univers israélite* noted that the government could now intervene and ban any political activity or social work that was not in accordance with French mores, especially "those which are not in accord with the responsibilities of one who has been shown hospitality."

85. For a discussion of the imprisonment of political refugees, see *L'Univers israélite*, February 24, 1939, and the report by Rabbi Joseph Sachs on Jewish aliens in Paris prisons, dated April 18, 1939, and contained in the archives of the ACIP, B135 bis, Consistoire, 1907–39.

86. For details on the demonstration, see *Affirmation*, June 23, 1939.

87. *Naie Presse*, April 30, 1939.

88. For information on the meeting, see *Naie Presse*, May 23, 1939.

89. According to Bielinky in an article in *La Terre retrouvée* on November 23, 1939, there were 10,000 volunteers registered at the end of August. The majority of them had probably also registered in April, when alien volunteers were first accepted into the French Army. According to an article in *Naie Presse*, April 23, 1939, Jews made up the largest segment of foreign volunteers.

90. The declaration denounced the registrations as "premature . . . which risk creating all sorts of problems." For information on the declaration, see *L'Univers israélite*, April 28, 1939.

91. The minutes of the meeting of April 25, as well as the two letters, can be found in the archives of the ACIP, B135 bis, Consistoire, 1907–39.

92. *L'Univers israélite*, August 25–September 1, 1939.

93. See, for example, the article by Chomsky on August 17, 1939.

94. Georges Kénig in *Naie Presse*, August 20, 1939.

95. On Liber's sermon, see Mandel, *Les Temps incertains*, p. 208; on the Fédération's statement, see *Pariser Haint*, September 2, 1939; on the Jewish Communists' statements, see Mandel, *Les Temps incertains*, p. 211.

96. *La Terre retrouvée*, September 10, 1939.

97. As Baron Robert de Rothschild stated in June 1939: "The community of Paris has certainly done its duty. As a result of the events of this past year, it had to assume a heavy burden in order to aid those unfortunates who seek asylum in our country, a country which could not and would not ignore their plight."

98. As Alfred Berl wrote in *Paix et Droit* in its issue of July 1939: "He [the Jew] should not avenge Israel for the unjust and atrocious persecution that it endures but rather aid in the defense of law against arbitrariness, of liberty against tyranny, of civilization which is threatened by the most frightening return to the barbarism of the caveman, to the cruelty of the savage only recently emerged from the darkness."

99. See also the editorial statement in *Naie Presse* on August 28, 1939.

9   Conclusion

The war did not mark the end of a Jewish settlement in Paris. The survivors of the deportation and extermination camps, as well as those who had remained in hiding in France, returned to reconstruct a community after World War II. In the 1950s the Jewish population of Paris increased significantly as a result of the large influx of Sephardic Jews fleeing North Africa during the struggle of Algeria, Morocco, and Tunisia for independence. By the 1960s North African Jews made up the bulk of the Jewish population in the capital. Today Paris Jewry is once again a thriving community, Numbering over 300,000, it is the largest Jewish settlement on the European Continent.

Yet 1939 did mark the end of the prewar Jewish community in Paris, that strange but fascinating admixture of western and eastern Jews found nowhere in such numbers in the world. A community of nearly 200,000 in 1939, Paris Jewry numbered no more than 80,000 in 1945.[1] Of the two groups, eastern European Jews were most severely affected by the war. Barely 20,000 of the nearly 100,000 immigrant Jews inhabiting the capital in 1939 returned from extermination camps or from asylum in other countries.[2] Their loss also meant the disappearance in Paris of the Yiddish culture that they had brought with them on their journey to the West. Today only vestiges of the once vibrant culture remain—a decaying "Pletzl" which is rapidly being taken over by newly arriving Arab workers, a number of small *shuls*, three Yiddish newspapers (*Naie Presse*, *Unzer Stime*, and *Unser Wort*, the latter a Zionist publication which began publishing after World War II) that barely break even financially, the Fédération and Farband, surviving more on the memories of the recent past than on hopes for the future.

French Jewry also took on a different character. Though far less affected by the Final Solution than eastern European Jews, native Jewry nevertheless faced a massive rebuilding effort after the war.

212

Aside from the physical destruction of synagogues and other consistorial buildings during the Nazi occupation of Paris, native Jews suffered a tragic loss of religious and administrative leadership. Of the sixty rabbis in the Consistoire central in 1939, seventeen were deported and two were shot. Important lay leaders in the Paris community, including Raoul-Raymond Lambert and Jacques Heilbronner, also met their deaths during the occupation. Through great effort and massive financial support from international Jewish relief agencies, the Consistoire de Paris was able to revive Paris religious life and reassume its position as the leading spokesman of Jewish residents in the French capital. Today the religious body is still the major native organization in the community, but its services now cater mainly to North African Jews. More and more, Jews from Morocco, Algeria, and Tunisia are assuming positions of authority in the various institutions affiliated with the religious organization.[3]

The postwar period also brought the first major coordination of effort between natives and immigrants. The creation of the FSJU (*Fonds social juif unifié*) in 1950, if not actually unifying the two groups, nevertheless served to coordinate the disposition of funds for the various social, educational, and cultural needs of the community as a whole. Its creation also marked the transformation of community social service from the voluntary and decentralized efforts of *dames patronesses* and *landsmenshaftn* to a centralized and coordinated program administered by trained professionals.

But the transition from the prewar to the postwar community was more than just a shift of population or a restructuring of institutions. The 1930s saw the growth of two separate communities in Paris, each with its own institutional structure, social stratification, and attitudes toward the larger society around them. Of particular importance were the differing views of Jewish identity and of the Jewish role in the Diaspora, which were given added urgency by the growing Nazi threat. After the war, the debate over the "Jewish question" was resumed. Some of the attitudes and beliefs posited by prewar Jewry were discarded; others were reinforced. But the intervention of the Holocaust and the creation of the State of Israel meant that no one would ever look at the "Jewish question" in quite the same way as Jews in Paris did in the 1930s.

In the previous chapters, I have tried to examine the Paris Jewish community as both a "case study" of prewar attitudes of European Jewry and an entity unto itself, a complex social grouping in the midst of the larger Parisian society. In a sense, the two approaches are intertwined. An answer to the central historical question surrounding Paris Jewry in the 1930s, the failure of natives and immigrants to establish a unified community committed to Jewish survival in the face of the enemy, can only be gleaned by examining the conflicting attitudes and beliefs of the two groups.

Of course there were many other differences that separated the two communities. Of prime importance was the social and economic gap that divided natives and immigrants. French Jews were almost completely *moyen* and *haut* bourgeois in makeup. Active in large industry, natives also were influential in the commercial and financial circles of Paris. Eastern European Jews, on the other hand, tended to concentrate in preindustrial artisanal trades. Though immigrants and natives could often be found in the same "Jewish" trade, the immigrant *façonnier* and worker in an *atelier* rarely had contact with the French Jewish *commerçant* and storeowner. Economic segregation was reinforced by geographical separation. While natives tended to settle in the richer western sections of Paris, eastern European Jews banded together in traditional Jewish areas in the center and the east. Under such conditions, it was rare that immigrants and natives met socially with one another. And without social contact among their members, the various native and immigrant organizations that sought unity could not possibly succeed.

Yet economic and social divisions provide only a partial answer to the problem of two communities. As we have seen, there were characteristics peculiar to the "Jewish" trades that made class hostilities much less marked than they might normally have been. As long as there was a belief in upward mobility in the Jewish community, the French Jewish merchant was looked upon by immigrant artisans more with envy than with hatred. Similarly, although class consciousness existed among French Jewry, the sense of Jewish communality, however limited, transmuted native class antagonism into a paternal condescension toward "unfortunate" coreligionists.

Natives and immigrants in the 1930s were quick to point accusing fingers at each others' organizations as the major obstacles delaying unity between the two communities.[4] It is undeniably true that by the mid-thirties there were signs of the development of a self-perpetuating bureaucracy in many of the Jewish organizations in Paris, jealously guarding the independence of their groups and vehemently opposed to any change that might bring about a loss of independence. Yet organizations were merely reflections of the varying beliefs and attitudes in the Paris community. Their continued existence depended upon the maintenance of deep ideological divisions within the community. Thus we are once again led back to the main divisive factor among Paris Jewry in the 1930s—the differing views of Jewish identity and of the Jewish response to Nazism.

In examining the attitudes of Paris Jewry, it is clear that the major factor dividing native from immigrant was not religious belief—after all, there were many eastern European Jews who were completely divorced from Judaism—but rather the historical and cultural perspective upon which the two groups based their commitment to Jewish life. For French Jews, Jewish identity was closely linked to the postrevolutionary French experience. By emancipating Jewry from centuries of oppression, France was said to have earned the right to share in the responsibility of bearing the messianic ideals of justice and brotherhood to the world. The intertwining of French ideals with the ideals of Judaism led to the creation of a new theodicy, one which could allegedly appeal to both religious and nonreligious Jews. Thus the men of the French Revolution, like God at Sinai, were said to have given the world a new Ten Commandments which if followed would lead to a world of contentment and happiness. In return, Jews were obligated, much in the same manner in which they thanked God and pledged to follow His Torah, to give thanks to those "enlightened" men who freed them from the slavery of obscurantism and superstition and to accede to their demands to assimilate. In this merger of national pride and religious dogma, it was not surprising that patriotic ceremonies often took on the character of religious ritual. Though publicly avowing the need to separate religious belief from secular affairs, French Jewry saw their Jewish identity largely as supportive of their efforts at integration into French society. In sanctifying *la patrie*, French Judaism also implied the supercession of Jewish identity by loyalty to the nation. In religious belief, as in all other aspects of life, natives were *Français israélites* rather than *Israélites français*.

Immigrant Jews arriving in Paris in the 1920s and 1930s found such ideas to be alien to their own experience. Traditionally, eastern European Jewry had defined itself against the larger society in which it found itself. Judaism and Jewish identity thus represented a form of self-defense against a hostile world. In the sheltered environment of the ghetto or *shtetl*, Jews remained relatively unconcerned with what went on about them. The *shtetl* had its own rhythm of life, only occasionally affected by changes in governments and governmental policies. Through centuries of daily living, a distinct culture developed that bore few similarities with the culture of the nation in which Jews lived. Subsumed in *yidishkayt*, eastern European Jews could not understand the differentiation made by French Jews between secular and religious concerns. Nor could they understand the process of individual assimilation so touted by French Jewry. Individualism could only flourish in a society steeped in liberalism. Even the emancipated Jew of the *Haskalah* (Enlightenment) or left-wing movements did not seriously believe that he would be accepted into an eastern European society which viewed Jews as a communal entity rather than as individuals. Whether intellectual or revolutionary, the eastern European Jew grew to understand that his hopes for integration into society could only be achieved through the liberation of the Jewish community as a whole.

This cultural tradition was not to be carried over in toto by immigrants coming to Paris. France was not Poland or Russia. Religious freedom was tolerated; individuals could rise on the economic and social ladder; a Jew could even become premier of France! Yet what remained after the concessions to a freer atmosphere was the sense of community and the desire to maintain *yidishkayt*. There were conflicting opinions among immigrants in Paris as to how much of *yidishkayt* should be retained. As we have seen, the Jewish Left sought to preserve only those progressive aspects of ghetto life that would be relevant to life in France. More traditional Jews wished to retain *shtetl* life in its entirety and indeed succeeded in recreating the *shtetl* in miniature in the "Pletzl." Yet whatever their particular attitudes, eastern European Jews all agreed that Yiddish culture was to be the basis upon which an immigrant community in Paris would be built.

It is difficult to say whether there would have been any significant change in immigrant attitudes toward Jewish identity if they had been allowed free access to French society. The events of the 1930s led eastern European Jews in Paris to profess contradictory beliefs. The frequent allusions made by both Fédération leaders and Jewish Communists to Jewish emancipation undoubtedly reflected a growing acceptance on the part of at least some immigrants of the myths of French Jewry. At the same time, however, the rise of anti-Semitism in Paris and the continued persecutions in central and eastern Europe also led to a reaffirmation of a "ghettoized" identity, often by sons and daughters of immigrants who would normally have been expected to rebel against their parents' parochialism. Even Jewish Communists, who had previously prided themselves in breaking with the "reactionary" religious ethos of eastern European life, began to have second thoughts in the late thirties and looked to religious tradition for solace in a period of despair. Events moved too quickly in the 1930s for immigrants in Paris to fully resolve their contradictory attitudes toward Jewish identity. On the eve of World War II, eastern European Jews seemed caught between an embryonic French Jewish identity, the product of the acculturation process of happier times, and the traditional defensive posture of the *shtetl* Jew, which seemed more appropriate in a period of persecution and despair.

The conflicting views of Jewish identity led to differing attitudes among natives and immigrants toward the appropriate response to Nazism and to anti-Semitism in general. Frenchmen first and Jews second, natives were never fully convinced of their obligations toward fellow Jews. The various relief programs instituted by the Consistoire and its affiliates in the prewar period were often grudgingly taken up by French Jews, less as sincere efforts to aid coreligionists than as means of disposing of troublesome elements that created an anti-Semitic backlash among Frenchmen. Beyond charitable works, there was little else in native activity that could be called a "Jewish" response. This is not surprising when one considers that French Jewish identity did not concern itself with Jewry as a group. The native's emphasis upon Judaism as a private affair may indeed have aided individual natives seeking to integrate themselves into French society, but it only hindered attempts to create an active Jewish response on the part of the community as a whole.

Of course, French Jews were only dimly aware of the tragic consequences of their limited Jewish identification. If they had ambivalent feelings about their Jewish identity, they had no such uncertainties in their attitudes toward France. As we have seen, France and Judaism were indistinguishable in the native view. French Jews thus could argue that the solution to the Jewish plight was ultimately bound up in France's adherence to the ideal of the Revolution of 1789. In the early thirties, reliance on the French government was an active policy of natives and not, as some critics have claimed, a mere rationalization for inactivity. Consistoire leaders frequently intervened with government officials; native rabbis were often consulted on matters pertaining to refugees; the government even provided certain benefits to French Jewish relief organizations. The willingness of French government leaders to aid natives in their relief efforts only bolstered the latter's belief that France was the true guardian of the oppressed of Europe.

The tragedy of French Jewry in the prewar period was that it continued to hold to the liberal myths of the French Revolution long after many Frenchmen had rejected them outright. The refusal of French Jewish organizations to mingle in politics made natives blind to the political changes that France was undergoing in the 1930s. While natives continued to guard their treasured belief in the politics of good will, Frenchmen were choosing up sides in the coming battle between democracy and totalitarianism. The fact that the battle took the form in France of a struggle between Left and Right led natives to dismiss it as mere political squabbling. When French Jewish leaders chose sides, they opted for the Right, mistaking its attacks upon the factionalism of parliamentary government for a renewed call for a *union sacrée* of all Frenchmen. Caught in the rapidly disappearing middle ground between a revolutionary Left and an anti-Semitic Right, French Jews looked vainly to the French government to stand above the political melee.

By 1938 native attestations of faith in the French government had become merely Pavlovian responses to the Jewish tragedy. Never committed to Jewish protest, French Jews now stopped interceding with French political leaders. The close ties between native leaders and government officials had all but deteriorated in the face of the growing realization on both sides that French interests and Jewish interests were in conflict. French Jews publicly expressed hope that government leaders would change their policies. In the religious weltanschauung that characterized native concerns in the waning months of peace, France had to resume its role as the bearer of the messianic ideal to the world. Yet the spiritual orientation of French Jewry only served to reinforce the hopelessness which natives felt when faced with a situation they were powerless to control. In a world of pragmatic diplomacy, territorial aggrandizement, and mass persecution, French Jews could only pray for divine intervention to save the world from catastrophe.

Unlike natives, immigrants faced few personal dilemmas when confronted with the oppression of their coreligionists. Eastern European Jews in Paris were quick to recognize the threat that Nazi racism posed for all Jews, regardless of personal affiliation. With the exception of older immigrants who had integrated themselves into the French Jewish community by the 1930s, eastern European Jewry never questioned the need for a Jewish response to what they regarded as the Nazi's declaration of war against all of Jewry. The problem for immigrants was choosing the correct response, that is, the most effective means by which the Paris community as a whole could counter anti-Semitism both within and without France.

In the course of the seven years between the accession of Hitler to power and the outbreak of war, immigrants in Paris made various attempts to mount a strong Jewish protest action in the capital. In every case these efforts met with failure. In part the failure resulted from the unwillingness of more influential native members of the community to take part in the action. Without the participation of Jewish "notables," Paris Jewry could not hope to bring the plight of Jewry to public attention. Equally important was the petty in-fighting among immigrant organizations that made it all but impossible to coordinate any action. Another factor was the anti-foreigner legislation of the 1930s, which threatened immigrants with expulsion and severely hampered the mounting of an effective campaign. Few immigrants were willing to admit the most important reason for the failure of Jewish protest—the impotence of a state-less people in a world of competing nation-states.

For a time, eastern European Jews were able to mask their disappointment by combining their emphasis on Jewish defense with an appeal for government intervention. The idea of governmental action to aid Jews was slow in developing within the immigrant community, for the bitter experiences of eastern Europe had led immigrants to doubt the sincerity of state officials. Yet although immigrants never fully accepted the natives' glowing picture of the French government's beneficence toward Jews, there were signs of a mellowing of their traditional hostility toward political authority. The repeated failure of Jewish protest campaigns convinced many eastern European Jews that Jewish action could only be successful if it were directed toward influencing governments to take international action to save Jewry. Immigrants were also caught up in the Popular Front movement which, upon its accession to power, seemed to bode well for an active governmental intervention to aid victims of Fascism. Faith in the Popular Front became so widespread in the immigrant community that when Blum's government fell in 1937, immigrant leaders were unable to rouse crestfallen eastern European Jews to resume Jewish protest action.

The so-called unity campaign of the mid-thirties represented an important turning point in immigrant attitudes toward the appropriate response to anti-Semitism. Originating during the period of Popular Front euphoria, the drive toward a unified community was envisioned by its most avid supporters as a buttress to French governmental and party efforts to aid European Jewry. Recognizing the futility of isolated Jewish protest, proponents of unity called for community support of sympathetic governmental leadership as the most effective means of countering the Nazi menace.

The collapse of the Popular Front in 1937 showed the facile nature of such arguments. No longer certain of government support and already convinced of the futility of Jewish action, the immigrants' search for community increasingly took on the characteristics of retrenchment and introspection in the face of Nazi persecution and world apathy. The fact that most immigrant leaders saw unity solely in terms of narrow self-interest, however, meant that the growing realization by individual Jews of Jewish isolation and abandonment would never be translated into a commitment to communal solidarity and survival. The events of the last two years of peace only reinforced the mood of despair. The popularity of the "return to the ghetto" idea in 1939, with its emphasis upon "optimistic" fatalism, showed that immigrants had indeed come full circle since their first halting attempts in the early thirties to accommodate themselves to their new homeland.

Of all immigrants in Paris, the Jewish Left experienced the most significant change in attitudes and thus the most crushing defeat of its hopes. Far more than any other eastern European Jews, Jewish Communists saw their settlement in France as a new era in Jewish history. No longer to be isolated into small illegal cells, Jewish revolutionaries were now to become an integral part of the international proletarian movement. It was not surprising, therefore, that with few exceptions Jewish Communists were quite willing to dispense with many of their sectarian beliefs that were nurtured in eastern Europe. With the advent of the Popular Front, the Jewish Left found itself in the enviable position of being the only group in the Jewish community with direct access to one of the parties of the government coalition. The success of the Jewish Popular Front in 1936 marked the culmination of Jewish Communist dreams of being both an active force in the developing immigrant community and full members in the French working-class movement.

The fall of the Popular Front in 1937 and the return of the PCF to more traditional working-class concerns brought a rapid end to these dreams. As xenophobic feeling spread among the French masses, it became clear that working-class organizations would do nothing to oppose it. The abolition of the Jewish subsection of the party in 1937 showed further that the French Left would not brook a movement in its ranks that placed too much emphasis upon narrow Jewish concerns. The attempt by Jewish Communists to integrate themselves into the French working-class movement while retaining an active role in the immigrant community thus ended in abysmal failure. The Jewish Left's decision to oppose the Nazi-Soviet Pact in August 1939 provided a final lesson of the incompatibility of Jewish and Communist interests in the 1930s.

The Paris Jewish community thus entered the war in disillusionment and despair. The dreams of building a strong and vibrant community had all but disappeared in the wake of the terrible calamities befalling Jews in the 1930s. Powerless to act and resigned to their fate, natives and immigrants fell back on traditional modes of defense that were diametrically opposed to one another. Though sharing a search for psychological and spiritual reinforcement within Judaism born of despair and fear, their differing evaluations of the meaning and significance of Jewish tradition only succeeded in deepening the rifts between the two groups. Thus while French Jewry returned to an emphasis upon the uniqueness of French Jewish history, eastern European Jews looked longingly to the ghetto which they had recently left. Caught between an irretrievable past and an uncertain future, the Paris Jewish community was only in the process of becoming when war broke out.

Notes

1. *Histoire des Juifs en France*, p. 423.
2. Grant, "Fun Keygenzaytiker Hilf," p. 11.
3. North African Jews are particularly numerous in the kosher butcher trade, Sephardic-run butcher shops comprising almost half of all Consistoire-approved meat markets in Paris and its suburbs. (Figures taken from a list of kosher butchers issued by the *Beth Din de Paris* in 1970.) Of the thirty-five Consistoire rabbis in Paris in 1970, at least fifteen were of Sephardic background (including Meyer Jaïs, Chief Rabbi of Paris). A list of rabbis in Paris can be found in the *Calendrier israélite*, issued annually by the Consistoire.
4. The individuals I interviewed in the course of my research all pointed to opposition organizations as the major cause of disunity in the 1930s. Thus Alperin was insistent that I make sure to note in the study that the Jewish Communists lay at the root of all the troubles befalling Paris Jewry before the war, while Kénig and Carol were equally insistent on blaming the Fédération and *Pariser Haint*.

Bibliography

I. Books

Arendt, Hannah. *Eichmann in Jerusalem: A Report on the Banality of Evil.* New York: Viking, 1963.
————. *Origins of Totalitarianism.* New York: World Publishing Company (Meridian Books), 1966.
Aubery, Pierre. *Milieux juifs de la France contemporaine à travers les écrivains.* Paris: Plon, 1957.
Bauer, Jules. *L'Ecole rabbinique de France, 1880-1930.* Paris: Presses universitaires de France, 1930.
Benda, Julien. *La Jeunesse d'un clerc.* Paris: Gallimard, 1936.
Berman, Léon. *Histoire des juifs de France des origines à nos jours.* Paris: Librairie Lipschutz, 1937.
Bettelheim, Bruno. *The Informed Heart: Autonomy in a Mass Age.* Glencoe, Ill.: Free Press of Glencoe, 1960.
Bloch, Jean Richard. *"& Co."* New York: Simon and Schuster, 1930.
Blum, Léon. *L'Histoire jugera.* Montreal: Editions de l'arbre, 1945.
————. *Souvenirs sur l'Affaire.* Paris: Gallimard, 1935.
Blumel, André. *Léon Blum, juif et sioniste.* Paris: Editions de La Terre retrouvée, 1951.
Byrnes, Robert F. *Antisemitism in Modern France.* Vol. 1. New Brunswick, N.J.: Rutgers University Press, 1950.
Cahen, Edmond. *Juif, non! . . . Israélite.* Paris: Librairie de France, 1930.
Centre national d'expansion du tourisme et du climatisme, ed. *Les Souvenirs israélites en France.* Paris, 1938.
Chavardès, Maurice. *Le 6 février 1934: La République en danger.* Paris: Calmann-Lévy, 1966.
Dalby, Louise. *Léon Blum: Evolution of a Socialist.* New York: Thomas Yoseloff, 1963.
Diamant, David. *Yidn in spanishn krig, 1936-1939.* Warsaw: OJFSNAJ, 1967.
Dreyfuss, J. H. *Israël et la France: Sermon prononcé le 1er jour de Pâques 5693 (11 avril 1933) au Temple israélite de la rue de la Victoire.* Paris: Consistoire israélite de Paris, n.d.

Eberlin, Elie. *La Double Tare.* Paris: Editions SNIE, 1935.

Elkins, Michael. *Forged in Fury.* New York: Ballantine Books, 1971.

Fontenelle, Bertrand. *M. Goldberg aimait Minet.* Paris: Les Nouvelles Editions, 1953.

Franckel, I. *Vi azoy tsu veren a Frantsoyz.* Paris: L. Beresniak, n.d.

Fridman, S. (Zosa Szajkowski). *Etyudn tsu der geshikhte fun ayngevanderter yidishn yishuv in Frankraykh.* Paris: Fridman, 1936.

Gary, Romain. *Promise at Dawn.* New York: Harper, 1961.

Grayzel, Solomon. *A History of the Jews.* Philadelphia: Jewish Publication Society of America, 1959.

Groos, René. *Enquête sur le problème juif.* Paris: Nouvelle Librairie Nationale, 192?.

Hertzberg, Arthur. *The French Enlightenment and the Jews.* New York: Columbia University Press, 1968.

Hilberg, Raoul. *The Destruction of European Jewry.* Chicago: Quadrangle Books, 1961.

Histoire des juifs en France, published under the direction of Bernhard Blumenkrantz. Toulouse: Edouard Privat, 1972.

Ikor, Roger. *Peut-on être juif aujourd'hui?* Paris: Editions Bernard Grasset, 1968.

Jehouda, Josué. *L'Antisémitisme, miroir du monde.* Geneva: Editions Synthèse, 1958.

Jellinek, Frank. *The Paris Commune of 1871.* New York: Grosset and Dunlap, 1965.

Kaplan, Jacob. *Les Temps d'épreuves.* Paris: Editions de Minuit, 1952.

Klatzmann, Joseph. *Le Travail à domicile dans l'industrie parisienne du vêtement.* Paris: Imprimerie Nationale, 1957.

Kornhendler, Yechezkel. *Alt Pariz.* Vol. 2. Paris: Oyfgang, 1948.

La Colonie Scolaire, ed. *Almanach juif, 1931.* Paris: La Nouvelle Generation, 193?.

Latour, Anny. *La Résistance juive en France, 1940–1944.* Paris: Stock, 1970.

Lazareff, Pierre. *Deadline.* New York: Random House, 1942.

Leksikon fun der nayer yidisher literatur. New York: Alveltlikhen Yidishn Kultur-Kongres, 1956–68.

Lerman, Y. *Far der Fartaydikung fun unzer folk.* Paris, 1938.

Levinger, Lee J. *A Jewish Chaplain in France.* New York: Macmillan, 1922.

L'Importance de la M.O.E. et les diverses immigrations: Bulletin spécial d'informations de la section centrale de la M.O.E. Paris: Parti communiste français, 1930.

Mandel, Arnold. *Les Temps incertains.* Paris: Calmann-Lévy, 1950.

Marrus, Michael R. *The Politics of Assimilation: A Study of the French Jewish Community at the Time of the Dreyfus Affair.*

New York and London: Oxford University Press, 1971.

Mauco, Georges. *Les Etrangers en France*. Paris: Librairie Armand Colin, 1932.

Maurin. *La Main-d'Oeuvre immigrée sur le marché du travail en France*. Paris: CGTU, 1933.

Micaud, Charles. *The French Right and Nazi Germany, 1933-1939*. Durham, N.C.: Duke University Press, 1943.

Millet, Raymond. *Trois Millions d'étrangers en France*. Paris: Librairie de Medicis, 1938.

Plumyène, Jean, and Lasierra, Raymond. *Les Fascismes français, 1923-1963*. Paris: Editions Seuil, 1963.

Rabi. *Anatomie du Judaïsme français*. Paris: Editions de Minuit, 1962.

Ravin, Jacques. *In Gerangl keygn natsishn soyne: Der Organizerter Vidershtand fun di yidn in Frankraykh*. Paris: Ofsnai, 1970.

Roblin, Michel. *Les Juifs de Paris*. Paris: Editions A. et J. Picard, 1952.

Roland, Charlotte. *Du Ghetto à l'Occident: Deux générations yiddiches en France*. Paris: Editions de Minuit, 1962.

Ruppin, Arthur. *The Jews in the Modern World*. London: Macmillan, 1934.

Schlewin, Baruch. *Yidn fun Belleville*. Paris: Farlag, 1948.

Schorsch, Ismar. *Jewish Reactions to German Anti-Semitism, 1870-1914*. New York: Columbia University Press, 1972.

Steinberg, Lucien. *La Révolte des justes: Les Juifs contre Hitler*. Paris: Fayard, 1970.

Suhl, Yuri. *They Fought Back*. New York: Crown, 1967.

Szajkowski, Z[osa]. *The Growth of the Jewish Population in France*. New York: Conference on Jewish Relations, 1946.

Trunk, Isaiah. *Judenrat*. New York: Macmillan, 1972.

20 Yor Naie Presse. Paris: Naie Presse, 1954.

Weber, Eugen. *Action française: Royalism and Reaction in Twentieth Century France*. Stanford: Stanford University Press, 1962.

Werth, Alexander. *France and Munich*. New York: Harper, 1939.

———. *France in Ferment*. New York: Harper, 193?.

———. *The Twilight of France*. New York: Harper, 1942.

———. *Which Way France?* New York: Harper, 1937.

Wischnitzer, Mark. *To Dwell in Safety: The Story of Jewish Migration since 1800*. Philadelphia: Jewish Publication Society of America, 1948.

Wormser, Georges. *Français israélites*. Paris: Editions de Minuit, 1963.

Yidisher Intersindikaler Komisie bay der CGT. *In Kamf far frayhayt*. Paris: OJFSNAJ, 1948.

Yidish Hantbukh: Pariz. Paris: Naie Presse, 1937.

II. Articles

"A Belleville." *Le Temps*, May 15, 1938.

Alperin, A. "Di Antisemitishe Propaganda in Frankraykh erev der milkhome." In *Yidn in Frankraykh*, edited by A. Tcherikover, 2:264–80. New York: YIVO, 1942.

———. "Yidishe Gezelshaftn un institutsies in Pariz in 1939." In *Yidn in Frankraykh*, edited by A. Tcherikover, 2:248–63. New York: YIVO, 1942.

"A Pieds joints." *Le Rire*, April 25, 1936.

Ariel, Joseph. "French Jewish Resistance to the Nazis." *Judaism* 18, no. 3 (summer 1969): 299–312.

"A Vort tsu di leyner." *Oyfn Shaydveg* 1, no. 1 (April 1939): 4.

Beauplan, Robert de. "Le Drâme juif." *La Petite Illustration*, February 4, 1939, pp. 3–32.

———. "Les Etrangers en France." *L'Illustration*, October 15, 1938, pp. 234–35.

Bielinky, Jacques. "Les Victimes de l'Hitlérisme à Paris." *Menorah*, March–April 1933, pp. 20–21.

Blumenkrantz, Bernhard. "Paris." In *Encyclopaedia Judaica* (1971), 13:103–9.

Bonsirven, Joseph. "Chronique du Judaïsme français." *Etudes*, January 5, 1933, pp. 64–82.

Cher, A. "Der Yidisher Gaystiker Krizis in sheyn fun der presse." *Oyfn Shaydveg* 1, no. 1 (April 1939): 201–17.

"Der Veg fun di gezelshaftn." *Tsen yor Farband fun yidishe gezelshaftn*, pp. 87–151. Paris: Farband fun Yidishe gezelshaftn, 1948.

Diamant, David. "Di Frantsoyzishe Kommunistishe Partey un di yidn." *Parizer Tsaytshrift* 9, nos. 26–27 (1961): 78–110.

Dobin, M. "Di Profesies fun di yidishe immigrantn in Pariz." *YIVO Bleter*, August–December 1932, pp. 22–42.

———. "Yidishe Immigrantn-Arbeter in Pariz." *YIVO Bleter*, January–May 1932, pp. 385–403.

Fink, Yaakov Yisroel. "Bamivkhan." In *Yahaduth Tzarfath*, pp. 57–70. Paris: Machberoth, 1951.

Grant, Alfred. "Fun Keygenzaytiker Hilf: Tsum Kamf farn natsionaln kiyum." In *Tsen yor Farband fun yidishe gezelshaftn*, pp. 9–41. Paris: Farband fun Yidishe gezelshaftn, 1948.

Hersh, L. "Yidishe Demografie." In *Algemayne Entsiklopedie: Yidn*, 1:331–86. Paris: Dubnow Fund, 1939.

———. "Yidishe Emigratsie far di letste hundert yor." *Algemayne Entsiklopedie: Yidn*, vol. 1. Paris: Dubnow Fund, 1939.

"Honneur à la mémoire des deux vaillants combattants." *Notre*

Voix, October 1942. Reproduced in *La Presse antiraciste sous l'occupation hitlérienne*, p. 55, edited by Centre de Documentation de L'Union des juifs pour la résistance et l'entr'aide. Paris: UJRE, n.d.

Jefroykin, Jacques. "Affirmation." *Oyfn Shaydveg* 1, no. 1 (April 1939): 224–26.

Jefroykin, Y. "Vu haltn Mir in der hayntiker velt?" *Oyfn Shaydveg* 1, no. 2 (August 1939): 14–26.

Krishtal, Isaac. "Der Arbeter-Ordn un zayn rol bay der antviklung funem Farband." In *Tsen yor Farband fun yidishe gezelshaftn*, pp. 67–70. Paris: Farband fun Yidishe gezelshaftn, 1948.

Lang, C. L. "Second Start in France." In *Dispersion and Resettlement*, pp. 21–23. London: Association of Jewish Refugees in Great Britain, 1955.

Lazareff, Pierre. "Les Oeuvres de bienfaisance et d'éducation." In *La Question juive vue par vingt-six éminentes personalités*. Paris: EIF, 1934.

"Les Israélites français veulent la paix au dedans et au dehors." *Le Matin*, December 3, 1938.

"Les Juifs." *Crapouillot: Numero spécial*, September 1936.

Lestschinsky, Jacob. "Yidishe Ekonomik." In *Algemayne Entsiklopedie: Yidn*, 1:387–440. Paris: Dubnow Fund, 1939.

———. "Yidishe Shtudentn nokh der velt milkhome." *YIVO Bleter*, January–December 1935, pp. 3–26.

Levinsky, M. "Frantzoyzer Verter inem Parizer Yidish." In *Yidn in Frankraykh*, edited by A. Tcherikover, 2:193–204. New York: YIVO, 1942.

Levitte, Georges. "A Changing Community." In *Aspects of French Jewry*, pp. 10–23. London: Vallentine, Mitchell, 1969.

Mandel, Arnold. "Di Yidn in Frankraykh." In *Algemayne Entsiklopedie: Yidn*, 4:613–50. New York: Dubnow Fund and CYCO, 1950.

Monikowski, J. "Vi azoy iz anshtann der Farband fun yidishe gezelshaftn." In *Tsen yor Farband fun yidishe gezelshaftn*, pp. 64–66. Paris: Farband fun Yidishe gezelshaftn, 1948.

Menes, A. "Unzer Veg un unzer goral." *Oyfn Shaydveg* 1, no. 1 (April 1939): 53–72.

———. "Yidn in Frankraykh." *YIVO Bleter*, January–May 1937, pp. 329–55.

"Paris." In *New Standard Jewish Encyclopedia*, edited by Cecil Roth and Geoffrey Wigoder. 4th ed. New York: Doubleday, 1970.

Peyret, Henri. "L'Immigration des Allemands chassés par le nouveau régime." *Le Temps*, November 30, 1933.

"Pour venir en aide aux juifs." *Le Matin*, November 19, 1938.
Poznansky, A. "Di Yidishe Gezelshaft amol un haynt." In *Tsen yor Farband fun yidishe gezelshaftn*, pp. 61-63. Paris: Farband fun Yidishe gezelshaftn, 1948.
Prissac, Jean de. "Quand Israël est libre." *Le Temps*, October 7, 1933.
Rawick-Lifschitz, M.; Gruss, Noe; and Halevy, M. A. "Périodiques juifs français du XXe siècle à la Bibliothèque Nationale et a la Bibliothèque de l'Alliance israélite universelle." In *Archives juives*, 4 (1967-68): 9-11, 18-24, 30, 42-43.
Riba, Raphael. "Yidisher Sotsialistisher Farband 'Bund' in Frankraykh." *Unzer Tsayt*, November-December 1947, pp. 159-61.
Ruppin, Arthur. "Yidishe Statistik." *Algemayne Entsiklopedie: Yidn*, 1:305-30. Paris: Dubnow Fund, 1939.
Sommer, Robert. "Hommage à notre cher Grand Rabbin." *Vendredi soir*, October 31, 1947, pp. 3-4.
———. "La Doctrine politique et l'action religieuse du Grand-Rabbin Maurice Liber." *Revue des Etudes juives* 125 (January-September 1966): 9-20.
———. "Les Préoccupations du judaïsme français." *Le Monde*, June 24, 1952.
Spector, Melekh. "Di Landsmanshaft-Patronatn in Frankraykh." In *Tsen yor Farband fun yidishe gezelshaftn*, pp. 71-73. Paris: Farband fun Yidishe gezelshaftn, 1948.
Szajkowski, Z[osa]. "1515 Yidishe Mishpokhes in Pariz." In *Di Yidishe Ekonomik* 2, nos. 9-10 (1938): 471-80.
———. "Tsu der Geshikhte fun yiddishn teyater in Pariz." *Gedank un leybn*, no. 3 (October-December 1946), pp. 174-84.
———. "Dos Yidishe Gezelshaftlikhe Leybn in Pariz tsum yor 1939." In *Yidn in Frankraykh*, edited by A. Tcherikover, 2:207-47. New York: YIVO, 1942.
Tcherikover, A. "Di Tragedie fun a shvakhn dor." *Oyfn Shaydveg* 1, no. 1 (April 1939): 5-28.
———. "Vegn 'Shaydveg' un vegn 'shlakhtfeld.'" *Oyfn Shaydveg* 1, no. 2 (August 1939): 8-13.
"Tsvay briv tsum Marshall Petain." In *Yidn in Frankraykh*, edited by A. Tcherikover, 2:295-303. New York: YIVO, 1942.
"Ver Fartaydikt di Ayngevanderter?" In *Supplement to Notre Drapeau*. Paris, 1938.
Wischnitzer, Mark. "Yidishe Alaynfarvaltung." *Algemayne Entsiklopedie: Yidn*, 1:563-84. Paris: Dubnow Fund, 1939.

III. Periodicals

The dates refer only to those issues I could uncover for the period
1932-40 in the course of research and do not necessarily denote the
complete run of the periodical.

Affirmation, January-August 1939
Arbeter Wort, 1934, 1936, scattered issues
Archives israélites, 1933-36
Bulletin de Chema Israël, March 2, 1934
Bulletin de l'Union patriotique de français israélites, December
   1935, December 1936
Bulletin de presse sioniste-revisioniste, 1935-38, scattered issues
Bulletin du Centre de documentation et de vigilance, 1937-39
Cahiers juifs, 1933-36
Chalom, 1933-34, scattered issues
Droit de vivre, 1933-39
Hantverker Vort, June 1938, January 1939
Hebdo-Pariz, April-November 1935, incomplete
Illustrierte Yidishe Presse, November 1934-March 1935, incomplete
Kadimah, 1933-39
La Conscience des juifs, August-September, November 1935; June
   1938
L'Ancien combattant juif, 1938, scattered issues
La Revue juive de Génève, 1932-39
La Terre retrouvée, 1933-40
L'Eclaireur israélite de France, 1934-38, scattered issues
Le Flambeau, 1934-37, scattered issues
Le Journal juif, 1935-36, incomplete
Le Populaire, 1933-39
Le Rayon, 1933-39
L'Humanité, 1933-39
Le Volontaire juif, 1933-35, incomplete
L'Univers israélite, 1932-39
Naie Presse, 1933-39, incomplete
Naye Zeit, 1936, incomplete
Paix et Droit, 1933-39
Pariser Haint, 1933-39, incomplete
Pariser Tageblatt, 1933-35
Samedi, March 1936-July 1939
Unzer Stime, 1936-39, incomplete

Unzer Hilf, 1937–39, scattered issues
Yidishe Presse Revue, September–October 1934
Yidisher Arbeter, May 1, 1936

IV. Reports

Association cultuelle dite Association consistoriale israélite de Paris. *Assemblée générale ordinaire, 1933, 1934, 1935.* Paris: Sécrétariat général, n.d.

Comité pour la défense des droits des israélites en Europe centrale et orientale. *La Défense des droits et de la dignité des réfugiés et apatrides, israélites et non-israélites, en France en 1934, 1935, et 1936.* Paris, n.d.

Fédération des sociétés juives de France. *Rapport de l'activité pour l'année 1934.* Paris: Imprimerie Polyglotte N. L. Danzig, 1935.

———. *Rapport moral et financier: Exercise 1935–1936.* Paris: ICC, 1936.

———. *Rapport général d'activité: Année 1947 et premier semestre 1948.* Paris: Imprimerie A. Montourcy, 1948.

HICEM. *Dix années d'émigration juive (1926–1936): Rapport présenté à la Conférence d'émigration juive les 20 juin–1 juillet 1936.* Paris: HICEM, n.d.

Les Etrangers de religion juive en France. A document edited by a specialist under the auspices of the Centre d'études de Lyon. Lyon: Centre d'études de Lyon, 1942.

Union patriotique des français israélites. *Compte rendu de l'Assemblée générale du 19 décembre 1934.* Paris: Imprimerie Georges Lang, n.d.

V. Unpublished Material and Archives

The archives of the Consistoire, the Bund, and YIVO listed below have yet to be officially cataloged. The numbering system I have employed thus represents only a temporary classification and is subject to change.

A. Alliance israélite universelle
   Manuscrit no. 586: Fonds Sylvain Halff
   1. Notes biographiques: Juifs de France, classées alphabétiques
   2. Fonds Sylvain Halff
      a. Sur le judaïsme français
      b. Menorah-1924
      c. Notes
         1. Quelques traductions de N. Ben Ezra
         2. Les addresses des principales personalités juives de Paris

3. La liste des rabbins, des membres de Commissions administratives de la communauté, dans les années 1936-38
d. Les Juifs et la guerre 1914-18

B. Archives of the Association consistoriale israélite de Paris

AA21	Déliberations du Conseil d'administration	1929-35
AA23	Déliberations du Conseil d'administration	1936-38
B127	Lettres reçues	1933
B128	Lettres reçues	1933
B129	Lettres reçues	1934
B130	Lettres reçues	1934
B131	Lettres reçues	1935
B132	Lettres reçues	1935
B133	Lettres reçues	1935-39
B134	Lettres recues	1939
B135 bis	Lettres reçues	1907-39
BB98	Lettres envoyées	1933
BB99	Lettres envoyées	1934
L	Juifs d'Allemagne	1933-34
NN	Inhumations	1931-42

C. Benguigui, Ida. "L'Immigration juive à Paris entre les deux guerres." Thesis submitted for a Diplôme d'études supérieures at the Faculté des Lettres et des Sciences humaines of the Université de Paris, 1965.

D. Bund Archives
Der "Bund" in Frankraykh. 1933-39.

E. YIVO Archives
1. Yidn in Frankraykh
   a. Khevre fun poylishe yidn
   b. Yidishe institutsies
   c. Frankraykh far der tsveyter velt milkhome
   d. Poaley-Tsiyon, tsionistn, arbetloze komitetn, Arbeter Ring
   e. Plitim, migratsie, hilf organizatsies
   f. Protokoln fun organizatsies
   g. Profesionale veraynen, bilike kikh, arbeter organizatsies
   h. Religeyze inyonim, materialn vegn zmiros yisroel
2. Bielinky Archives
   a. Arts, actualités
   b. Personnel
   c. Correspondance un farshidenes, 1938-40
   d. Manuscrits
   e. Untitled folder
   f. Bielinky materialn
   g. Fédération: Correspondance et farshidenes
   h. Articles-manuscrits

i. Le Renouveau

VI. Interviews and Personal Correspondence

Alperin, A. An editor of *Pariser Haint* in the 1930s. January 21, 1971.

Berg, Roger. Editor of the *Journal des Communautés*. July 6, 1972.

Carol, W. A former Jewish trade union leader in Paris. August 4, 1970.

Kempinsky, Hillel. Head archivist at the Bundist archives. January 17–20, 1971.

Kénig, Georges. An editor of *Naie Presse* in the 1930s. June 25, 1970.

Lerman, Y. A Jewish Communist militant in Paris in the 1930s. August 5, 1970.

Mandel, Arnold. Writer. July 10, 1972.

Rabi (Wladimir Rabinovitch). Writer. Personal Correspondance, July 22, 1972.

Taumann, M. Secretary of the Association des anciens combattants engagés, volontaires juifs, 1914–18. June 14, 1970.

Wormser, Georges. Treasurer of the Consistoire de Paris in the 1930s. July 10, 1972.

Index

Acculturation of immigrants, 61–63, 216–17
Action française, 38 n. 11, 104
Affirmation, xii, 51, 191–93
Aliens, legislation relative to, 15–16, 145 n. 122, 153, 176, 182–83, 184–85, 199
Alliance israélite universelle, 28; archives and library, xiii, 39 n. 17; attitude toward Jewish protest, 84–85, 107, 139 n. 25; contacts with Fédération des sociétés juives de France, 125, 150, 151
Alperin, A.: on Jewish Communists, 141 n. 52, 221 n. 4; on Jewish protest, 108–9, 139 n. 23, 139 n. 25, 173; on Jewish voters, 141 n. 53; on world leaders, 106, 107–8, 139 n. 19, 177, 180–81; on Yiddish culture, 69 n. 63
Alsace-Lorraine, 7 n. 6, 7 n. 8, 26
Amarti, 99 n. 53, 109, 140 n. 33, 140 n. 34, 187
Anschluss, 158, 172–75
Anticommunism: among French Jews, 76, 79–80, 97 n. 33, 98 n. 48; among immigrants, 114–16, 128, 143 n. 94, 162
Anti-Semitism: in France, 74–75, 182, 205 n. 5, 207 n. 40; among French workers, 130–31, 145 n. 119, 146 n. 133, 170 n. 45, 182, 188, 207 n. 141; and Nazism, 46, 73–74, 93 n. 2; in Paris, 175, 179–80, 206 n. 29, 206 n. 34; in Rumania, 171–72
Arbeter Ring, 42 n. 38. *See also* Bundists
Arendt, Hannah, xv n. 1
Asch, Sholem, 141 n. 47
Ashkenazim, 1–2, 6, 26
Association consistoriale israélite de Paris. *See* Consistoire de Paris
Association des israélites traditionnels, 168 n. 14
Austria, Nazi occupation of. *See* Anschluss

Bankers, Jewish, 11–12
Belleville, 5; Jewish identity among residents of, 20 n. 8, 55, 179; living conditions in, 16; novel about, 70 n. 70; and riots of February 6, 1934, 142 n. 76; strikes in, 142 n. 77; and outbreak of World War II, 202–3
Berl, Alfred, 93 n. 2, 96 n. 23, 101 n. 81, 211 n. 98
Berl, Emmanuel, viii, 207 n. 36
Berman, Léon, 150
Bermann, Rabbi David, 65 n. 17
Bernhard, Georg, 124
Bernheim, Léonce, 112, 140 n. 45
Bielinky, Jacques, xvi n. 5, 41 n. 32, 65 n. 17, 66 n. 27, 98 n. 45, 137 n. 1
Bigart, Jacques, 7 n. 5, 150
Birobidjan, 59, 68 n. 52, 69 n. 56
Bloch, Abraham (Rabbi), 79, 97 n. 31
Bloch, Edmond, 79, 81, 98 n. 44, 114–15, 117, 141 n. 59, 144 n. 104
Blum, Léon: anti-Semitic attacks upon, 81; attitude toward Jews and Judaism, 66 n. 31, 92, 101 n. 85, 146 n. 141, 207 n. 42; Consistoire contacts with, 82–83, 98 n. 45; Jewish attitudes toward, 55, 95 n. 16, 98 n. 46, 106, 131, 138 n. 17; participation in Jewish protest, 170 n. 49; ties to native community, 63 n. 3
Boycott of German products, 83, 107–8, 118, 123–24, 139 n. 25, 139 n. 27, 139 n. 28
Boy Scouts, Jewish, 38 n. 13
Brenot, Marcel, 146 n. 135
Brocanteurs, 13, 26
Bundists: activities, 41 n. 36; archives, xvi n. 5; attacks upon Communists, 43 n. 46, 56, 132–33, 146 n. 136, 170 n. 46, 170 n. 47, 186; Communist attacks upon, 195; on Jewish identity, 55, 58, 67 n. 47, 200; on Jewish protest, 118, 120–21, 133, 186; number in

236   Index

Jews, 53, 140 n. 38; on the Jewish Left
and the Jewish Popular Front, 144 n.
97, 144 n. 102, 155; on Jewish protest,
108, 112; as leader of the Fédération
des sociétés juives de France, 39 n. 24,
40 n. 27, 111, 126, 169 n. 38; on
political noninvolvement, 110, 113,
124, 141 n. 51, 156
Jefroykin, Jacques, 193–94
Jewelry and watchmaking, Jews employed in, 18
"Jewish policy," 90–91, 102 n. 88, 109,
208 n. 52
Jewish Popular Front, 110, 121–36, 143
n. 86, 143 n. 90, 144 n. 98, 144 n.
102, 146 n. 135, 153, 155, 163, 169
n. 31
Jewish subsection of the Parti communiste français, xiii, 33, 120–21;
abolition of the, 134–35, 146 n. 135
"Jewish" trades, 5, 13–14, 20 n. 9, 188,
214; class consciousness in, 17–18,
43 n. 48, 122; number of Jews employed in, 14, 21 n. 20; strikes in, 17,
35, 119, 129–30, 142 n. 77, 145 n. 111,
145 n. 112, 145 n. 118, 208 n. 63;
union affiliation in, 17, 35–36, 43 n.
46, 146 n. 129. See also Façonniers,
Jewish
Judcovici, Ben-Zion, 40 n. 27, 110, 124,
144 n. 102

Kaplan, Rabbi Jacob: on Judaism and
France, 74, 94 n. 7, 179, 198; associa-
tion with right-wing groups, 78, 96 n.
27, 98 n. 48; on Zionism, 52–53
Kaufman, A., 153
Kehila, idea of, among immigrants, 47,
153–57, 168 n. 16
Kénig, Georges, 146 n. 135, 204, 221
n. 4
Klal yisroel, 17, 58–59, 118, 122
Knout, David, 208 n. 67
Korn, F., 122, 143 n. 88, 145 n. 120
Kosher butchers and slaughterhouses in
Paris, 25, 221 n. 3
Kremer, A., 189–90, 191
Krystalnacht, 183, 185

Lambert, Raoul-Raymond, 66 n. 28,
213; on Léon Blum, 98 n. 46; on
Consistoire and right-wing movements, 81, 97 n. 41; on French

government, 101 n. 79, 172; on immigrants, 150–51, 152, 205 n. 5; on Jews
and France, 52; on Jewish protest,
89–90, 99 n. 58, 180, 196; on Nazi
anti-Semitism, 74
Landsmanshaftn in Paris, viii, 3, 29–30,
31, 39 n. 21, 122, 153, 169 n. 31
La Rocque, Colonel de, 77, 80–81, 96
n. 24, 184
Laval, Pierre, 15, 89
League of Nations, Jewish attitudes
toward, 107, 139 n. 22
Lebecq, Georges, 78
Lecache, Bernard, 27, 65 n. 19, 91,
144 n. 104, 164–65, 170 n. 53, 174,
205 n. 13. See also Ligue inter-
nationale contre l'antisémitisme
(LICA)
Left, Jewish. See Bundists; Communists,
Jewish
"Legal Status" campaign, 178
Lerman, Y., on CGT, 43 n. 43; on
Jewish culture, 60; on Jewish protest,
127, 145 n. 123, 170 n. 45, 205 n. 11;
on dissolution of Jewish subsection,
134–35, 146 n. 135; on return to the
ghetto, 194–95; on strikes in the
"Jewish" trades, 132
Lévi, Rabbi Israël, 98 n. 45, 138 n. 10
Lévy-Wogue, Fernand, 94 n. 4
Liber, Rabbi Maurice, 98 n. 45, 138 n.
10, 198, 202
Liberal professions, Jews in, 11
Libraries, Jewish, in Paris, 30, 32, 39 n.
17, 62, 67 n. 67
Licht, David, 68 n. 52
Ligue internationale contre l'anti-
sémitisme (LICA), 26–27, 50–51, 102
n. 94, 170 n. 48, 170 n. 49; on
Anschluss, 174; attitude of Jewish Left
toward, 118; native Jewish response
to, 82, 83, 95 n. 18; relations with
Popular Front, 91–92; protest action,
98 n. 42, 102 n. 91, 141 n. 54, 206
n. 29, 207 n. 41; and unity effort,
164–65, 170 n. 53. See also Lecache,
Bernard
Ligue nationale contre l'antisémitisme,
208 n. 53
Linke Poalé-Sion, 120–21, 143 n. 80
Lirik, N., 108–9

Main d'oeuvre etrangère (MOE), later
Main d'oeuvre immigrée (MOI), 43 n.